Answers to Life:

Truths We Fail to Admit to Ourselves

Robert Foster Russell, Ph.D.

I have chosen to capitalize throughout the book pronouns that refer to God the Father, God the Son, or God the Holy Spirit. Such capitalization may not appear in the original text of quoted scriptures.

I have used bold print at various locations throughout the book to emphasize certain portions of quoted scriptures. The bold print may not appear in the actual biblical text.

All stories about individuals are true. Where appropriate, the names of the parties have been changed. Otherwise, they are used by permission.

www.xulonpress.com

Table of Contents

Introduction

There is a tempest of rage brewing in our young people. Too often they have been cheated and exploited, not only by the commercialism of this consumer age, but by the educators and sociologists who have stripped them of values, family relationships, and the sense of a greater purpose in life. I see too many young men and women whose virtue has been abused and whose faith in partnership and commitment has been shattered. I truly fear for their future. [1]

— Billy Graham

A few winters ago, my family went with a group of friends to Crested Butte, Colorado. We went there simply to spend some time together in fun and fellowship. The town of Crested Butte is a small, picturesque place—no traffic lights, just one four-way stop intersection. On Main Street are several interesting retail establishments and a few quaint restaurants. The surrounding, beautiful mountains provide excellent skiing and spectacular views.

Late one afternoon in the midst of our vacation, I was skiing by myself. My friends had already retired for the day, and I was just enjoying some peaceful time on the mountain. As I boarded the next chairlift—a slow, two-person model—I was seated next to a young man who was obviously a local. At this resort, perhaps more than any other, the locals are clearly distinguishable from the tourists. The locals generally wear earth tones and somewhat worn ski clothing that has an occasional patch made of duck tape. They sometimes cruise on alpine skis, but they prefer snowboards or the challenge of telemarking[2] with cross-country skis on downhill slopes. The locals are generally friendly and helpful, but they primarily tolerate the tourists because of their financial contributions to the resort, which keeps it operating for those who really know what they are doing.

My newfound friend was a snowboarder, probably about 21 years old, and a cordial gentleman. He stated, "I live to snowboard." He worked at night in the laundry operations of one of the local hotels where he earned just enough money to survive. He spent every day snowboarding and had not missed a day on the mountain since he arrived in Crested Butte. This was his second season at this location; previously, he made his winter abode at another ski resort in California. He was attracted to Crested Butte by its reputation for having some of the best extreme (dangerous) skiing terrain on the continent. If he was like most of the other locals, he probably spent his summers hiking or mountain biking, or maybe he headed for the coast and spent the summer surfing at a beach resort.

It was obvious from chatting with the young man that he truly enjoyed (almost worshiped) snowboarding. The sport provided him with great joy and excitement. He was not about to ditch his lifestyle for a 9:00 to 5:00 job and a house in the suburbs. He clearly preferred the simplicity of his current life. At his age, who could blame him? He was in that unusual stage we experience when our bodies are strong, our responsibilities few, and life is great as long as there is one more day of excitement just around the corner. However, I could not help wondering how he would deal with deeper issues like aging, suffering, or dying. I wondered about his family and whether or not his parents truly cared about his daily life. Had they overlooked him to climb the corporate and social ladders of success? I wondered if he had observed their lives and concluded they were artificial, superficial, and not for him. My new friend's life certainly seemed exciting, but it also appeared empty. He had the look of a person who was content, even happy, but all the while longing for something more.

Isn't there more to life?

We live in a rapidly changing, ever-progressing world, yet in the midst of this development there exists an enormous void. The void is clearly visible in the eyes and hearts of many young people, as well as in the lives of numerous adults. The void is caused by a lack of meaning and purpose in life. It is a result of people looking for answers but finding only empty, temporal solutions. It is disillusionment with technology and change, accompanied by a desire for immutable, reliable principles upon which to base life and find meaning.

The modern, rational age promised breakthrough answers to the problems of humankind, and it did dramatically improve the standard of living for many people. Nonetheless, modernism brought additional complexities, previously unimaginable horrors, and threats to the continuity of human life. Thus, we have moved into a postmodern era in which people have renewed the search for answers beyond the physical realm.

Modernism has failed because it sought only to solve the physical problems of human beings. In reality, the search for answers requires a broader perspective that considers the psychological, philosophical, and spiritual aspects of life. It requires recognition that the fundamental aspects of human life have not changed throughout history. Human beings have always struggled to survive, persevere, and find meaning and purpose in life. Perhaps that is why the author of Ecclesiastes wrote in approximately the 3rd or 4th century B.C., "What has been will be again, what has been done will be done again; there is nothing new under the sun" (Ecclesiastes 1:9).

Environmental, physical, and relational obstacles have created difficulties for every generation, yet more significantly, the search for purpose in life has plagued every individual. The pace of contemporary life leaves little time to reflect upon questions regarding meaning and purpose. In the context of our current world, the deeper, critical questions of life seem to get pushed aside. We have no time for contemplating the complexities of life; rather, we're off to the next business meeting, sports event, or social gathering. We substitute the temporal satisfaction of our busy agendas for a more profound understanding and acceptance of the basic principles of life.

Our abilities to gather and transmit information have risen exponentially; we can instantaneously communicate with distant parts of the world. However, we exchange a few moments of information sharing by means of some technological device for deeper, more meaningful interaction. In fact, many of our busy activities are transient endeavors that serve to numb our already overtaxed minds. Our lives have become shallow, artificial, superficial . . . empty. **We are a world society that yearns to ask:** *Isn't there more to life?* Somewhere in our vast array of technology, information, and knowledge isn't there someone with deeper, more satisfying answers?

The proposition of this entire book is that there are universal truths which can be relied upon by all, and which provide essential meaning to life. Such truths have stood the test of time. The generations who have passed before us have found them reliable, and those who will succeed us will also find them pertinent. If this were not the case, the truths would not really be meaningful to us.

These universal truths are nearly self-evident, yet they are easily and often overlooked. In fact, many of the beliefs and principles of life applied by our contemporary societies are transient—they lack eternal value. Most societies of the world seem increasingly and collectively to turn a deaf ear to the voices of those 'crying in the wilderness'—crying for answers regarding the elementary and essential issues of life. Instead of building our lives around immutable principles, we have developed societal mores that promote immediate gratification, materialism, and individual fulfillment at the expense of others.

Despite widespread economic prosperity at the outset of the 21st century, scores of people throughout the world realize that something is amiss in our cultures. Regardless of our respective belief systems, we sense a deep need for a fundamental shift in direction. We seem to be plunging into an abyss with no hope of avoiding the fall. Consequently, from virtually every corner people are calling for change. Many individuals assail the lack of values and morality that afflicts numerous societies. Some seek institutional answers to societal problems; others look to change the institutions themselves. We are quick to blame governments, business organizations, and educational institutions. We fault bureaucracies, failed leaders, and any other scapegoat that has a prominent and proximate position.

Yet, if we look clearly at our points of blame, we will see a mirror standing in the way. It poignantly reflects our blame back upon ourselves. The reason is clear: **the behavior of institutions is a function of the values of the individuals who compose the organizations**. No government, business, or other institution has ever spelled the success or failure of a society. Rather, people make the decisions, form the systems, and foster prosperity or decline. The responsibility for our actions is our own.

I have never met a small child who did not immediately look for an excuse when caught with his or her 'hand in the cookie jar.' However, the act was the responsibility of the child and no one else. Whereas the decline of various societies throughout the world has been a collective undertaking, the ultimate responsibility for the decay rests squarely upon the shoulders of those of us who have forsaken, ignored, or simply overlooked the essential values of life. We have failed to transmit to our youth the fundamental truths of life. **What is worse, we have failed to even admit the truth to ourselves!**

Chapter 1

Give Me an Answer!

A few years ago, I encountered a young man with a much different background from that of my aforementioned snowboarding friend; however, he demonstrated some of the same characteristics. Hereafter I will call him Ben Luking, which is not his real name. Ben had grown up in a farming community in Virginia where he had been a good student and athlete (football, soccer, etc.) while in high school. I came to know him quite well during his years in college; he even worked for me during his senior year. He continued to be a reasonably good student and athlete during his collegiate experience. In addition, Ben had a cordial, friendly personality that helped him easily make friends.

As his senior year wound to an end, Ben and I talked more and more about his future. He had dated a charming young woman since high school, and there was some possibility of marriage in the future. He was also exploring the possibility of graduate school to earn a MBA degree, and he had some job opportunities wide open before him. All in all, Ben appeared to have his life together, and his future appeared bright.

Just weeks before Ben graduated, he revealed some interesting news to me. Upon graduation, he planned to go to Montana to be a real cowboy for the summer. He was going to work for a ranch where he would literally herd cattle most of the time. His work hours would be daylight to dark, and his living quarters would be a dusty trailer. Ben's plan for the summer meant he would forgo a good job opportunity. In addition, his girlfriend, while agreeable, was not thrilled about the adventure.

I found his course of action rather curious, so I asked Ben why he planned to undertake this adventure, especially in light of the fact that it might mean permanently losing a good job opportunity that was before him. He responded partly by saying that he just wanted to do something different and fun before he settled into the normal routine of life. Such opportunities don't come along later in life when there are responsibilities like children, careers, and mortgages to maintain. However, part of Ben's response was simply that he was uncertain about what to do in life. He was confused and thought the summer respite would be good. Indeed, many hours on horseback probably would provide time to think through his desired course in life.

Given Ben's confusion, I asked him one direct question: "Ben, what is the meaning and purpose of life?" He responded quite truthfully with an answer that probably represents the perspective of the vast majority of young people today. Ben sighed, his shoulders drooped, he shook his head and said, "I don't have any idea." Ben had jumped through all the right hoops up to this point in his life. He was the all-American boy who was about to complete a good college education, had a good relationship with a member of the opposite sex, and had everything to which to look forward. Nevertheless, something was missing! Like my snowboarding friend in Colorado, Ben had the appearance of a person who was confident and happy, but he too yearned for something more.

The Tip of the Iceberg

I believe both Ben Luking and my snowboarding friend are representative of a large portion of society. In many people, probably the majority, there are busy minds, active bodies, and empty spirits. Josh McDowell calls the teenage portion of this group "The

Disconnected Generation."[1] However, teenagers are not the only ones who hold their lives loosely together with a superficial philosophy. Whether it be the subculture of a resort community, the organizational structure of a Fortune 500 company, or simply the daily routine of a marriage that is more functional than meaningful, countless individuals have accepted lifestyles and viewpoints which address few long-term questions and yield little that is eternally valuable. Whether occupied with work, family matters, recreational activities, or just our favorite television show, we seem too busy to address deep issues.

Perhaps our lives are so full of activities that we simply do not take the time to ponder and resolve the critical questions of life. On the other hand, maybe we are so busy because we have brushed upon the questions but have failed to come up with sufficient answers. Conceivably, our excessive activities simply mask our uncertainty and frustration. Maybe many of us have given some thought to the deeper issues of life, yet have only developed tentative, insufficient philosophies that carry us from one day to the next. **The result is a great spiritual vacuum in our culture**. Countless individuals are searching and crying for answers but most remain unfulfilled. Like the two young people I previously described, emptiness is clearly visible on their weary faces.

I believe the road to deeper, richer meaning in life is paved with difficult questions that ultimately cannot be avoided. We must face our fears and uncertainties, seek deeper truth, and convey reliable principles to the next generation. Simply busying ourselves with the affairs of life is not a sufficient response to the deep yearnings of our souls.

The Meaning and Purpose of Life?

I am a professor at a private college where we have classes small enough to allow the professors to get to know each student relatively well. Each semester I encounter a wide array of students who generally fit into a few academic categories. First, there are the students who seem to have a genuine purpose. For whatever reason, something motivates these students to do their best work, gain as much as possible from their college experience, and prepare themselves for future endeavors. Some of these students may be driven by a sense of responsibility, honor, and integrity. Others in this same group may come from backgrounds that have been less than desirable (broken or dysfunctional families), and they have a deep need to prove themselves. It is not easy to discern the motivating factor, but it is easy to identify which students are strongly motivated. They may not always be the students who earn the best grades, but they are clearly dedicated to their work.

The second group of students I encounter are those who want to graduate and make something of their lives but not at the expense of missing out on today's enjoyment. This 'just get by' group always seems to be a large segment. They may be highly capable students, but they generally settle for mediocre grades. They simply lack deep motivation. They tend to focus more on simple, short-term pleasures than on long-term goals.

The third category of students consists of what I refer to as the 'defiant ones.' This group tends to be in open defiance of the status quo. They make up their own rules as they go, rather than abide by the policies that may be established by the college or by a particular professor. Some of these students seem to be peacefully enjoying life and are almost oblivious to the disastrous consequences of their behavior. Others in this group are clearly angry or resentful. The defiant ones often do not last more than a few semesters, but occasionally some of them manage to eke out a degree. The motivating factors behind the students in this group are hard to discern, but the lack of positive motivation is evident.

When I first started teaching, I found it difficult to understand the students in the last two categories. It was clear they only halfheartedly wanted to be in the educational setting. Why were they incurring the high cost of a college education? Why were they investing four years of their life? Why did they not attempt to do their best possible work? The answers to these questions eluded me until I began to look at deeper issues.

A few years ago, I began conducting what I refer to as 'The Meaning and Purpose of Life' tangent. It is one of many tangents I now purposely incorporate into my classes. The tangents tend to stimulate discussions about real-life issues. They have great academic and personal value, even if they are indirectly related to the subject matter of any given course. Alumni tend to remember more from the tangents than they do from the primary course material. In the meaning and purpose of life tangent I simply ask students to anonymously write on one page what they believe to be the meaning and purpose of life. I collect the work, summarize it, and use it as the basis for a subsequent discussion.

Almost universally, the responses can be easily divided into four distinct categories. The category that has historically contained the most responses has been the one that relates to work and career issues. The students state that meaning in life is to be found through one's work and the accomplishments and achievements that accompany the work. They believe they will be remembered for what they have done in life. This category was very popular in the 1980's and early 1990's but has somewhat waned in recent years.

The second popular category relates to relationships and family issues. Since most of the students are single, the responses often mention finding the right person and settling down to have a family. The students perceive that these relationships will provide meaning and purpose in life. Many students seem to have an idealistic hope of finding true love that will fulfill the desires of their hearts.

The third distinct category generally has fewer respondents but is still significant in size. This spiritual group has been steadily increasing in size in recent years. This group mentions some aspect of a relationship with God as the source of meaning and purpose. The members of this group often vary greatly in their perception of what it means to relate to God, but the central theme is still the same.

The fourth category that is usually significant in size includes the group of students who admit they genuinely have no idea what life is about. I call this group the 'honest ones.' They are just like my young friend, Ben Luking, whom I mentioned earlier. They are intellectually astute people who are on paths toward significant careers, but they have no real comprehension of the deepest essence of life.

I began using the meaning and purpose of life tangent because I sensed an emptiness in most of the students, and I wanted to do something to stimulate discussion about some of life's deeper issues. These discussions are often the highlights of the semester. Unfortunately, our discussions almost always reveal an even greater sense of emptiness and uncertainty than was present in the written responses. We discuss real statistics that relate to the categories. For example, only about one-half of all workers across the United States indicate they are satisfied with their jobs.[2] Many, if not most, would rather be doing something different. Then there are the sad statistics which indicate that one-third of all marriages in the United States dissolve within ten years and approximately 50 percent end in divorce within 20 years.[3] If meaning and purpose in life are to be found primarily in work or relationships, then the majority of people are disappointed, confused, and frustrated. Our discussions about the category relating to God also reveal uncertainty. Many of the students have some measure of faith but most have little depth in their understanding of God. It is clear that many are riding the tide of their parent's faith. With some obvious exceptions, most have not yet developed a personal understanding of God.

The end result of our discussions is that a lot more students end up in the category of those who admit they genuinely have no idea about the meaning of life. Their written responses had often included what they hope will provide meaning, but they maintain no real confidence in their responses. While the late-teen to early-twenties years are often times of uncertainty, it is grievous that so many young people traverse through this season of life with no real sense of purpose, meaning, and direction.

Over the years of conducting the tangent and working with students and other persons in various settings, I have come to one rather disturbing conclusion: **Most of the people in our society are genuinely unsure about the purpose of their existence and the meaning of their lives.** Most fit in the 'honest ones' category of those who admit they are clueless. This sad fact is particularly true among the younger generations. They are suffering from inadequate leadership. They may have received sophisticated educational training and been exposed to many technological marvels, but they lack depth. Like the people described in II Timothy 3:7, they are "always learning but never able to acknowledge the truth."

They are desperately in need of the type of leadership that imparts wisdom and nurtures their souls.

The apparent emptiness of most students sheds much light on their academic performance. As I look back over the academic categories, it becomes much easier to understand the students who fall in the 'just get by' and 'defiant ones' categories. On the whole, they do not have a sufficient understanding of the purpose of their existence, and as a result, they lack sincere motivation to make something more meaningful come from what seems like a meaningless endeavor. In other words, they have no sense of purpose and no personal goals; therefore, they are mostly treading water.

As the years pass, it seems that each class of students is a tad more unsure, a bit emptier, and a little more lost than the previous group. In addition, they are an increasingly angry lot of people. Of course, there are periodically bright spots—students who appear to have a clear sense of purpose and who encourage their peers. Nonetheless, we have nearly an entire generation of young people (and probably an equally large number of older adults) who are crying for answers. Unfortunately, many people do not have answers, and many are not even sure what constitutes the appropriate questions.

Philosophies of Life

Various philosophies of life attempt to show humankind the pathway to meaning and purpose. There have always existed certain generally accepted modes of behavior that have dominated every generation. For example, some people have always expected to find meaning through achievements, the accumulation of wealth, or the acquisition of power. In addition, there are a large number of religions that have attempted to show the way to meaning by providing doctrines about beliefs and behaviors.

Whether by conscious choice or by default, we are all abiding by one or more of these philosophies. Our chosen beliefs and resulting behaviors become our own personal religions. Even the atheist has accepted a philosophy that carries with it certain beliefs that inevitably affect the choices he or she makes in life. The very ideas and behaviors of denying or avoiding God become a religious philosophy in and of themselves.

Popular ideology in today's world is to accept all philosophies as being right for the given individual. That is, you believe what you desire to believe and I will have my own beliefs. As long as we do not tread on one another's sacred ground, we can all be happy. It is the postmodern doctrine of tolerance. Unfortunately, this view is a hopeless, utopian approach to life. Certainly, not all of the secular and religious philosophies of the world can be equally true. In fact, many are in direct opposition to one another on the most basic of issues. For example, Christianity claims that Jesus is divine—that He is God, whereas Islam merely acknowledges Jesus as a teacher and prophet but certainly not divine. It is therefore imperative that thinking individuals address the critical questions of life in order to discern the truth from among all the various possibilities.

Life's Great Questions

The first great question of life is simple but crucial: ***Is there a God?*** All the world's endeavors hinge upon this one great question. If there is no God, then life is simply what we can observe. The only purpose of human existence is being fulfilled in our daily activities. There is no reason to believe that our decisions have significance beyond the present. If the answer to the first question is no, then perhaps all other questions are moot. However, if the answer to the first question is yes, life takes on a much different flavor. For if there is, in fact, a God, then every moment of our current lives has purpose and eternal value. The decisions we make, our modes of behavior, and the least of our words and thoughts are of immeasurable significance.

There are three basic positions with regard to the first question: 1) theism, 2) atheism, and 3) agnosticism. Theism is a belief in a God or gods in some form. Atheism is a belief that there is no God. Agnosticism is a "belief that there can be no proof either that God exists or that God does not exist."[4]

The vast majority of the world's population is theistic. Christians (Catholics and Protestants together) constitute the largest single theistic group, representing about one-third (33%) of the world's population. Muslims are the second largest group, accounting for almost one-fifth (19.6%) of humanity. Hindus and Buddhists taken together also represent about one-fifth (19.3%) of the populace. Nonreligious persons (non-practicing theists, atheists, agnostics, etc.) constitute 12.7% of the world's citizens. Chinese folk-religionists account for 6.4% of the world's inhabitants, but no other single religious sect accounts for as much as four percent of the world's population. Judaism represents less than one percent (.2%) of the world's total population, but it has played a prominent role in world history.[5]

For those who conclude there is no God, the only questions they face are those that revolve around how they may choose to expend their lives. The questions are purely humanistic in nature. However, those who maintain a theistic perspective face additional questions of life that extend beyond their individual existence. For such persons, the second great question of life is: ***Who is God?*** Surely, if there is a God and He has significant responsibility for our very existence, then it must be possible to know about this God to some extent. Furthermore, it may be possible not only to know about God but also to know Him personally. The third critical question of life is a logical extension of the second. If there is a God and if He can be known, then the third question is simply: ***Do I know God?*** Depending upon how one responds to this question, he or she might also ask: ***How can I know God?***

Major World Religions

It is beyond the scope of this book to compare and contrast all of the religions and philosophies of the world. However, if we look at Hinduism, Buddhism, Islam, and Christianity, we encompass the primary religious beliefs of the majority (nearly 72%) of the world's population. Let us take a brief look at the basic tenets and contrasting points of these major religions.

Hinduism: Hinduism is a complex, polytheistic religion in which participants worship one, a few, or many gods (or none at all) and fashion for themselves an individual style of worship.[6] The key tenets of Hinduism are *karma* and *reincarnation*. Karma is the accumulation of good or bad that results from one's life. By doing good works a person develops good karma, but bad deeds lead to karma demerits. Hindus believe karma attaches to their souls and determines their state of existence in the next life. Reincarnation provides Hindu believers with multiple opportunities to develop good karma as they work through each life and ascend to higher planes of existence.[7]

According to Hindu teachings, there are four legitimate ends to human life: 1) righteousness (*dharma*), 2) material success (*artha*), 3) love or pleasure (*kama*), and 4) emancipation (*moksha*).[8] Dharma is obtained by adhering to the moral law and developing moral virtue. Artha may not only mean economic success but also political success. Kama is the Indian god of love and reflects an emphasis upon sex as a human good. Moksha is the ultimate or supreme goal of Hindus. It is release from the reincarnation cycle and deliverance from the human condition. According to Hindu beliefs, Moksha yields an existence that is far beyond human understanding. There are three paths to moksha: 1) personal devotion, 2) works, and 3) knowledge.[9]

Hindus believe there are many paths to the same goal. Thus, God, god-likeness, or divine realization can be found through many religious experiences.[10] This is why Hindus are open to borrowing practices from other religions as a part of their own experience. Nonetheless, the core of Hinduism still rests upon the responsibility of the individual to work to accumulate good karma and thus determine his or her fate by means of personal actions.

Buddhism: Buddhism was born in Hinduism, but Buddha rejected some of the tenets of Hinduism, particularly the idea that a person's spiritual journey is a predetermined matter of birth. Buddha believed a person from any caste could reach the ultimate goal (*nirvana*) in a single lifetime, rather than going through a series of reincarnated states as required in Hinduism.[11] Like Hindus, Buddhists believe that actions lead to good or bad karma, which determines one's reincarnated state. Ultimately, when individuals have accumulated sufficiently good karma, they reach nirvana—a transformed mode of human consciousness in the eternal realm.[12]

Buddha professed that human suffering is the outcome of past bad karma, which resulted from wrongful cravings or actions. The way to overcome bad karma is through dharma, which in Buddhism incorporates truth, law, and right thoughts and actions.[13] The pathway to achieving right thoughts and actions includes wisdom, ethics, and mental discipline.[14] Buddhism is both a polytheistic and atheistic religion because it allows for worship of many gods but does not emphasize their significance in the road to nirvana. It is a highly humanistic religion because of its emphasis upon personal actions that yield nirvana.[15]

Monotheism: Unlike Hinduism and Buddhism, which are polytheistic religions, Christianity and Islam are monotheistic because they both speak of belief in one God. Both Christianity and Islam maintain that God created the world and that He created the first human being, named Adam, whose descendants included Noah, Shem, and Abraham.[16] Christians, Jews, and Muslims all trace their heritage to Abraham, the Old Testament patriarch of Israel. However, Christians and Jews establish the heritage through Abraham's son, Isaac, who was born to Sarah, whereas Muslims trace the lineage via Ishmael, the son of Abraham born to Hagar.[17]

Islam: Muhammad initiated Islam between 560 and 632 A.D. Its roots in Judaism and Christianity are revealed by the fact that Islam incorporates aspects of both the Hebrew Old Testament and Christian New Testament.[18] However, Muhammad argued that the Hebrew and Christian Bibles had become distorted. Therefore, he wrote the *Koran*, which purported to contain the perfected scriptures.[19] Islam teaches that God, known to Muslims as *Allah*, has provided humanity with the means to know good from evil through the prophets and the *Koran*. Therefore, on the impending judgment day people will be held accountable for their actions.[20] There are "five pillars of Islam," which are: 1) pronouncing a confession of faith in *Allah*, 2) performing the five daily prayers, 3) fasting during the month of Ramadan, 4) paying the alms tax, and 5) performing, at least once in life, the major pilgrimage to Mecca.[21]

Christianity: Christian faith primarily focuses upon the life, death, and resurrection of Jesus Christ. In fact, the dividing point between Christianity, Islam, and other religions is the very nature of

Jesus Himself. The historical authenticity of Jesus is well established, not only by evidence within Christianity but also by independent sources.[22] The great debates of history do not regard the validity of Jesus' existence; rather, they concern His divinity. Islam accepts the life and teachings of Jesus, but denies His divinity by denying the doctrines of the Incarnation and the Trinity.[23] Jesus is seen as a prophet and good teacher within the beliefs of Islam. Likewise, Judaism denies the divinity of Jesus. While the heritage of Christianity is traced through the Old Testament scriptures of Judaism, most Jews are still looking for a messiah (deliverer) to fulfill the Old Testament prophecies. Hindus and Buddhists might simply see Jesus as a good teacher or one among many gods. They would not see Him as the atoning sacrifice for the sins of all humankind.

Only Christians (including Messianic Jews) believe that Jesus was and is the Messiah prophesied in the Old Testament. According to Christianity, His virgin birth and bodily resurrection from the dead affirm Jesus' messianic role and His divine nature. Unlike Hinduism, Buddhism, and Islam, which place the burden of performance on the individual, Christians believe that salvation and eternal life are gifts of grace provided by God through Jesus. Christians believe that Jesus' crucifixion served as the atonement for all sin and the substitution for the death that each person deserves as a consequence of his or her personal sin. Therefore, the gifts of salvation and eternal life in heaven are received by professing faith in Christ.

Answers to Life's Questions

Most of the world's religions and philosophies focus on what humankind must do to ascend to higher levels. The emphasis is upon personal achievement, self-improvement, and/or self-induced righteousness. Whether it be self-actualization, personal fulfillment, entrance into heaven, or finding inner peace, most theories place the burden of finding true meaning and purpose squarely on the shoulders of each man and woman. **There is only one philosophy of life that places the burden of each human being's current and future destiny not on the individual but upon God Himself.** It is the only approach that provides a coherent and sufficient understanding of the entire process of life. **Fundamentally, all of the answers to life are to be found in *genuine* Christianity**. I emphasize the word genuine because there have been many forms of Christian thought and practice, not all of which have been faithful to the life and teachings of Jesus. In many cases, human beings have contrived rules and regulations that are purportedly Christian but that really profane the truths of Christianity. For example, the medieval church sold "indulgences" to sinners so they could buy "satisfaction" for their sins.[24] Furthermore, many endeavors have been undertaken in the name of Christianity that have clearly been outside of the will of God (e.g., anti-Semitism and slavery).

Ultimately, the responses to the great questions of life boil down to two basic philosophical positions. The first possibility is that through their own volition human beings can achieve rightness with God, assimilation with the gods, or a god-like state. This is the position of Hinduism, Buddhism, Islam, and every other significant religion of the world, except Christianity. The second position is that human beings are helpless to rectify their situation. They are mired in their own sinfulness, incapable of rectifying their lives and approaching God's nature. Therefore, they are dependent upon God to rescue them from the bondage of their existence. Only Christianity adheres to the latter position. Because of the unique proclamation of Christianity, I am convinced that any person who seeks the truth with an open heart and mind will ultimately be drawn by the Spirit of God to recognize the divinity of Jesus and the reality of Christianity. There the individual will find conclusive answers to the great questions of life:

Yes, there is a God. "For since the creation of the world God's invisible qualities—His eternal power and divine nature—have been clearly seen, being understood from what has been made, so that men are without excuse" (Romans 1:20).

His name is Jesus. Anyone who genuinely searches for God will ultimately come to Jesus. Jesus is not just part of God; He is fully God in His being. "For in Christ all the fullness of the Deity lives in bodily form" (Colossians 2:9).

He can be known. "The Jews gathered around Him, saying, 'How long will you keep us in suspense? If you are the Christ, tell us plainly.' Jesus answered, 'I did tell you, but you do not believe. The miracles I do in my Father's name speak for me, but you do not believe because you are not my sheep. **My sheep listen to my voice; I know them, and they follow me.** I give them eternal life, and they shall never perish; no one can snatch them out of my hand. My Father, who has given them to me, is greater than all; no one can snatch them out of my Father's hand. I and the Father are one' " (John 10:24-30).

Conclusion

Perhaps our greatest failure as a society is our lost comprehension of the real truths of Christianity. In many western nations, especially in the United States, Christianity flourished among our ancestors. However, within the turbulent pace of our contemporary world we have managed to displace truth with hedonism and materialism. Consequently, the whole purpose of this book is to set forth basic principles that are drawn from the tenets of Christianity. The principles are not really new; in fact, they are ageless. Nevertheless, they have become muddled in today's culture. Therefore, they need to be revisited with a fresh, invigorated perspective.

Chapter 2

The Reality of Death

Dick and Berniece were a wonderful couple—pillars of the church we attended together. They had retired from regular, full-time employment but made very productive use of their time. They were usually present for most of the events held at the church. They attended Bible studies, participated in various programs, and even served as leaders of the church's evangelism program. Moreover, Dick and Berniece were the church members who were most actively involved in visiting people in their homes, at the hospital, or wherever God might lead the couple. Whenever the pastor needed someone to make a special visit, he would call Dick and Berniece. Dick was a warm, kind gentleman who could develop a friendly conversation with almost anybody. He had the ability to convey love by simply shaking your hand. Berniece tended to be more quiet, but she always shared a warm smile. I rarely saw Dick without Berniece and vice versa; they were truly a unified couple.

One Saturday afternoon Berniece and a relative decided to go on a brief shopping trip to a nearby store. She and Dick were planning to go to the church that evening to participate in a prayer vigil in support of a special speaker who was coming to the church. Consequently, she planned to be gone only a short while and then return home to prepare dinner. When she got ready to leave, Dick was seated at a table reading. He loved to read anything that would help him gain greater understanding of the Lord. Berniece kissed him and left for the shopping trip.

When Berniece returned home, she noticed that Dick's bicycle was not in the garage. He often went for a bike ride as a means of exercising and relaxing. Berniece set about preparing a simple meal and awaited Dick's return so they could eat. She did not begin to worry until she realized it was approaching the time to leave for the church. Surely Dick would remember the time and return home soon. A little while later a neighbor stopped by and indicated he had heard that emergency personnel had been called to care for someone who had apparently had a heart attack along the roadside only a couple of miles from Berniece's house. Worry turned to fear for Berniece. Sometime later, another gentleman knocked on Berniece's door; she recognized him as a detective who worked for the local police department. He asked Berniece for a picture of her husband. After looking at the picture, he indicated he had difficult news to share. Dick apparently had a heart attack while bicycling, and he had collapsed alongside the road. Despite the efforts of rescue personnel, he never regained consciousness and was pronounced dead at the emergency room of the local hospital.

In the brief span of an afternoon, Berniece's world was shattered. Dick had been a good husband; he was the desire of Berniece's heart. Suddenly he was gone. It seemed impossible. Berniece was overwhelmed by all the pain of being separated from Dick for the rest of this life. She seemed in shock at first, but after a few days, the reality of her loss began to set in. She had friends and family who helped all they could, but no one could offset the agony.

The Question of Meaning

Despite the lightning-fast pace of modern life, one event continuously brings us back to the question of meaning. The perplexing event is death. Death places everyone, regardless of position, status, wealth, or stature on the same plane. Since death itself is the most striking aspect of life, any philosophy that ignores the issue of death is by definition incomplete. Finding deeper, richer meaning in life begins with developing a sufficient understanding of death.

From our perspectives, it is hard to imagine a world in which there would be no threat of death. However, just consider for a moment what it would be like to live in a world that did not possess that possibility. Certainly, many aspects of life would be much different and probably much simpler. Given the typical desires of humanity, it would be reasonable to assume that most people would live life with the purpose of continually improving their respective positions. That is, we would naturally tend to work to improve our family, home, career—our lot in life. For whatever we acquired and improved, we would retain forever, unless we chose to convey it to someone else. Life would be a never-ending process of growth and expansion.

Many of us do live just as if death will never come. We pretend to have a 'forever of tomorrows' to alter our circumstances, or to face life's difficult questions. Perhaps that perspective results from the fact that God has "set eternity in the hearts of men" (Ecclesiastes 3:12). Nevertheless, death does stare us unremittingly in the face. The life of every living organism seems to follow a consistent pattern: beginning, development, growth, maturity, decline, and ultimately death. This life cycle may differ greatly in duration for each organism, but it is nonetheless a constant for all. Therefore, the question naturally arises: ***Does it make sense to live this life as if there is no death?*** Should we simply push the thought from our consciousness and eat, drink, and be merry? Or is it wiser to keep the realization in the back of our minds as we contemplate the true value of the endeavors we undertake? Perhaps a genuine understanding of death is the prerequisite to true life. My argument is simple: **Until a man or woman is prepared to face death, he or she is not truly prepared to live**.

We Know Not When

On a quiet Saturday afternoon several years ago, I was busy doing a few simple chores around my home. The doorbell rang and I found a tall, handsome gentleman wearing a priest's collar standing at the front door. He looked harmless enough, so I invited him in for a visit. Identifying himself as Darrell Golnitz, he explained that he was a Lutheran priest who lived a short distance from my home. He was simply going door to door trying to meet his neighbors and inviting them to visit his church.

Something about this man was different. He looked physically strong and yet kind and warm. He seemed genuinely interested in me. While he may have been no different from many other empathetic people, I knew that deep in this man's spirit he was special. We began a conversation that lasted much of the afternoon. I explained about the difficulties of my own life, which had brought me to the point of searching for God. He shared some of his insights into the nature of God and some of his personal experiences. What he did not know was that I was still wrestling with some of the wounds of my pre-Christian life, and talking with him was very helpful. He apparently found me a bit intriguing. He rarely had the opportunity to talk in depth with someone who had become a Christian as an adult. Most of his parishioners had been in the church most of their lives. They had generally gone through the formal procedures of the church to learn about and profess Christianity. For him it was a unique opportunity to learn how God's Spirit could draw a young man into His kingdom. We parted company, but we both knew that God had a special purpose in this meeting.

I did not talk with Darrell for quite some time after that day, but I did become aware of the location of his home. It was clearly visible from the road I traveled each weekday to and from work. During the next couple of years, I from time to time uttered a short prayer for Darrell when I passed his home or when I happened to encounter him in our community.

My prayers for Darrell and his family quickly took on a new intensity when I learned that Darrell's 13-year-old son, Darren, had been diagnosed with a rare type of cancer. Every day when I passed the Golnitz home, I prayed for Darren's healing. Often my heart was stirred with empathy for the family, and I would be in tears by the time I finished praying. I truly expected that God would bring about a miracle and the young boy would recover.

During the following months, I heard various reports about

Darren's condition. He apparently had a very positive approach to the situation and remained active in a number of fun activities despite undergoing chemotherapy. A little more than four months after the diagnosis Darren underwent an extensive surgery that removed the primary tumor. The family and community of supporters were very hopeful. However, hope was put to the ultimate test just a few weeks later when the family learned that additional tumors had invaded his pleural cavity and it was filling up with fluid.

Dream Makers, an organization that helps dreams come true for persons who are suffering, made it possible for Darren and his family to attend the World Series of Major League Baseball in California. The five of them (Darren, dad, mom, brother and sister) had a wonderful journey. Darren received special treatment from some of the baseball players and enjoyed seeing the Golden Gate Bridge and the Pacific Ocean.

Nevertheless, two days after his return from the World Series, Darren died. He said goodbye to his family members and fell into a peaceful sleep in his mother's arms. Despite the prayers of many in our community who had come to know and love the Golnitz family, Darren died before reaching his fourteenth birthday. It had only been about six months since his diagnosis.

The pain of the Golnitz family was shared by many of their friends, Darren's classmates, and churches in the area. Perhaps the deepest pain was born by Darrell. Here he was a Lutheran Priest—a man of faith. He was supposed to lead others to know and trust God, but could he still trust? Where had God been in this situation? How could something like this happen . . . why did it happen?

The Why Question

To gain a proper understanding and acceptance of death, we must begin by addressing the 'why' question. We must satisfactorily deal with the question: ***Why does death even exist?*** This is perhaps the most perplexing question in the entire human experience. Theories that attempt to explain the existence of death may derive from a rational perspective or from supernatural explanations. Whatever the case, developing an understanding of this most daunting question is essential to gaining a trustworthy perspective on life itself.

It would be natural to seek an explanation through some scientific insight into the physiological changes that take place in the body and lead to death. In fact, a 1981 Presidential Commission addressed this question and concluded that death occurs when there is: 1) irreversible cessation of respiratory and circulatory functions and/or 2) irreversible cessation of brain activity.[1] However, such definitions only look at the physiological consequences of death. Science is rather limited in its ability to explain the existence of death as a known reality for all creatures. Certainly, science can explain how certain diseases or injuries adversely affect the body and how these factors lead to the cessation of normal bodily functions. Nonetheless, medical science is often unable to define the reasoning behind the development of certain ailments.

While progress is being made in understanding various physiological issues, medical science is only capable of deferring, not eliminating, death. According to Dr. Jack McConnell, former Corporate Director of Advanced Technology at Johnson & Johnson, some of the most advanced genetic research currently underway has the potential to make incredible breakthroughs that will lead to substantially longer life spans and remarkably healthier lives. Even so, the most hopeful of these advances still falls short of being able to eliminate death. There seems to be some mysterious, incomprehensible aspect of life that ultimately leads to death.[2]

The inability of science to fully understand death is due to the fact that the ultimate cause of death is not physical: it is spiritual. Science, as we know it, is not capable of analyzing the spiritual realm with any significant insight. In order to understand the ailment that leads to death, we must move to a higher plane of wisdom and understanding.

Not only must we move from the physical realm to the spiritual realm to understand death, but we must also set aside our preconceived notions about cause-and-effect, fairness, and even meaningfulness. There may be natural spiritual laws that are as reliable as the physical laws of nature, but they do not necessarily follow the same dimensions of logic. Consider the following situation, which occurred during Jesus' life on Earth:

> As He [Jesus] went along, He saw a man blind from birth. His disciples asked Him, "Rabbi, who sinned, this man or his parents, that he was born blind?"
>
> "Neither this man nor his parents sinned," said Jesus, "but this happened so that the work of God might be displayed in his life. . . ."
>
> Having said this, He spit on the ground, made some mud with the saliva, and put it on the man's eyes. "Go," He told him, "wash in the Pool of Siloam." So the man went and washed, and came home seeing. (John 9:1-3,6-7)

Interestingly, when the disciples first saw the man, their response was to ask who sinned to cause the blindness. They applied the rational law of cause-and-effect and concluded that someone's sin was responsible for the impairment. However, Jesus made it clear that no one's specific sin caused the situation. Rather, the person was born into a world filled with many calamities, and the man was allowed to suffer this difficulty so that the glory of God might be displayed through his life. This response did not make sense in the physical realm, but through Jesus' spiritual eyes, it was clearly understandable.

Humans have a great need to make sense out of what is very difficult to understand. If we cannot formulate some reasonably logical explanation, the stress of the unknown and inexplicable becomes overwhelming. Consequently, our tendency is to develop cause-and-effect conclusions about situations when in fact a causal relationship may not exist.

When a person who is older in years dies, we find it somewhat easier to accept his or her death. We can review the person's life and note the many contributions made to society. We surmise in our minds that there was meaning in the person's life and somehow dying at an old age after an active life carries with it some measure of fairness and completeness. The loss is still painful, but at least we can develop some measure of understanding about the situation. However, when a young person dies or when a young person suffers some severely debilitating ailment, we are left without understanding. **The real problem is that our logical, rational approach to life is insufficient to fully explain the death of anyone at any age**. Death of an older person may be somewhat easier to accept, but it is no more logical than the death of an infant. For approximately the last 200 years, western civilization has been dominated by modern, scientific thought. Such rational influences have yielded enormous technological advances, both good (transportation and communication) and bad (armaments and weapons of mass destruction). However, understanding the critical issues in life, such as death, requires not only rational thought but also supernatural, spiritual insight.

Spiritual Understanding

About five months after Darren Golnitz died, I participated in a weekend retreat called a Walk to Emmaus with approximately 50 other men. It was a spiritual retreat in which we spent three days in study, prayer, fellowship, and fun. I was asked to be one of several leaders of the event and was appointed to present to the group a teaching entitled 'The Body of Christ.' Unbeknownst to me, Darrell Golnitz was scheduled to be on the retreat. He had been invited to participate in such a weekend at a previous time but had to cancel because of the death of his son. Darrell was not part of the leadership of this particular event. Instead, he came to receive whatever God might have in store for him at this juncture in his life.

As the weekend unfolded, most of my attention and prayers were focused on Darrell. He was obviously very distraught. That strong, handsome gentleman who had appeared at my front door a few years earlier now looked weak, withered, and deeply wounded. I had prepared an outline for my teaching. Nonetheless, as the time approached for me to speak, I continually found myself being drawn to Darrell, and I believed the Lord was giving me a completely new set of ideas about what to say.

I began the talk as I had originally planned, but I soon began to allow the Spirit of God to take me in another direction. I told the men about the time this priestly looking fellow showed up at my front door and how that afternoon I told this complete stranger my life story. I described some of the difficulties of my own life and talked about what a wonderful difference God had made. I did not understand all the difficulties that I had gone through, but I certainly could see how God was in the process of taking the rubble and ashes of my life and turning them into gold and silver. I spoke about how God had blessed me through a certain priest (Darrell Golnitz), who had appeared out of nowhere. I indicated that the priest had been the 'Body of Christ' to me.

Subsequently, I explained how I became aware of the condition of Darrell's son and how God had called me to pray diligently for this young man. Until this particular day, Darrell had been unaware of my concern for his family during their most difficult of periods. The mood of the whole group was very somber as I talked about the time preceding and following the death of Darrell's son.

I concluded the talk by referring to a special section of the Bible. I believed the Lord had directed me to this scripture in order that I might deliver it directly to Darrell. It was from chapter 38 of Job. Up to that point in the book, Job had suffered great personal losses, including financial ruin, the death of family members, and the loss of his health. Two basic discussions had been taking place in the book of Job. First, Job's friends had been telling him about all the cause-and-effect reasons why he was suffering so severely. Meanwhile, Job kept declaring his righteousness before God and requesting an audience before the Almighty. Finally, in chapter 38 we find God Himself speaking to Job. Portions of His statements are as follows: "Who is this that darkens my counsel with words without knowledge? . . . Where were you when I laid the earth's foundation? Tell me, if you understand. . . . Have the gates of death been shown to you? Have you seen the gates of the shadow of death? . . . Do you know the laws of the heavens? Can you set up God's dominion over the earth?" (Job 38:2, 4, 17, 33).

God's reply is not so much a harsh rebuke to Job as it is a loving declaration of His omnipotence. He is fully aware of Job's situation. God did not bring the condition upon Job to punish him for his sin. Nor could Job vindicate himself by his own righteousness and thus alleviate the difficulties of his circumstances. Rather, God had permitted Satan to attack Job in order that higher spiritual purposes might be accomplished. It was God's intention that through suffering Job would come to understand the nature of life and the character of God more clearly. **Before Job's suffering took place, he *knew about God*, but through this process, he had come to *know God*.** There is a tremendous difference!

Eventually, Job replied to God, "I know that you can do all things; no plan of yours can be thwarted. You asked, 'Who is this that obscures my counsel without knowledge?' Surely I spoke of things I did not understand, things too wonderful for me to know. You said, 'Listen now, and I will speak; I will question you, and you shall answer me.' My ears had heard of you but now my eyes have seen you. Therefore I despise myself and repent in dust and ashes" (Job 42:2-6).

Job's suffering transformed him. Before his time of great suffering, Job lived an upright life, but he was not without sin. Job's understanding of the true nature of God was limited. Through his suffering he came to understand and trust God in a deeper, more complete way. Furthermore, he came to recognize that he lacked the righteousness he thought he had possessed. He came to despise himself and repent of his melancholy words.

Darrell Golnitz received with a tender heart the words God had given me to speak. Somehow, God had spoken directly to the deepest recesses of his soul. Immediately after the talk, Darrell returned with me to our prayer chapel where we cried and prayed together. Darrell and I had additional conversations at various points throughout the weekend, but I did not try to relay words of wisdom. I just tried to comfort him and reassure Darrell that God still had His eyes and hands on the Golnitz family. My role was simply to be a vessel of encouragement. Primarily, it was the Spirit of God who was ministering to Darrell and giving him renewed faith and hope.

God's ways are certainly not our ways: "For my thoughts are not your thoughts, neither are your ways my ways, declares the LORD. As the heavens are higher than the earth, so are my ways higher than your ways and my thoughts than your thoughts" (Isaiah 55:8-9). He did not allow Job to suffer for rational reasons but rather to accomplish a more important spiritual purpose. He did not allow Darren Golnitz to die purposelessly. Rather, God is continuing to accomplish for many people His higher spiritual purposes through both circumstances. In fact, during that Walk to Emmaus weekend God laid a new cornerstone in Darrell's life. God renewed his hope and began a new process of bringing eternal meaning and purpose out of the events of his life.

Our Interdependency

In order to gain some level of wisdom and insight into God's ways, we must recognize that we are interdependent, not independent, people. God is not simply working to accomplish His ultimate purpose in our individual life; rather, He is operating simultaneously in the lives of everyone. It is impossible for us to understand all the ramifications of the events of our days for the lives of other people. Nonetheless, they are very profound.

Berniece, whose situation I described earlier, is still a widow, and she must struggle with the difficulties of loneliness and solitude. Yet God daily works in and through her. He is transforming her into the complete person He desires her to be.

The Golnitz family will always miss an important member of their family while they remain on this earth. Yet Darren's life story is not complete. God continually uses Darren's life and death in and through the Golnitz family to accomplish eternal purposes of immeasurable worth.

There must be a 'why' to what God is doing. He must have higher goals than we can rationally and easily comprehend. Yes, we must ask: *Why does death occur?* Nevertheless, to understand its existence we must gain wisdom. We must develop the ability to see the world and life with spiritual eyes. We must gain God's perspective on life and His viewpoint regarding death.

Chapter 3

Our Ailment

⌐ ⌒ ⌐ ⌐

Fundamentally, we are born with a condition that is worse than any common illness. It is more devastating than cancer, heart disease, or any other known ailment. It is so serious that it is always life threatening and leads to death in one hundred percent of the diagnosed cases. It may seem unfair or unjust that we are born with such a condition, since we had no choice in the matter. Yet the truth is still evident. But what is the disease, can it be detected early and treated before it reaches its advanced stages, and most importantly, is there a cure? The answers are both yes and no. Yes, it can be detected early and treatment can lessen the symptoms and effects of the disease, but sadly, there is no known cure. Inevitably, in every case it leads to death; there is no escape.

The disease seems tough to diagnose, yet everyone who is afflicted—which includes everyone—is vaguely aware of the existence of the ailment. It is not purely a physical disease, although the symptoms of the disease can be seen in the body. It is not purely a mental ailment, yet the disease certainly affects the mind. The origin of the disease and its resident position is in the human *will*. The disease is . . . *sin*.

The question naturally arises: **What is sin?** Essentially, it is a condition that dwells in the mysterious recesses of the soul of each person. Sin results from the desire to set oneself above God. It is an attempt to live apart from God and outside His perfect will. It is a desire to be the master of our own fate, the controller of our own destiny, ruler of our own world. Sin is not just an action; it is a spiritual condition that inhabits the core of humans. It is an integral part of our very nature. **The sin nature of human beings predetermines death of the human spirit and leads to death of the human body**. The Apostle Paul referred to this circumstance in Romans 5:12: "sin entered the world through one man, and **death through sin**, and in this way **death came to all men, because all sinned**."

Had sin never entered this world, there would be no such thing as death. Unfortunately, sin opened the eyes of human beings to the reality of evil. As a consequence, our souls are attracted to thoughts and behaviors that are unholy and ultimately self-destructive. From God's perspective, it was necessary to pronounce judgment upon the sin nature of human beings: "And the LORD God said, 'The man has now become like one of us, knowing good and evil. He must not be allowed to reach out his hand and take also from the tree of life and eat, and live forever'" (Genesis 3:22).

Real Freedom

In creating humans, God set out to create beings in His image—beings with whom He could have fellowship. He desired to express love and have those He created love Him in return. God's desire was and is for unconditional, pure love. Such love can only exist in the context of freedom. Therefore, freedom is a natural law that flows from love.

If created humans were to be truly free, they had to be free to the extent that each could refuse or reject relationship with God. Therefore, because of His love nature, God chose to set humans free. God's ultimate divine plan for all creation will be fulfilled (He never lost His omnipotence). Nonetheless, within the confines of the completion of His ultimate will, humans have freedom. This freedom resides in the will of each individual.

Sin could not exist in humankind if it were not for freedom of the will. That is, if men and women were mere puppets of God, it would be impossible for them to sin. Their will would be absolutely determined by God. However, God in His infinite wisdom chose to create humans in His own image.[1] In so doing, He gave them the capacity to love. True unconditional love (*agapê* love) can only exist in the context of freedom. Therefore, in creating the condition whereby humans could express the highest form of love, God inevitably created the possibility that they could sin. God foreknew that sin would result under this condition, but His love and eternal purposes were of greater significance. That is, He desired to create beings He could love and who could love Him in return. To accomplish this eternal goal, He had to release the will of humankind to freedom. He knew the costs, but His eternal purposes will be accomplished despite the difficulties that result from sin.

Certainly, God is sovereign over the entire world. However, in His perfect wisdom and love, He has chosen not to control the will of humankind. In reality, human beings can control little in their lives other than their wills. We did not determine when we were born, and we have little influence over when we will die. The family, economic conditions, social position, even the location we were born into were totally out of our control. Yet these beginning circumstances largely influence, if not dictate, the course of our respective lives. We may undertake many endeavors that are designed to overcome our circumstances, but we find as soon as we conquer one aspect of life another part spirals out of control. We live in a constantly changing world in which it is difficult to maintain complete and absolute control over our lives for even a single day. We admire persons who ascend to high positions in any given field because it appears that from their lofty perch they are in control of their lives. However, the ability to control life is fleeting. Power and wealth can only sustain a temporary hiatus from the complexities of life. Regardless of our status, we are not immune to the difficulties related to interpersonal relationships, aging, health problems, and a host of other challenging circumstances.

Despite an inability to control our outward circumstances, and perhaps even our own bodies, we always remain in control of our will. We are like the little boy who was told to sit down by his teacher. He did sit but stated that in his heart he was still standing. We too may be physically sitting but our wills may remain in the standing position. People who have faced great physical and mental persecutions have been able to persevere by resolving in their own will not to capitulate to their oppressors. The will of humankind is so strong because God has granted absolute freedom in this arena. Therefore, it is in the will where a person chooses to accept or reject God.

People the world over cherish freedom. Something in all our souls yearns to be truly free. But what is freedom? Is it license to do anything our hearts desire? Is it freedom from the demands of life, such as the periodic drudgery of work? Is it the opportunity to indulge our greatest passions or the ability to pursue personal happiness to its utmost degree?

Unfortunately, most of us perceive freedom as the ability to do whatever we desire. Yet it is this freedom to do whatever we desire that is the core of our problem. The will left uncontrolled naturally gravitates toward sin. Every person is born with not only the capacity to sin but also the propensity to sin. We are born with a *sin nature*. The sin nature is simply the inclination of every human being to disobey the holy, righteous, and perfect will of God.

The sin nature is an inherited condition. Just as some professional athletes have inherited exceptional physical characteristics from their parents (e.g., Bobby Bonds and Barry Bonds), we all have inherited the sin nature. We freely participate in and affirm the condition. Had we been born without this condition, we would have quickly created it. We are not innocent, for we have all confirmed the sin nature by our own cooperative volition. The question is not if we will sin but when and to what extent.

Given the freedom that God has granted to the will of each person and the propensity of each person to attempt to live apart from God, the inevitable consequence is "bondage of the will."[2] That is, rather than experiencing true freedom in which we love unconditionally, we become slaves to our own desires and passions. We seek to find love, meaning, and purpose in our lives through other people, in things we acquire, or through feats we achieve. We undertake a self-centered journey to satisfy our senses but eventually find only boredom and emptiness.

We sin because we deceive ourselves into believing that the sinful behavior will improve our condition and give us a more pleasurable and meaningful life. Sin is pleasurable for a season; its temporary pleasures lure us to justify the sin and deny the accompanying guilt. However, the real consequences of sin are always harmful and destructive on a long-term basis. Whereas obedience to God's will yields ongoing blessings, sin leads to shame.

The existence of sin in the nature of humans leads to the outworking of many types of transgressions. The reality of sin is easily observable. One need only read the front page of a newspaper to be reminded of the constant barrage of deceit, thievery, and outright murder that pervades every society in the world. Furthermore, in briefly studying history, we find that landmarks in time often occur when sin has come to the forefront on a grand scale, resulting in wars and unimaginable atrocities against humankind. Yet sin is not simply at work outwardly in societies; it taints the smallest of our thoughts and actions. While you may not have committed a significant outward crime, your thoughts have not been pure and holy. "For all have sinned and fall short of the glory of God" (Romans 3:23). All of us need deliverance from sin.

Death is a natural consequence of sin, but from God's perspective, it is not a condemnation: it is a gift. For if we could not experience physical death, we would be forever condemned to dwell in a sinful body in a sin-filled world. From God's perspective, allowing humankind to live eternally in a sinful condition is the equivalent of sentencing a person to eternity in a maximum-security prison with no possibility of parole. The person would have a form of life but would be without true freedom and locked in eternal bondage to his or her captor. This judgment would be worse than death itself. From God's perspective, physical death is given in order that we might be completely and perfectly set free from our sinful nature.

You see, real freedom is not license to behave without bounds; nor is it living in a society in which all are free to act in any way their hearts desire. That type of freedom simply leads to licentiousness and social chaos. **Real freedom is liberation from bondage**. In society it is freedom from tyranny, but in individuals it is freedom from our own sinful natures. In essence, **real personal freedom is**

holiness. Such freedom yields liberty, which is the freedom to act coupled with the personal ability to exercise restraint. It is a personally and socially responsible form of freedom. It is the type of freedom that facilitates genuine love.

The Depth of the Problem

I attended high school with a young man, whom I will call Eddie, whose future none of us would have ever guessed. His story is a matter of public record, but his real name is omitted here in order to minimize any additional pain to his family. My purpose in including his story is to bring some good out of what is otherwise a very tragic situation.

Eddie was a somewhat tall, handsome young man. His family was normal in all respects; both of his parents were employed in respectable positions in the community. He walked with a bounce in his stride that seemed to indicate a fairly high degree of happiness. He often smiled and was generally a pleasant person. Eddie played on the basketball team, was a good student, and had a number of friends. He often socialized with other students who were active in sports or leaders of various organizations. He was neither a loner or recluse nor odd in any way. Eddie occasionally drank alcoholic beverages when running around with the cool crowd, but he was only a social drinker and was not active in drug use. Overall, Eddie seemed like a normal young man, with an above average intellect and a bright future.

After high school, Eddie attended a highly selective university. He graduated and began a career in sales. Before he reached age 30, he had already been promoted to the position of Vice President of Sales and Marketing for a sizable company. During this time, Eddie married, and the couple had two children. They owned a large home in a prestigious neighborhood and seemed to be on the road to achieving the American dream.

Despite Eddie's apparent success, something went awry in his perspective on life. According to published reports, Eddie developed a lifestyle that was bound to end in catastrophe.[3] During his days as a salesman, he had learned to enjoy the high life. Apparently, he took advantage of big expense accounts and heavy personal borrowing to acquire expensive items, take lavish trips, and gamble extravagantly. In so doing, he incurred some hefty gambling debts. In addition, Eddie was apparently involved in various inappropriate relationships outside of his marriage.

Approximately four years into his marriage, Eddie wanted out of the relationship. Yet for some inexplicable reason, he chose not to divorce his wife. Instead, he chose a course of action that would have been unimaginable to anyone who knew Eddie as a younger man. He chose to poison his wife. Maybe he had gotten into extreme financial difficulties and was lured by the more than $300,000 worth of life insurance policies he had taken out on his wife. Whatever the cause, Eddie undertook a bizarre course of action. Over a period of several months, he repeatedly poisoned his wife with arsenic. Yes, arsenic—it seemed like a storyline out of a poor movie, but it was true. She sought medical treatment for the ensuing ailments but died believing she had Guillain-Barre Syndrome, a disease with symptoms similar to arsenic poisoning.

I suppose that because of the mystery surrounding the cause of her death, an investigation ensued. Eddie cooperated with the police in the investigation; perhaps he thought his actions would not be exposed. Nonetheless, his deeds were soon uncovered. The police stated, "He didn't have the element of a criminal mind, and that's why he made so many mistakes." Eddie had no criminal convictions, except for a drunk driving charge while he was in college. Yet at age 30, he pled guilty to first-degree murder. Eddie was sentenced to life in prison and will not be eligible for parole until he is at least 50 years old.

Eddie's astonishing actions are hard to understand. He caused enormous pain and suffering for his wife, his wife's family, his own extended family, his friends, and even his own children. How could a young man with such great potential squander his life in such a reckless fashion? If he wanted out of his marriage, why didn't he just seek a divorce? Certainly, psychologists could theorize about the environmental or social causes of Eddie's actions. In fact, in our culture it has become popular to blame everybody and everything (except ourselves) for our actions, but ultimately Eddie had total responsibility for his undertakings. We are not merely victims of our circumstances; we are creatures who are responsible for our actions. The question that most people want to ask is: What was different about Eddie that made him go too far—what made him snap?

He is Not Unique

The sobering fact is that Eddie differs from the rest of us on only a few dimensions. He *fully acted* upon his own self-indulgent, self-centered thoughts. He set himself not only above God but also above all creation. Furthermore, Eddie believed he could do whatever he desired to satisfy his own self-seeking passions. Eddie lacked the self-control necessary to keep his sin from becoming a matter of public concern.

Sadly, however, Eddie is like the rest of us in many other ways. In actuality, each of us has fallen far short of the holy standard of God. While it is true that different sins have different effects and consequences, from a spiritual standpoint, sin is sin. What we consider the smallest of sins is still enough to deeply darken our souls. "We all, like sheep, have gone astray, each of us has turned to his own way" (Isaiah 53:6). While most of us exercise enough self-control to avoid public admonishment for our sins, we are all guilty of sinning against God and against His creation.

If Eddie was truly different, then we would see only a few similar situations in our world, and they would be explainable because of unusual circumstances. However, actions similar to Eddie's are observable everywhere and all the time. Countless people demonstrate the ruthless self-centeredness that leads them to disregard the rights of others, even to the extent of taking other persons' lives. How else do we account for the mother who murders her own child or the social group that attacks another sect? Or what about a nation that adopts a philosophy which leads to a holocaust against an entire ethnic group? Can these events be explained by rational deduction or environmental influences? Sure, there are from time to time crimes of passion that result from anger or rage. These are at least somewhat understandable, but most atrocities are committed by people who are acting out of their own contemplated volition. Obviously, the Nazi guards at concentration camps were under some duress to commit crimes against humanity, but could they not have chosen a different course of action? The very fact that they were willing to commit horrendous forms of murder rather than face death themselves is simple evidence of the depravity of humankind.

We are so self-centered and self-protective that we willingly sacrifice the lives of other people to protect our own lives. We all possess the capacity to commit atrocious acts. Under stressful circumstances, with the wrong influences, and with skewed motives any of us could be compelled into behaviors we never imagined were possible. According to the Apostle Paul, we do the very things we don't want to do, even though we don't want to do them:

> I do not understand what I do. For what I want to do I do not do, but what I hate I do. And if I do what I do not want to do, I agree that the law is good. As it is, it is no longer I myself who do it, but it is sin living in me. I know that nothing good lives in me, that is, in my sinful nature. For I have the desire to do what is good, but I cannot carry it out. For what I do is not the good I want to do; no, the evil I do not want to do—this I keep on doing. Now if I do what I do not want to do, it is no longer I who do it, but it is sin living in me that does it. (Romans 7:15-20)

Perhaps you are like many people who believe they are not capable of committing atrocious crimes against their fellow citizens. For such persons, one of two circumstances exists: 1) either Christ has already come into their lives and broken the power of sin over them, or 2) their own pride blinds them from seeing the depravity of their own being. If Christ has come into their lives, then their sin nature has been crucified with Him, and they are new creations. The power of sin to keep them in bondage has been broken. Indeed, by the power of the Holy Spirit they do have the capacity to avoid sin. (This is not to say that Christians cannot commit abominable acts. They can and do. They still have control of their own will and can disregard the work of the Spirit in them. Nonetheless, sin no longer has dominion over the Christian.

Therefore, the prevalence of sins among Christians *should* be reduced.) On the other hand, if Christ has not entered into the spirit of an individual, that person does in fact possess the capacity to sin in ways that he or she may not believe are possible.

The example of the tragic developments of Eddie's life is extreme. Thankfully, by the grace of God most of us do not commit horrendous crimes. Nevertheless, Eddie's situation does poignantly reveal the problem of our sin-filled condition. We are all capable of acts of depravity. You see, **ultimately Jesus came as the Lamb of God not just to save us from our sins but, more importantly, *to save us from ourselves*.** He came to give us a miraculous escape from our own sin natures.

Western societies have managed to dispel the idea of human depravity. We have replaced this realistic view of humans with an idealistic perspective. We have become comfortable with the idea that each of us is basically good. We believe (or want to believe) that deep within us is a fundamentally good person who, given appropriate nurturing, will develop into a positive, contributing member of society. This line of reasoning assumes that those who develop into persons who are damaging to society are not at fault. Their environmental circumstances cause them to make wrong choices; therefore, they may be excused for their behavior. They are still fundamentally good; they just need reprogramming.

While we do possess some potentially marvelous characteristics, we must recognize the reality of the sin nature that dwells within us. We have amazing skills, unique abilities, and wondrous traits, but we are not basically good. At our core is a potentially wretched self-centeredness. It is nothing less than sin, which is the underlying cause of most of the problems of our lives.

Nothing is more important for the renewal of our society than a recognition and understanding of the truth about sin. Preceding generations have from time to time known their own sinful weaknesses, but modern life has masked the condition of our souls. **It is an understanding of the sin nature that seems to be lost in our culture.** In order to find meaning in life and understanding of death, we must first come to the end of ourselves, recognize our own sinful nature, and admit our inability to escape our condition.

Chapter 4

Pride—the Primary Barrier to Truth

~ ⌒ ⌒ ~

Most of us recognize a need for something more meaningful in our lives than the mundane activities of our daily existence. Nonetheless, a barrier exists that prevents us from seeking deeper truth and living life with greater eternal purposes in mind. **This most basic of barriers is PRIDE.** It is pride that often stands between us and the fullness of life that God has intended for us to know. Psalms 10:4-6 states, "In his pride the wicked does not seek Him [God]; in all his thoughts there is no room for God. . . . He says to himself, 'Nothing will shake me; I'll always be happy and never have trouble.'"

Pride is at the heart of the ancient conflict between good and evil. Satan's conflict with God arose from his prideful desire to set himself above God:

> How you [Satan] have fallen from heaven, O morning star, son of the dawn! You have been cast down to the earth, you who once laid low the nations! You said in your heart, "I will ascend to heaven; I will raise my

throne above the stars of God; I will sit enthroned on the mount of assembly, on the utmost heights of the sacred mountain. I will ascend above the tops of the clouds; **I will make myself like the Most High**." (Isaiah 14:12-14)

The same conflict that exists between good and evil, as well as between God and evil, exists in the hearts of men and women. In essence, pride is at the root of our friction with God. As defined in chapter three, sin is the desire to set oneself above God; it is an attempt to live apart from God. The underlying cause of this desire to live without God is pride. "This is what the Sovereign LORD says: 'In the pride of your heart you say, 'I am a god; I sit on the throne of a god in the heart of the seas.' But you are a man and not a god, though you think you are as wise as a god'" (Ezekiel 28:2).

Of course, there are some types of pride that are appropriate. The Apostle Paul spoke of taking pride in other people who were responsible, diligent, and full of love.[1] However, the type of pride he referred to was one that results from self-sacrificing goodness. This is not the pride that is pervasive in our society. Rather, we are overcome with the type of self-centeredness that yields conceited, self-aggrandizing pride. Henry Fairlie called it "Superbia" and characterized it as pride that causes disobedience, boasting, hypocrisy, obstinacy, self-centeredness, and arrogance.[2]

Arrogant pride takes on many forms. While it is sometimes bold and brash, it is often subtle, cunning, and manipulative. For example, Muhammad Ali, who won the world heavyweight boxing championship three times, was known to be rather boastful. When he was in his heyday as a professional boxer, he boldly proclaimed that he was "The Greatest" in the world. However, his proclamation may have been as much a manipulation of the media and the public as it was a genuine boast.[3] Pride may be observed in what individuals say or do, or simply reside in the hidden recesses of our hearts. Pride inevitably shows itself in boasting. This type of pride is the antithesis of godly humility. "For everything in the world— the cravings of sinful man, the lust of his eyes and the boasting of what he has and does—comes not from the Father but from the world" (I John 2:16).

Pride is certainly not limited to outward actions or statements. **Pride is a condition of the heart**. It may vehemently exist in a person who outwardly appears warm, charming, and loving. Only God knows the hearts of human beings; He knows better than we ourselves the extent of the prideful condition of our hearts.[4]

Pride carries with it many dangers. Consider these excerpts from the book of Proverbs: "When pride comes, then comes disgrace" (Proverbs 11:2). "Pride only breeds quarrels" (Proverbs 13:10). "Pride goes before destruction, a haughty spirit before a fall" (Proverbs 16:18). "A man's pride brings him low, but a man of lowly spirit gains honor" (Proverbs 29:23).

Pride causes men and women to believe they can control their own fate. In our pride we believe we can withstand anything or overcome any difficulty. However, God knows our weaknesses and breaking points far more clearly than each of us. While a given sinful activity may not be a temptation for you, it could be the most vulnerable point for another person. In our pride we often play with fire believing we are strong enough to avoid trouble, but inevitably pride makes us weak. It is pride that causes us to spurn discipline, to ignore wise teaching, and to seek after that which endangers our souls.

Modern-Day Pride

A few generations ago people generally recognized pride as a dangerous and undesirable trait. For centuries it was viewed within Christianity as one of the 'seven deadly sins.'[5] However, our contemporary social tendencies actually promote pride. It seems that humility has lost its respectability, and pride has supplanted its position. Public figures no longer seem to be concerned about their moral character but only about their image. They may be liars and swindlers, but so long as they maintain popular support, they consider themselves successful. They thrive on the pride of popularity.

Examples of the exaltation of pride are prevalent in various sports. While professional sports are really no different from any other arena of endeavor, they are so visible that they represent well the underlying currents of our society. It is interesting that persons are paid enormously high salaries to do such things as hit a portion of a carcass and a few other bound ingredients with a piece of wood. Is not the pounding of a nail into wood by a skilled carpenter a more socially valuable activity? Would not the financial resources be better used to teach and feed the children?

Let me quickly point out that I do not deride the men and women who play professional sports. Who can blame them for applying their skills in fields that provide such lucrative financial rewards? The men and women who play the sports are not the problem. Sports at all levels of play provide great utility to individuals and to society. They serve to channel the energies of young people into constructive, character-building avenues. They refresh participants and help to keep their bodies physically fit. Even spectators reap the rewards of enjoyment and relaxation. Nonetheless, our society has moved far beyond these perceptions of sports and turned them into something of an altogether different nature.

The extravagance of professional sports is symptomatic of a society gone awry. The multi-million dollar salaries of professional athletes would not exist if it were not for the hunger of society to create idealized heroes. While the vast majority of the population cannot ascend to the upper echelon of professional sports, many people identify with and personalize the accomplishments of their heroes. Average individuals may not be able to personally achieve fame and fortune, but they can vicariously do so through the heroes they appropriate for themselves. It is a means to buildup and indulge our own pride. It is evidence of a society that has pride as its core problem.

Let us consider just a few of the words that can either directly or indirectly define this type of pride: conceit, haughtiness, arrogance, egotism, brashness, smugness, vanity, immodesty, and snobbishness. These terms describe the type of pride that is fueled by the accolades of other people. Persons who are in some way or another empty, or are in need of greater meaning in their lives, are naturally drawn to the praises of others. Somehow the acclaim given us by other persons seems to fill the void, at least temporarily. It fuels our belief that we can independently make our lives meaningful, that we are in control, and that all the difficulties which befall other people will not affect me, because I am different—I am special. We can observe persons seeking after the accolades of people in countless situations. It may be the businessperson who believes one more promotion and a slightly better title will provide the answers, or perhaps the athletic coach who sacrifices everything to win the championship. It may simply be the young woman who dresses provocatively to attract the attention of the men with whom she works. The praises of other people lull our own pride into a sense of false confidence and self-deification. In essence, we begin to believe our own imagined press clippings. We become overwhelmed with the type of pride that attempts to set itself above God.

In a society in which the pride of most individuals is yearning for adulation, professional sports appear to provide the ultimate source of fulfillment. Where else can a person be paid an exorbitant salary and literally have thousands of fans cheer wildly over the least of their accomplishments? What is more, many of those spectators have paid (sometimes outrageous prices) just to have the opportunity to watch the person play. The vast majority of workers are modestly paid (or underpaid), and the only people reviewing their work are not spectators but inspectors who are making sure it is done right. Would not most individuals desire to work in an environment that mimics professional sports?

We are a society of individuals who idolize and worship professional athletes. It is not because we so truly love the person-athlete, but because we identify with the athletes, and their performances reflect back on our own pride. In other words, we vicariously experience the successful life of the athlete. A professional athlete who is on top of his game has the world in his hand. Reebok (the shoe manufacturer) once ran a line of commercials that delineated the exploits of various professional athletes and concluded by having the athlete declare, "It's My Planet." There is some temporary truth to the statement. As a society, we literally turn professional athletes into figures of worship—momentary conquerors.

Nevertheless, watch the commercial value of athletes decline as they age or their performance simply declines. Fan support shifts rather quickly from last year's champion to this year's up-and-comer. Attendance figures at professional games are highly correlated with the won-loss records of the participating teams. Poor performers do not enhance our pride.

Pride motivated actions are not confined to professional athletics. Alumni of universities tend to put great pressure on schools to fire coaches who are not winners. The alumni want to be identified with winners because it reflects upon them individually. I once observed an alumnus of a particular university who mentioned almost nothing about his alma mater during football season when the school's team was in last place in the conference. However, the following winter the school's basketball team won the national championship. Immediately thereafter his chest was blazoned with T-shirts that hailed his alma mater. Of course, he is no different from the alumni at most other schools. He was simply basking in the momentary pride of being a vicarious victor.

Professional athletes are generally young men and women who because of their age are especially susceptible to the temptations of pride. Almost anyone would find it hard not to become self-admiring in the context of the glamour of professional sports. However, the professional athletes who have aged or suffered a few injuries begin to show the signs of true humanity. They have reached a position that countless others yearn to have, yet they know there is a degree of emptiness that is still present. Sure, the vagaries of their positions often defer a confrontation with reality, but they cannot eliminate it.

Take, for example, the situation with Michael Jordan (perhaps the greatest basketball player yet to have lived) and his father. Immediately after his team's victory in the final game of the 1996 NBA playoffs, Jordan's attention was diverted. Despite his return to the pinnacle of success, his attention was on his father, who had been murdered in 1993. His father had simply pulled to the side of the road to rest while on a trip. He was accosted by two hoodlums and murdered.[6] Countless young people around the world have wanted to 'Be like Mike,' but Michael Jordan's life is not without difficulties. He must face the same tough questions about death and meaning as everyone else. His worldly success, enormous fortune, and worldwide fame have not and cannot insulate him from the complexities of life.

The Deceitfulness of Riches

Perhaps the place where pride is most exalted is in the context of wealth. The United States of America has experienced immense material prosperity, as have some other nations of the world. The standard of living has risen substantially above what existed just a few decades ago. Items that were once considered luxuries are now considered necessities. Yet in all our material prosperity, we are not satisfied. We seem to covet more and more. It could easily be argued that the god of many of the developed nations of the world is materialism.

Throughout history wealth has always been a great lure. Thousands of people have sacrificed their integrity, their families, and even their lives in their quest for wealth. Riches provide such a strong temptation because they appeal to the pride of each human being. Part of what makes professional sports so attractive is the adulation of fans, but another lucrative aspect is the large amount of money that can be involved. It appears that to achieve the status of professional athlete extraordinaire is to achieve the ultimate position in life. Nonetheless, the adulation of people and material wealth are fleeting rewards. Proverbs 23:5 says, "Cast but a glance at riches, and they are gone, for they will surely sprout wings and fly off to the sky like an eagle."

Great wealth is appealing because it appears to provide an escape from some of the difficulties of life. For those whose work is drudgery, wealth seems to provide the pathway to freedom. Others seek wealth in order to acquire possessions, which they expect will yield happiness. Still others see wealth as the ticket to social status and acceptance. Some people even perceive wealth as a cushion against illness. They assume they can afford the best medical treatment and will therefore be able to avoid or minimize physical difficulties. Some people have even used their wealth to secure methodologies, such as cryogenics, whereby their bodies can be preserved until a cure is found for the ailments they face.

Wealth appeals to the pride of humans because it gives the illusion of allowing people to control their own destiny. Wealthy persons perceive they can control their own life, as well as the lives of other persons. King David of Israel spoke of such a man in Psalms 52:6-7: "The righteous will see and fear; they will laugh at him, saying, 'Here now is the man who did not make God his stronghold but trusted in his great wealth and grew strong by destroying others!'"

I happened to see an interview on television with Charles Barkley,[7] who at the time was among the premiere professional basketball players in the NBA. The interviewer was questioning Mr. Barkley about the prospects of being traded to another team. Mr. Barkley replied that he would only be willing to play for a select few teams, and if one of those teams did not agree to his terms, he would simply not play at all. He went on to say that he was one of the few people in the world who could control his own situation. I assume he was implying that his wealth and status allowed him to control his future. His statements caused me to be stricken with thoughts about how little control Mr. Barkley or anyone else really has over his own life. Sure, he may have been able to veto an undesirable trade, and he could afford not to work, but his days, like ours, are numbered. Mr. Barkley, like all the rest of us, is subject to the authority of Almighty God. Mr. Barkley is just a public figure who represents countless other like-minded persons who fallaciously believe they can self-determine their own future. Consider God's words to the nation of Edom, an adversary of Israel, spoken through the prophet Obadiah: "The pride of your heart has deceived you, you who live in the clefts of the rocks and make your home on the heights, you who say to yourself, 'Who can bring me down to the ground?' Though you soar like the eagle and make your nest among the stars, from there I will bring you down, declares the LORD" (Obadiah 1:3-4).

The Hardships of Wealth

Because wealth of any magnitude feeds our pride, it can be very dangerous. Wealth does allow a person to temporarily defer some difficulties or circumvent some obstacles. However, wealth tends to lull us into a false sense of security. Somehow the amassing of financial resources and material possessions gives us the illusion of meaning in our lives. However, real meaning can easily be forfeited to the deceitfulness of riches. The story of the 'rich young ruler' clearly portrays the problem of riches:

> As Jesus started on His way, a man ran up to Him and fell on his knees before Him. "Good teacher," he asked, "what must I do to inherit eternal life?"
>
> "Why do you call me good?" Jesus answered. "No one is good—except God alone. You know the commandments: "Do not murder, do not commit adultery, do not steal, do not give false testimony, do not defraud, honor your father and mother."
>
> "Teacher," he declared, "all these I have kept since I was a boy."
>
> Jesus looked at him and loved him. "One thing you lack," He said. "Go, sell everything you have and give to the poor, and you will have treasure in heaven. Then come, follow me."
>
> At this the man's face fell. **He went away sad, because he had great wealth**.
>
> Jesus looked around and said to His disciples, "How hard it is for the rich to enter the kingdom of God!" (Mark 10:17-23)

This man stood face to face with God incarnate. He had the wisdom to ask Jesus one of the greatest questions in all of life: "What must I do to inherit eternal life?" Yet he failed to respond with an eternal perspective. His heart was deceived by wealth; he could not see that his choice was one of eternal value versus short-term pleasures. Wealth had blinded him to the truth of life. Jesus had this type of person in mind when He told the parable of the sower in Matthew 13. In the parable He indicated the seed being planted was the message about the kingdom of God. Some seed takes root and grows, but much seed never bears fruit. In particular, the rich young ruler can be seen in the seed that fell among the thorns: "The one who received the seed that fell among the thorns is the man who hears the word, but the worries of this life and the deceitfulness of wealth choke it, making it unfruitful" (Matthew 13:22).

It is interesting that in the Book of Mark the story of the rich young ruler comes just after the following scripture: "People were bringing little children to Jesus to have Him touch them, but the disciples rebuked them. When Jesus saw this, He was indignant. He said to them, 'Let the little children come to me, and do not hinder them, for the kingdom of God belongs to such as these. I tell you the truth, anyone who will not receive the kingdom of God like a little child will never enter it.' And He took the children in His arms, put His hands on them and blessed them" (Mark 10:13-16).

Have you ever noticed how little money really means to very young children? They have no comprehension of where it comes from, and they certainly do not desire to hoard it. If you were to hand my toddler a $20 bill, his response would be to taste it or tear it into pieces. As children get a little older, they begin to see that money is useful for acquiring desirable things, but it really takes several more years for the deceitfulness of riches to affect children. Kids tend to value relationships with their parents, siblings, and friends more than they value money. However, by their teenage years their perspective begins to change. Most adults are probably closer than they imagine to having the heart of the rich young ruler than the heart of a child.

Not only can riches blind a person to eternal truth, they can also create great burdens in this life. "A man's riches may ransom his life, but a poor man hears no threat" (Proverbs 13:8). In a world that so hungers for riches, it is hard for many people to understand the burdens of wealth, but they can be quite real.

The time taken out of one's life to invest in endeavors that garner riches can be costly. Many children would far prefer to have more of their parents' time and less of their purchased possessions. Numerous marriages have run aground because one spouse loved money over his or her marriage partner. For example, J. Paul Getty (1892-1976) was the person who built Getty Oil Company into a large, profitable operation.[8] He loved the excitement of prospecting for oil and worked continuously to find the next big oil strike. However, "throughout his life, Getty had put a financial value on everything, even love and companionship."[9] On the road to becoming one of the world's richest men, he left in his wake a great amount of agony. He had five failed marriages and witnessed various difficulties with the children he fathered. For example, Getty adored his chronically ill son, Tim, but saw him infrequently because his son lived in New York while Getty lived in Europe. A few weeks before Tim's twelfth birthday, Getty called him and asked him what he wanted as a gift. The boy replied, "I want your love, Daddy, and I want to see you." Tim died a few weeks later without seeing his father.[10] It was one of many difficult moments in Getty's life brought on by his insatiable desire for wealth.

Most people may find it hard to comprehend, but wealth can actually be a curse. On the one hand, it insulates persons (at least temporarily) from some of the harsh realities of life. On the other hand, it can also prevent a person from enjoying the natural privacy that is common to most of us. Many prominent and wealthy persons have found it difficult to enjoy some of the simple pleasures of life because their lives have become fodder for public discussion and review. They are often hounded by the news media, stalked by deviant individuals, and otherwise barred from leading normal lives.

The deceitfulness of riches can affect anyone, regardless of income or accumulated wealth. I once knew a woman who played the state lottery every week. She seemed to be compulsive about participating. She indicated she was afraid not to play. She feared that the one week she did not play would be the week she would have won the big one. Such compulsion was indicative of a gambling addiction. She had a modest income and was hoping the lottery would provide her with a ticket to happiness. Unfortunately, what was really occurring was her state government was taking advantage of her weaknesses and playing upon her fears (most lotteries are effectively a tax on the lower income segments of society). In the meantime, she held a false sense of hope about a perceived answer to life. She was not wealthy, but nevertheless she was subject to the deceitfulness of riches. You see riches can provide a source of deceit to even the most destitute of persons.

Riches will inevitably fail. They may fly away in the midst of a few bad decisions, or they may simply prove to be empty sources of meaning. "Whoever trusts in his riches will fall, but the righteous will thrive like a green leaf" (Proverbs 11:28). Even if one is deceived into believing riches provide the answers to life, accumulated wealth will fall far short of usefulness on the date of one's death. "For the sun rises with scorching heat and withers the plant; its blossom falls and its beauty is destroyed. In the same way, the rich man will fade away even while he goes about his business" (James 1:11). At that point, the rich man and the poor man are on equal terms. "Rich and poor have this in common: The LORD is the Maker of them all" (Proverbs 22:2).

Humility - The Solution to Pride

Perhaps the dominant characteristic of the soul of people throughout the world is that of pride, which is manifest in self-centeredness, conceit, and vanity. Most of us do not consciously recognize the prevalence of pride in our lives, but it is ever so real. We tend to perceive pride when it exists in a person who clearly demonstrates vainglory (extreme conceit, boasting, and arrogance). But what we fail to realize is that we all exist in a state of pride—some more than others. Only the persons who have completely denied themselves are without pride. This side of heaven, we can only approach such a level of modesty. Still yet, the goal of the wise man should be humility, not pride.

Near the beginning of this chapter I referred to the first segments of two scriptures from Proverbs 11:2 and 13:10, but notice the later portions of each scripture:

"When pride comes, then comes disgrace, but **with humility comes wisdom.**"

"Pride only breeds quarrels, but **wisdom is found in those who take advice.**"

The antithesis of pride is humility. Humility carries with it a certain degree of modesty and recognition that we are merely human. All people, regardless of the magnificence of their abilities, have limitations that preclude them from viewing life as God sees it. The humble person seeks God's perspective, which yields wisdom. Wisdom is of great value; it is to be greatly desired:

Get wisdom, get understanding; do not forget my words or swerve from them. Do not forsake wisdom, and she will protect you; love her, and she will watch over you. **Wisdom is supreme; therefore get wisdom.** Though it cost all you have, get understanding. Esteem her, and she will exalt you; embrace her, and she will honor you. She will set a garland of grace on your head and present you with a crown of splendor.

Listen, my son, accept what I say, and the years of your life will be many. I guide you in the way of wisdom and lead you along straight paths. When you walk, your steps will not be hampered; when you run, you will not stumble. Hold on to instruction, do not let it go; guard it well, for it is your life. (Proverbs 4:5-13)

Wisdom breeds holiness and godliness. Therefore, the person of utmost reason seeks humility and wisdom. For ultimately, "the eyes of the arrogant man will be humbled and the pride of men brought low; the LORD alone will be exalted" (Isaiah 2:11).

Chapter 5

The Triune Human Being

⌒ ⌒⌒ ⌒⌒ ⌒

H aving faced the reality of death and having begun to recognize the deep internal problems of humanity, we must also gain an understanding of the complex nature of each human being. In so doing we can develop a comprehension of the source of our deepest problems. Furthermore, we can begin to seek answers to the difficulties that plague us.

The common perception of humans is that we are physiological and psychological beings. One goal of our enlightened age has been to scientifically study these arenas in an attempt to understand and eliminate many of the difficulties of human life. We can study the body with a high degree of specificity and develop a relatively sophisticated understanding of how it functions. Science has made enormous progress in this area; the severity of many of the physical ailments of humanity has been reduced. We can also study the mind, emotions, and feelings, but we are much more limited in our ability to comprehend what takes place in this realm. In fact, the foundational principles for theories regarding psychological function are generally developed from isolated, controlled studies. When the theories are applied to real people in dynamic environments, the concepts inevitably become speculative.

While the study of the physiological and psychological aspects of humankind is good, it is also inadequate. One of the problems with limiting our perspective to these areas is that humans are in fact three-dimensional. Every human being consists of three basic dimensions: 1) body, 2) soul, and 3) spirit. At the core of our being is a spirit that is distinct from our soul and body.

The spirit is the inmost part of an individual; it is that part of our being which can relate directly to God. The soul is our unique person; it consists of our mind, our will, and our emotions.[1] The body is obviously the outer part of our being; it is primarily a housing for the other components. During normal human life the body, soul, and spirit are inseparable and somewhat indistinguishable. All three parts are coexistent, interdependent, and complementary. However, at the point of death, the body as we know it will not continue. The spirit and soul of each person will evacuate our earthly body and enter into eternity where we will receive a new body. "So will it be with the resurrection of the dead. The body that . . . is sown a natural body, it is raised a spiritual body" (I Corinthians 15:42-44).

Several scriptures speak of the distinction between body, soul, and spirit:[2]

> May your whole **spirit, soul, and body** be kept blameless at the coming of our Lord Jesus Christ. (I Thessalonians 5:23)

> For the word of God is living and active. Sharper than any double-edged sword, it penetrates even to dividing **soul and spirit**, joints and marrow; it judges the thoughts and attitudes of the heart. (Hebrews 4:12)

> Do not be afraid of those who kill the **body** but cannot kill the **soul**. Rather, be afraid of the One who can destroy both **soul** and **body** in hell. (Matthew 10:28)

The following diagram is an adaptation from the original work of Dr. Charles Solomon.[3] It provides a conceptual image of the spirit, soul, and body:

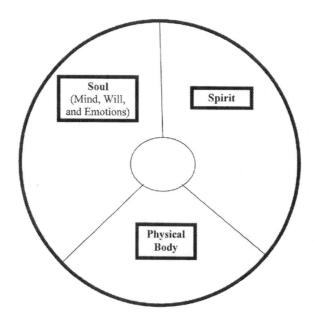

Contemporary culture tends to place a great deal of emphasis on the body, or upon the mind, but often pays little attention to the spirit. We can turn almost anywhere in our culture and see how the body is excessively emphasized. Whether it be television advertisements, the local health club, or the business office, we often impart the idea that true value is measured by physical appearance. In fact, adults and children who are perceived as exceptionally good looking tend to receive beneficial treatment in various settings.[4]

Another portion of our society tends to overemphasize the soul by viewing the mind as the most critical aspect of life. We believe that if we can develop the mind through study and training then we can alter almost anything. Without doubt, the human mind is most amazing; it is capable of wondrous activities. Nonetheless, our over reliance on the mind leads to a mistaken belief that the answer to everything is more research, study, and education.

An emphasis on education and development of the mind is very important. It is also vital to train and condition the physical body.

Both the mind and body tend to atrophy from lack of use. Nonetheless, an unbalanced emphasis upon either the mind or the body without an emphasis upon the spiritual dimension of human beings entails a profound and perilous omission. Coming to an understanding of the condition of the spirit is critical to the eternal development of each individual.

The Condition of the Human Spirit

Had sin never entered the world we would commune on a personal basis with God. "God is spirit" (John 4:24), and accordingly, our relationship with Him would be spiritual. However, because of our sinful nature we are separate from God and lacking in fellowship with Him. Because God's very nature is perfect and holy, He simply cannot be in union with our unrighteousness. Consequently, the point of our separation from God is in our spirit.

Let us examine the spiritual condition of persons both prior to knowing and after coming to know Christ by analyzing Ephesians 2:1-5:

> As for you, you **were dead in your transgressions and sins**, in which you used to live when you followed the ways of this world and of the ruler of the kingdom of the air, the spirit who is now at work in those who are disobedient. All of us also lived among them at one time, gratifying the cravings of our sinful nature and following its desires and thoughts. Like the rest, we were by nature objects of wrath. But because of His great love for us, God, who is rich in mercy, **made us alive with Christ even when we were dead in transgressions**—it is by grace you have been saved.

This scripture indicates that prior to coming to know Christ, people are dead in their transgressions and sins. Consequently, the question arises: *How can a person who is physically alive be dead in transgressions?* Perhaps this scripture indicates that a person who has sinned will at a future time physically die in his or her transgressions. However, the scripture subsequently stipulates that a person who has received Christ has been made alive with Him. If it were true that the scripture was referring only to future physical death, then those who accept Christ would never experience death of the body. But of course we know that all persons, whether Christian or not, do experience bodily death. Consequently, it is not possible that this scripture is referring only to physical death at some future point in time. Rather, the scripture is referring to something that is currently dead.

The next logical step would be to consider whether the scripture is referring to death of the soul. However, it is clear that the soul is not dead in each person we see walking around. If this scripture is referring to death of the soul, it can only be referring to some future death. The scripture is conceivably saying that the soul of a person who has sinned will die at a future time—that the soul will cease to exist when the body ceases to exist. Thereby, the scripture referring to 'being made alive in Christ' would indicate that the soul will not die but will come alive with Christ at the point of physical death. According to this reasoning, the souls of non-Christians would die at the point of physical death, but the souls of Christians would experience newness of life after death. However, this line of reasoning is incompatible with other scriptures which indicate that the soul of every person, whether Christian or not, continues after the point of physical death. Consider the following scripture:

> There was a rich man who was dressed in purple and fine linen and lived in luxury every day. At his gate was laid a beggar named Lazarus, covered with sores and longing to eat what fell from the rich man's table. Even the dogs came and licked his sores.
>
> The time came when the beggar died and the angels carried him to Abraham's side. The rich man also died and was buried. **In hell, where he was in torment, he looked up and saw Abraham far away, with Lazarus by his side.** So he called to him, "Father Abraham, have pity on me and send Lazarus to dip the tip of his finger in water and cool my tongue, because I am in agony in this fire."

But Abraham replied, "Son, remember that in your lifetime you received your good things, while Lazarus received bad things, but now he is comforted here and you are in agony. And besides all this, between us and you a great chasm has been fixed, so that those who want to go from here to you cannot, nor can anyone cross over from there to us." (Luke 16:19-26)

This scripture clearly indicates that persons who have died physically still have an existence whether in heaven or in hell. It is apparent that the soul of each person continues to exist.

The scripture in Ephesians simply cannot refer to either the soul or the physical body. The only logical interpretation of this scripture, which is consistent with other scriptures, is to conclude that the passage is referring to the spirit as being dead in trespasses. That is, **prior to knowing Christ each of us is spiritually dead in our trespasses and sins**. According to theologian George Ladd, "When Paul says that people are in their human situation dead but made alive in Christ, he must mean that they were spiritually dead, i.e., their spirits did not enjoy a living relationship with God."[5] Since sin has pervaded all of humankind, the spirit of each person is dead prior to being made alive in Christ.

Because God designs us as beings who are to have spiritual fellowship with Him, this condition of being spiritually dead leaves us in a hopelessly lost state. We are confined to a life that is thoroughly incomplete. Within us is a great void. Where there should be an alive, vibrant, active spirit, there is only emptiness.

The latter portion of the Ephesians scripture is referring to persons who have accepted Jesus into their lives as having been made spiritually alive in Christ. On this point George Ladd stated, "to be made alive means to be quickened in spirit so that they enter into living fellowship with God."[6] The sins of the person have been wiped away, the Holy Spirit has come to dwell within the individual, and the spirit of that person has been made alive for the first time. According to Romans 8:10-11, "if Christ is in you, your body is dead because of sin, yet **your spirit is alive because of righteousness**. And if the Spirit of Him who raised Jesus from the dead is living in you, He who raised Christ from the dead will also **give life to your mortal bodies through His Spirit, who lives in you**."

Self-Centeredness - The Consequence of a Dead Spirit

The natural consequence of being separated from a perfect relationship with God is that we turn inward. We are spiritually alone; therefore, we seek to find meaning and purpose within ourselves. As a result, we very naturally function with a self-centered perspective. Pride and self-centeredness are nearly one and the same. At the root of pride is a self-orientation. As a consequence, we naturally become prideful in believing that we can find meaning and purpose in life within the confines of our own abilities.

In addition to attempting to find real life within ourselves, we also attempt to extract life from other people. Whether we are consciously aware of our sinful condition or not, we are aware of our unmet needs. We often attempt to fill these voids via other people. God did design us to be relational beings, and our desires for relationship are fitting. Unfortunately, when human beings are in a spiritually empty condition, they are not capable of entering into relationships in the manner God intended.

God's perfect plan is that each person would first find his or her greatest fulfillment in life through relationship with Him. In fact, God Himself desires to be both the source of life and the fulfillment of life for each one of us. Human beings who are in a perfect spiritual relationship with God are then prepared to enter into perfect relationships with other people; such a state will exist in heaven. However, in this world, because of the fallen nature of humankind, either we have no relationship with God or we have a relationship that is perfected in some ways but progressing toward perfection in others. As a consequence, individuals who have not yet entered into a totally perfected relationship with God will naturally attempt to extract from other people some of the aspects of life that only God can provide. The result is that earthly human relationships fall short of eternal perfection, even for those who fellowship with Christ.

In fact, if we could walk in perfect union with God, we would be givers of life to other people; we would have no need to extract from them. Out of us would flow rivers of living water from which other persons could find nourishment.[7] Instead, we are somewhat like parasites. We attach ourselves to others, and at least part of our motivation can be to extract life from them.

Not only do we attempt to extract life from others, but we also blame them for personal problems that really exist in our relationship with God. For example, in Genesis chapter four we read of the story of Cain killing his brother Abel.[8] Both Cain and Abel made offerings to God, but "the LORD looked with favor on Abel and his offering, but on Cain and his offering He did not look with favor. So Cain was very angry, and his face was downcast. Then the LORD said to Cain, 'Why are you angry? Why is your face downcast? If you do what is right, will you not be accepted?'" (Genesis 4:4-7). Cain's anger was really directed at God, but his response was to vent his anger upon his brother by murdering him. Somehow he made the erroneous assumption that by eliminating his brother he would look better in the eyes of God. Instead, his jealous action only worsened his position in life and his relationship with God. Much of the murder and mayhem in our world today results from this same problem. Countless people are fundamentally angry with God over their lot in life (or because God has refused to be their puppet), and they vent their anger on other humans in a misguided attempt to gain control of life and better standing before God.

Without a spiritual relationship with God, we have no compass, we have no direction—we simply do not know how to live the life that is before us. Stuck in our spiritually empty, prideful, self-centered condition, we will naturally entertain thoughts and undertake behaviors that are sinful. This emptiness of spirit and self-centered condition gives rise to the sinful nature of humankind. We sin because we know no other way to live; our own sinful nature keeps us in bondage to sin. Consider Paul's words from Romans 8:5-8:

> Those who live according to the sinful nature have
> their minds set on what that nature desires; but those who
> live in accordance with the Spirit have their minds set on
> what the Spirit desires. The mind of sinful man is death,

but the mind controlled by the Spirit is life and peace; **the sinful mind is hostile to God. It does not submit to God's law, nor can it do so**. Those controlled by the sinful nature cannot please God.

Prior to the point of salvation, one's overall condition might be graphically portrayed as follows:

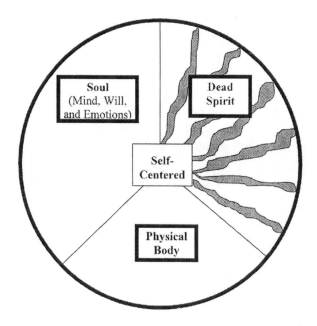

This condition carries with it many difficulties. Because we lack the source of internal strength that only God can provide, we may well experience thoughts and feelings of inadequacy, inferiority, insecurity, and fear.[9] Furthermore, we may suffer physical ailments that are either a direct or an indirect result of our spiritual condition. Medical science has determined that stress can cause or exacerbate many illnesses.[10] The most stressful situation in all of life is to attempt to live with meaning and purpose apart from God.

People in a spiritually dead condition may not only suffer from anxiety but are also likely to live with a profound sense of loneliness. Such persons may or may not be consciously aware of the depth of their loneliness, but it will nevertheless motivate much of their behavior. It is hard to recognize and describe the profound reality of loneliness until one has come to experience the joy and fullness of a personal relationship with Christ. It is the same as a married person describing to a single person what it means to experience marriage. No matter what the choice of words, the description of marriage will be incomplete—it must be experienced.

Most people attempt to compensate for their loneliness by developing varying degrees of interpersonal relationships. Yet emptiness will still persist, driving some of us to bounce continuously from one relationship to another. We often blame others for the way we feel when in fact the problem is ours, not that of the other person. Our internal feelings of loneliness and emptiness cannot be fulfilled by external relationships. They can only be eliminated by means of an internal relationship.

As we progress through life, one of two basic occurrences will take place: 1) we will either recognize the emptiness within and seek relationship with God, or 2) we will amplify our self-orientation. If we seek God, then a transformation process begins to take place that will continue throughout the remainder of our lives. If we choose to ignore God, then our spiritual, mental, emotional, and perhaps even our physical condition will worsen and become more complex.

Chapter 6

Fear and the Development of Walls

⌢ ⌣ ⌢

I am blessed to live in a somewhat rural location, and I enjoy watching the various animals that scurry around outside our home. In addition to the neighborhood dogs and cats, I have observed deer, rabbits, my neighbor's cows, foxes, turtles, frogs, an assortment of snakes, skunks, horses, squirrels, birds of various sorts, wild turkeys, groundhogs, and chipmunks. (No bears yet, but they have been observed in the region.)

Among these animals, my favorites to watch are the gray squirrels. They are most amazing creatures that have several very wonderful abilities. They are extremely quick and very agile; in a split second they can scamper up a tree, leap from one flimsy limb to the next and then race back down the trunk of the next tree. Squirrels seem to like company, and they love to play. It is common to see two or more squirrels chasing each other around the yard, up and down trees at unbelievable speeds, and occasionally up the side of our screened-in porch (which invariably leaves a few unwanted holes). Sometimes I think it would be nice to be a squirrel just for one day. I would frolic from one tree to the next all day long.

However, not everything about a squirrel's life is attractive. I have observed a characteristic in squirrels that seems to be present in all living creatures but is more visibly pronounced in these animals. They appear to live in a constant state of fear. As I watch the cute little animals, I notice they are in perpetual motion. Either their body is moving or their head is moving, but they are rarely still. They are constantly checking for anything that may pose a threat to their existence. Sometimes I would like to chat with the squirrels and tell them to just relax. Nevertheless, it seems they will never slow down; they simply appear to have no peace.

While most of us do not resemble squirrels in our actions, we are from time to time beset with fear. Unfortunately, fear is often a logical reaction to the environment in which we live. It is an environment that includes many perils, including the threat of rejection.

A World of Rejection[1]

If the world were filled with persons who had been spiritually perfected, we would experience continual, unconditional love from everyone we encounter. Every person would be in perfect relationship with God and would transmit to other people the love of God. Of course, this kind of situation will only exist in heaven. In this world most people are not yet spiritually renewed; most are spiritually dead.

Persons who have not yet chosen to seek meaning outside of themselves will tend to function in self-centered modes. Primarily, they will undertake thought patterns and behaviors that gratify the sinful nature. Paul writes of such persons in both Galatians and Romans:

> The acts of the sinful nature are obvious: sexual immorality, impurity and debauchery; idolatry and witchcraft; hatred, discord, jealousy, fits of rage, selfish ambition, dissensions, factions and envy; drunkenness, orgies, and the like. I warn you, as I did before, that those who live like this will not inherit the kingdom of God. (Galatians 5:19-21)

Since they did not think it worthwhile to retain the knowledge of God, He gave them over to a depraved mind, to do what ought not to be done. They have become filled with every kind of wickedness, evil, greed and depravity. They are full of envy, murder, strife, deceit, and malice. They are gossips, slanderers, God-haters, insolent, arrogant, and boastful; they invent ways of doing evil; they disobey their parents; they are senseless, faithless, heartless, ruthless. Although they know God's righteous decree that those who do such things deserve death, they not only continue to do these very things but also approve of those who practice them. (Romans 1:28-32)

However, the problem does not originate only within people who are not yet Christians. Those who have been born of the Spirit are involved in a transformational process whereby their minds are being renewed. While they have been spiritually justified and regenerated by the work of Christ in their hearts, they have not yet reached full perfection in all aspects of life. Such persons are still learning to think and act like Jesus. Consequently, even the most spiritually mature Christians will occasionally undertake actions that are damaging to others.

As a consequence of the selfish acts of many people around us, we inevitably encounter situations that frustrate the most basic desires of our hearts. Instead of enjoying the fruits of the love of other people, we oftentimes find ourselves searching for relief from the agony that comes our way. Our most simple and basic attempts to love others can be painfully rebuffed.

We are creatures who were designed to give and receive unconditional love. In fact, **the most basic desire of the heart of each human being is to love and be loved**. This is so because "God is love" (I John 4:8), and we are created in His image.

Unfortunately, the sin-filled condition of humankind makes an environment of perfect love impossible. We live in a world in which self-centered people are seeking after their own gratification through whatever means they deem appropriate. This self-pleasing process often results in extensive anguish for other people. The result is that instead of living in a world of perfect love, we live in a world that is predominated by various forms of rejection.

Rejection takes on many forms. It can be overt, direct, and very painful. Rejection can also be subtle, even unintentional, but still damaging. Rejection takes place at all levels of society. We can observe it in the ways little children relate to one another, or we can watch it take place when an adult loses his or her job.

Rejection can begin at an early age. Infants who are abandoned experience profound rejection. Unwanted children may sense coldness from their parents. Physically or emotionally abused children suffer extensive rejection. Even wanted children may inadvertently experience slighting from their overworked caretakers. All families are dysfunctional to some extent (some much more than others); therefore, all children experience some form of rejection. Even the best of families incorporate human flaws that result in temporary problems.

The opportunities to experience rejection multiply as we progress through life. Any of us may experience sibling conflict, inadequate parenting, performance-based acceptance, or various forms of discrimination. For example, have you ever observed how small children in the typical school setting can be very cruel to one another? One child is ridiculed for being overweight while another is derided for being too skinny. A child might win social points for being a fast runner, but his peers will find some flaw to attack. His ears might be considered too big, or he might be chided for being short. The school setting can be a no-win situation for all but a few children. Even the grading systems of most schools have rejection built into them. The allotment of grades will generally follow a normal distribution,[2] which results from comparative grading. Consequently, the majority of children will not receive the highest possible grade. Therefore, every time grades are issued the majority of students experience some degree of rejection. Adequate performers may begin to see themselves as inadequate in some form or another. (This is not to say that all grades should be equivalent. Justice requires that they be based on effort and resulting performance. Nonetheless, many students experience rejection via the typical system.)

Adolescence brings with it completely new forms of rejection.

Just as young people are attempting to find their identity apart from their parents, they must face the difficulties of the early stages of the sorting and selection process that takes place between the sexes. Modern dating brings with it many perils and ample opportunities for rejection. The maturation process between adolescence and young adulthood may be the most treacherous stage of life. During this period, young people make critical decisions about relationships, education, and career, yet they are often confused, afraid, and bewildered by the demands of life.

The list of potential points of rejection continues to grow as the stages of life change. It could be denial of an application to a preferred school or the inevitable mound of rejection letters that accompany most job searches. It could be a promotion that went to another person or betrayal by someone once considered a close friend. Whatever the situation, dreams are inevitably tempered by reality. Even the most successful people eventually encounter a situation in life that is bigger than what they can handle independently (illness, broken relationships, etc.).

Perhaps the most intense form of rejection in our culture is divorce. Experts at the University of Washington School of Medicine ranked stress-inducing events in a hierarchy and placed divorce second only to the death of a spouse.[3] However, the death of a spouse does not leave the survivor with the deep sense of personal rejection. Rather, the surviving spouse may have felt intensely loved by the departed partner. The loss is very painful, but in most cases (suicide being the exception), the dying person did not choose to leave his or her spouse.

Conversely, divorce is nothing short of pure rejection. The spouse who initiates the divorce is clearly stating (whether intentional or not) that his or her marriage partner is not sufficient. The instigator of the divorce infers that someone or something else can better provide satisfaction. If an adulterous relationship spawns a divorce, the rejection is even worse. The departing spouse is implicitly stating that someone else is clearly superior and preferable.

Rejection wears many uniforms and it omits no one. Although some people seem to avoid severe rejection, others are magnets for pain. Inevitably, a world that is populated by sinful, fallen people will impose its wrath of rejection upon all of its inhabitants. Even God is not immune to the fury of rejection.

The Rejection of God

God Himself has experienced rejection more profoundly than any of us. First, Israel rejected God when the nation tired of being a theocracy and desired a king like other nations:

> So all the elders of Israel gathered together and came to Samuel at Ramah. They said to him, "You are old, and your sons do not walk in your ways; now appoint a king to lead us, such as all the other nations have."
> But when they said, "Give us a king to lead us," this displeased Samuel; so he prayed to the LORD. **And the LORD told him**: "Listen to all that the people are saying to you; it is not you they have rejected, **but they have rejected me as their king**. As they have done from the day I brought them up out of Egypt until this day, forsaking me and serving other gods, so they are doing to you." (I Samuel 8:4-8)

Of course, all of us have rejected God. In our desire to be our own god, we have acted to reject God just like the Israelites. We have all committed idolatry by worshiping other gods. We may not call them gods, but in place of the one true God we have worshiped money, possessions, other people, and countless other items that have captivated our hearts and minds.

God received His most profound rejection when He came to dwell among us in the form of Jesus. He was mocked, cursed, beaten, scourged, and crucified by the demands of His own people. He came with the incarnate message of the love of God, but creation received Him not. Instead, He suffered the most humiliating and defiling of deaths. The prophet Isaiah foretold the rejection Jesus was to experience: "He was despised and rejected by men, a man of sorrows, and familiar with suffering" (Isaiah 53:3).

Every one of us needs to soberly examine the fact that we individually put Jesus on the cross as much as did the Jews and Romans who actually participated in His trials and crucifixion. It was not the physical acts of soldiers that nailed Jesus to the cross, but rather the spiritual consequences of our sins forced Him to go there. There was no other way for God's creation to be reconciled to Himself, except that He create the bridge of reconciliation by making Jesus the sacrificial lamb for all of our sins. "He was pierced for our transgressions, He was crushed for our iniquities; the punishment that brought us peace was upon Him, and by His wounds we are healed" (Isaiah 53:5).

Part of the mystery of God's handiwork is that He takes the most dismal circumstance and turns it into a wondrous situation. So it was with Christ's crucifixion, for in voluntarily going to the cross Jesus became the cornerstone of all creation. He was rejected in the process, but by this same process, He became the dividing point of all humankind. God laid " 'a stone in Zion, a chosen and precious cornerstone, and the one who trusts in Him will never be put to shame.' Now to you who believe, this stone is precious. But to those who do not believe, 'The stone the builders rejected has become the capstone, and a stone that causes men to stumble and a rock that makes them fall' " (I Peter 2:6-8).

Clearly, God's response to rejection is not like ours. We turn inward, become self-protective, and harbor anger or bitterness against those who have rejected us. Because God's very nature is that of perfect love, He does not turn inward but maintains continuous unconditional love for His creation. God is continuously experiencing rejection from His creation, but He is slow to anger.[4] Rather than harboring bitterness, He expresses continual forgiveness.

In comparison to God, our ability to deal with rejection is very limited. God's response to rejection is rooted in love. In contrast, our sinful condition impairs our ability to respond in love to any form of rejection. Instead, we seek remedies that in themselves are self-serving.

Walls and the Fear-Pride Continuum

We can surmise that we live in a world mostly filled with self-centered, fearful, spiritually dead people who inevitably impose extensive rejection upon one another. It is no wonder the front page of most every newspaper is filled with stories of the cruelty and barbarity of humanity! Such a world inevitably leads to many personal and social problems. Humans must deal with the complexities of life, but that is not an easy task.

The soul of each human being is a fragile and delicate entity. People easily sense rejection and pain from the slightest of actions by others. Sometimes even the unintended and unconscious actions of others lead to deep personal wounds and internalized rejection. I once witnessed a friend of mine become angry with another person over a rather minor issue. I made the mistake of talking to him a few minutes later about an unrelated matter, and his response to me was cold, short, and gruff. He was probably oblivious to the negative effect his comments and actions had on me. It took me several days to overcome the very negative emotions I had experienced and to forgive his actions. In the great scheme of life, it was a minor incident, but it was exemplary of the types of events that routinely have an adverse effect on our potentially fragile souls.

Given that they live in a difficult environment, persons who are spiritually empty will inevitably build *walls* around themselves. That is, they will develop patterns of thinking and modes of behavior that are self-protective. The more threatening the external world becomes, the higher and thicker the development of an individual's *wall*. The ultimate purposes of walls are to hide our weaknesses, cover our iniquities, and defend against rejection from the world. **The underlying emotion that drives the creation and development of our wall is** *fear,* **and the state of mind which necessitates the wall is** *pride.*

God has several important goals for every human being. **First, He desires that each person would receive salvation via belief in Jesus the Christ.**[5] "For God so loved the world that He gave His one and only Son, that whoever believes in Him shall not perish but have eternal life" (John 3:16). **His second primary goal is that each person be conformed to the image of Jesus.** "For those God foreknew He also predestined to be conformed to the likeness of His Son, that He might be the firstborn among many brothers" (Romans 8:29). Of course, these two goals are prerequisites to God's ultimate goals of preparing individuals for eternity and bringing them into the kingdom of heaven.

Pride and fear work as two powerful forces to stand between us and the goals that God has for our lives. They serve as a continuum of tensions that pull us away from fellowship with God and out of His will. Fear and pride are in continuous strife with our souls. Sometimes they work as opposite forces of tension. Imagine a seesaw with fear resting at one end and pride at the other. If one decreases, the other increases, and vice versa. If Satan cannot scare us into fear, then he will deceive us into functioning out of pride.

In addition, pride and fear are not always opposites of one another. They can just as easily work in tandem. When fear is strong, it may cause us to develop a veneer of pride that serves a self-protective purpose. Fear causes us to hide from being the persons God intended, and pride causes us to desire to be our own god. Pride leads to sin, which has as its consequence fear and death.

Before a person accepts Christ, pride and fear work hand in hand to keep us from coming to know God. They are Satan's primary tools of deception. "The god of this age [Satan] has blinded the minds of unbelievers, so that they cannot see the light of the gospel of the glory of Christ, who is the image of God" (II Corinthians 4:4). Until we humble ourselves and begin to fear God more than humans, we cannot find real spiritual truth.

Even after one becomes a Christian, fear and pride continue as our biggest barriers to walking fully with God. They prevent us from being the image of Christ. Fear and pride are so deeply ingrained in our souls that God must perform a miraculous transformation in us in order to accomplish His will for our lives. However, before we can begin to be free from fear and pride, we must come to recognize how they work their way into our lives in the form of *bricks* in the walls we build around us.

Fear and the First Wall

Fear and the first wall entered the world concurrently. They were both the result of sin. Had there been no sin, fear and walls would not be aspects of our lives. Let us examine the following scripture to see just how quickly walls began to be invented after the first sin:

When the woman saw that the fruit of the tree was good for food and pleasing to the eye, and also desirable for gaining wisdom, she took some and ate it. She also gave some to her husband, who was with her, and he ate it. Then the eyes of both of them were opened, and they realized they were naked; so **they sewed fig leaves together and made coverings for themselves**.

Then the man and his wife heard the sound of the LORD God as He was walking in the garden in the cool of the day, and **they hid from the LORD God among the trees of the garden**. But the LORD God called to the man, "Where are you?"

He answered, "I heard you in the garden, and **I was afraid because I was naked; so I hid**."

And He said, "Who told you that you were naked? Have you eaten from the tree that I commanded you not to eat from?"

The man said, **"The woman you put here with me—** she gave me some fruit from the tree, and I ate it."

Then the LORD God said to the woman, "What is this you have done?"

The woman said, **"The serpent deceived me**, and I ate." (Genesis 3:6-13)

Immediately following Adam and Eve's sin, they experienced fear, and they began to invent walls. First, they covered themselves, then they hid among the trees, and lastly, they blamed someone or something other than themselves for their sins. Each of these actions constituted a *brick* in their newly constructed walls.

We develop walls in the patterns of Adam and Eve. First, we adorn our bodies with various items, which are designed to portray us in the best possible way. Second, we hide ourselves from the world by becoming involved in various activities ranging from our jobs to church duties. The activities are somehow supposed to make us feel significant to others and hide our weaknesses. And third, we blame others for our shortcomings. The person at fault might be our spouse, our parents, our boss, even a stranger, but we do not often accept the blame for our own sins. (In fact, it is popular in modern society to explain away aberrant behavior as the consequence of environmental influences, rather than to accept responsibility for deeds that are consequences of our personal decisions.) Of course, over a few thousand years of wall building, we have added quite an array of options to the repertoire of walls that are available. Nonetheless, fear is still the driving force that stimulates the wall construction process.

Modern Types of Walls

An individual's wall can consist of many different protective thoughts and modes of behavior (bricks). It consists of anything or anyone, other than God, upon which we depend for acceptance and self-fulfillment. Walls may result from mental, emotional, or spiritual problems but will eventually affect all three areas. There are extreme, blatant types of walls, and there are some walls that are very faint. Sometimes individuals are not aware of the depth of their walls, but others can easily see their self-protective maneuvers. In other circumstances, it is the wall possessor who is fully aware of its existence, when others have no idea.

The wall of every single person is different because "each heart knows its own bitterness, and no one else can share its joy" (Proverbs 14:10). Thoughts or behaviors are not automatically bricks that fit into walls. Instead, a given behavior may be a part of one person's wall but simply a normal behavior for another individual. **The motivating factor that causes the behavior determines whether or not it is a potentially damaging action**. For instance, two different people may keep their homes in a very neat, clean condition. One person may do a good job maintaining the home in order to honor God and bless his or her family members. That person may truly enjoy the process of maintaining the home. The other person's motivation for maintaining an immaculate home may be a personal sense of insecurity and fear. Perhaps this person fears the rejection of family members or even strangers who may criticize the home's condition if it is anything less than perfect. For this person, maintaining the home may be a compulsive, anxious endeavor, which serves as a large brick in his or her wall.

It is impractical to attempt to identify all of the various types of walls that may exist, but let us consider a few categories and examples of walls. (You can use your own insight to speculate about other walls that may exist in people's lives.) Three basic categories of walls include: 1) severe, 2) common, and 3) subtle behaviors and thoughts. *Severe walls* are fairly easy to identify. They include items such as alcoholism, drug addiction, repetitive violent or criminal behavior, occult activity, racism, ongoing sexual promiscuity, addiction to pornography, compulsive gambling, belligerent rebellion, and other obvious attempts to escape from, control, or defend against reality. Severe walls might even involve psychotic thoughts and behaviors. Severe walls are clearly the most debilitating because they seriously interfere with normal human life and can be very destructive both to the individual harboring the walls and to other people.

Common walls are very interesting because they are thoughts or behaviors that are a normal part of life for many people. In fact, because they are so common, it is difficult for most people to identify the negative aspects of such walls. Common walls may include such encumbrances as an excessive concern about personal appearance, an inordinate performance or achievement orientation, an over reliance on skills (athletic, musical, etc.) to define one's identity, workaholism, messiness, compulsive neatness, perfectionism, the hoarding of financial resources, uncontrolled spending, and/or materialism. Common walls might also include undue dependence upon someone or something, being a loner, a domineering or controlling spirit, argumentativeness, denial, and religiosity. Many of these areas include normal, valid aspects of life that are emphasized to such an extent that they become controlling or inhibiting factors. For example, everyone needs relationships, as well as time alone, but excessive dependency on either of these can become a brick in the wall. It is not only the excessiveness of the behavior that creates the wall but also the underlying motive behind the behavior. Some people play sports for exercise, stress reduction, and simple fun; others might participate in the same sport in an attempt to prove they have worth and to lure others to value them. For the latter participant the sport becomes part of a common wall.

Subtle walls are by definition less demonstrative and often hard to discern. They are nonetheless just as prominent and potentially inhibiting as the more extreme forms of walls. Subtle walls might include judgmentalism, excessive intellectualism, inflexibility, withdrawal, false politeness, unnecessary self-criticism or criticism of others, bitterness, vengefulness, indifference, and a host of other shrewd ways in which individuals function in a defensive or manipulative manner. Subtle walls grow out of our self-protective attitudes toward other people. We erect barriers of protection that allow us to either retreat from social interaction or maintain a lofty sense of superiority. While subtle walls may be far less visible to other persons, they can still damage or stymie relationships and prevent individuals from experiencing the fullness of life.

In addition to the various types of walls that exist for individuals, numerous walls exist for groups. In essence, the factors that motivated the development of individual walls for members of any given group serve to facilitate the development of *group walls*. Any subset or subculture, ranging from a group of cheerleaders to a street gang, can develop group walls. Most longstanding groups tend to develop an internal culture where accepted members find some measure of security. The group serves as both a physical and psychological form of self-protection from the rest of the world. Threats to the group vicariously become threats to the individual members. Destructive groups can fall victim to the worst forms of "groupthink"[6] where they deem all other groups inferior and may even seek to annihilate them. Like individual walls, group walls can become very powerful mechanisms that can inflict enormous pain and suffering both within the group and upon external parties.

Walls and the Human Condition

Having come to understand the triune nature of people and now having come to recognize the reality of walls, we can graphically represent the human condition as follows:

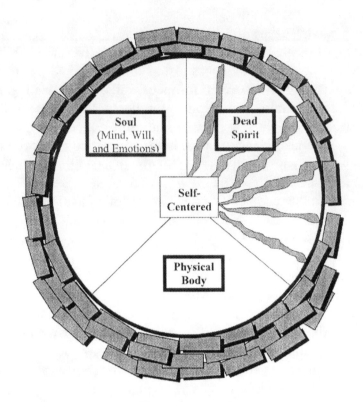

Oftentimes hiding behind either a group wall or individual walls are people who are not only spiritually empty but also full of uncertainty and fear. One would think that they desire to stop crouching behind the wall, but **men and women fear leaving the refuge of their walls** because they fear being exposed to other people and especially to God. "This is the verdict: Light has come into the world, but **men loved darkness instead of light** because their deeds were evil. Everyone who does evil hates the light, and will not come into the light for fear that his deeds will be exposed" (John 3:19-20). Humans fear that their weaknesses, ineptitude, and sinfulness will be open for all to see and bring with it overwhelming rejection. Of course, with respect to God such hiding is fruitless because God knows the inmost thoughts of all people.[7]

Removing the Fear Bricks

God's desire is that we would live in love. In order to accomplish this type of life, fear and pride must be conquered and our walls must be dismantled. Whether they are aware of it or not, persons who have not yet accepted Christ are entrenched behind their walls and are subject to the whims of fear and pride.

The prerequisite to God's great work in our lives is humility. As we yield our will and humble ourselves before Him, then He is free to accomplish His marvelous purposes in our lives. God waits patiently for us to walk in humility. The Lord declares: "This is the one I esteem: he who is humble and contrite in spirit, and trembles at my word" (Isaiah 66:2).

As we humble ourselves, Christ's principles and thoughts enter our lives and increasingly fill our minds and hearts. As a consequence, the grip of fear is broken. "For you did not receive a spirit that makes you a slave again to fear, but you received the Spirit of sonship" (Romans 8:15). Furthermore, Christ conquers the greatest fear—the fear of death.[8]

The only fear that is acceptable in the presence of the Spirit of God is fear of the Lord Himself. This type of fear is a reverent fear of the majesty and awesome power of God. It is a type of fear that leads to blessings. The "fear of the LORD" constitutes: 1) "a fountain of life," 2) "the beginning of knowledge," and 3) "the beginning of wisdom" (Proverbs 14:27, 1:7, 9:10). This type of fear facilitates the transformation process, for it is a part of realizing the fullness of one's salvation. "Therefore, my dear friends . . . continue to **work out your salvation with fear and trembling**" (Philippians 2:12).

It is interesting how often in scripture God encourages us not to fear but to trust in Him. "For the eyes of the Lord are on the righteous and His ears are attentive to their prayer, but the face of the Lord is against those who do evil. **Do not fear what they fear; do not be frightened**. But in your hearts set apart Christ as Lord" (I Peter 3:12,14-15). Therefore, it is incumbent upon every mortal human to recognize: 1) the wantonness of their spiritual condition, 2) the futility of their manufactured walls, and 3) their need to step out from behind fear and pride. Until individuals reach such a point of recognition and truly desire personal transformation, they will not and cannot experience the fullness of life. Fortunately, God has a plan for the transformation of every willing human being. The only prerequisite is our cooperation.

Chapter 7

The Transformation Process

~ ᕙ᷈ ᔭ᷈ ᠸ

The transformation process has a magnificent and profound beginning. It is inaugurated by God as He endeavors to woo each individual into fellowship with Himself. The salvation process is not the mere recital of some prescribed statements. Rather, it is a genuine internal work of the Holy Spirit in conjunction with the repentant heart of an individual. The process by which salvation takes place primarily transpires in the spiritual realm. It is a mysterious event that is inaugurated by God's will and work, affected by the prayers and activities of other people, and dependent upon the submission of our own pride and free will. Working within the constraints He established, God is continuously endeavoring to draw each person into spiritual communion with Himself. By His choice and design, He does not force us into fellowship; we are not puppets. Rather, God seeks to lovingly offer salvation to all people. "The Lord is not slow in keeping His promise, as some understand slowness. He is patient with you, not wanting anyone to perish, but everyone to come to repentance" (II Peter 3:9).

Not only does God freely extend His offer of reconciliation, but He also initiates the process by which it takes place. First, the Holy Spirit draws each individual into understanding truth and recognizing the divinity of Jesus. "Therefore I tell you that no one who is speaking by the Spirit of God says, 'Jesus be cursed,' and **no one can say, 'Jesus is Lord,' except by the Holy Spirit**" (I Corinthians 12:3). Once a person's mind and heart begin to open to the Spirit of God, then God Himself provides the means of reconciliation in the form of His son. **Jesus said, "No one comes to the Father except through me"** (John 14:6). "Salvation is found in no one else, for there is no other name under heaven given to men by which we must be saved" (Acts 4:12).

Consequently, the triune being of God Himself is constantly at work in people's lives. The transformation process is a pure act of grace and love on God's part. We must participate in the process as receivers of God's offer of salvation, but we are responding to grace, not originating or creating the process. Our only action is to exercise our will in choosing to receive God's offer.

God will not force us to accept His free offer of salvation. We must humble ourselves and come to some recognition of our own depravity and emptiness. As we begin to yield our will and swallow our pride, our hearts become contrite, broken, and pliable. This allows the Holy Spirit to undertake three great works in our inmost being. **First, He brings us to the point of repentance**. At this point we have a vivid perception of our sinful condition and our categorical loneliness. All of us are aware that there is a God: "The wrath of God is being revealed from heaven against all the godlessness and wickedness of men who suppress the truth by their wickedness, since what may be known about God is plain to them, because God has made it plain to them. **For since the creation of the world God's invisible qualities—His eternal power and divine nature—have been clearly seen, being understood from what has been made, so that men are without excuse**" (Romans 1:18-20). Consequently, the point of repentance is not the point at which we realize there is a God; it is the point at which we admit that we have sinned against His creation and against God Himself.

As we begin to confess our sins in humility, the Holy Spirit brings forth **His second great work. He reveals to us the truth about Jesus**. (Of course, some persons might first come to understand the truth about Jesus and subsequently work through the process of repentance from sin.) The Holy Spirit brings us to understand, in a way that was not possible to understand by our own finite minds, that

Jesus is God. He was actually born into this world, and He died on a cross to take away our sins and become the means of reconciliation between God and man. The Holy Spirit reveals that God in His infinite love conceived, undertook, and carried out the very process by which sinful people would be transformed into holy and pure beings. At this point, the response of the individual is simply to accept the atoning work of Jesus as the sufficient covering of his or her sin.

Through this process of repenting from our sins and accepting Jesus into our hearts, we open the door to allow God to accomplish in our lives His eternal purposes for our very existence. **God consummates the salvation process by means of the third amazing undertaking of the Holy Spirit. God Himself comes to dwell within the very being of each person who has accepted Him.** In so doing, He brings life to our dead spirits. "He who unites himself with the Lord is one with Him in spirit" (I Corinthians 6:17). In the matter of just an instant of time, we are transformed from spiritually dead people into persons who are literally alive in Christ (and He is alive in us). We do not become gods as some would falsely teach, but rather we come into perfect fellowship with God, and He comes to live in and through us.

If as you read this book your heart is being stirred and you realize that you are a sinful person who is in need of forgiveness, then you also need to recognize that the Holy Spirit is speaking to you at this very moment. There may be many times in your life when the Holy Spirit will bring you close to the point of accepting the grace of God, but none of us knows what it means to forgo the opportunity when the Spirit is clearly speaking to us. We may have subsequent opportunities to accept Christ, but we may forfeit immense rewards in the meantime. If you now recognize your own sinful condition, then repent of your sin and accept Jesus into your life . . . it is that simple. The Holy Spirit is present just where you are; you do not even need another person; God clearly knows your thoughts and hears your words. You may use the following prayer as a guide to help you repent of your sin, accept Jesus as your savior, and invite the Holy Spirit to come and dwell in your inmost being:

> **God, I recognize that I am a sinner. I have sinned against other people and I have sinned against you. I confess my sins now and I repent of my sinful ways.** (*Name the specific sins which come to your mind and turn them over to Christ.*) **I realize that Jesus died on the cross to take away my sins, and I now accept Jesus as my Savior. I thank you for making me a new creation in Christ. I invite your Holy Spirit to come and dwell in me, and I ask you to become not only my Savior but also my Lord. Thank you for giving me a new life! Amen!**
>
> If you prayed this prayer and received Jesus as your savior, then you need to act on your decision. First, determine in your will to seek God with all your heart. Second, share your decision to accept Christ with trustworthy family or friends. Third, begin to read the Book of John in the New Testament of the Holy Bible and continue to study all of the Scriptures. Fourth, become actively involved in a church that teaches that Jesus is God and which upholds the truth of scripture. Fifth, profess publicly your new faith (as God leads). Sixth, invite the Holy Spirit to take control of your heart and mind, so you might increasingly become the likeness of Christ. And lastly, enjoy embarking on the most meaningful and purposeful journey in all of life!

The Initiation of Change

When Christ comes to dwell within a person via the Holy Spirit, the transformation process has begun. It is an inside-out process. That is, God begins by transforming one's inmost being and then works through the individual in order that the outside world might observe the inner work. As defined in the following scripture, the process is one of being changed from fearful, prideful people to people who walk in love:

> **God is love**. Whoever lives in love lives in God, and God in him. In this way, love is made complete among us so that we will have confidence on the day of judgment,

because in this world we are like Him. **There is no fear in love. But perfect love drives out fear**, because fear has to do with punishment. The one who fears is not made perfect in love.
We love because He first loved us. (I John 4:16-19)

Let us begin examining the process of transformation by reviewing one man's story. I first saw Matt when he and his family began to attend our church. They were an attractive group (father, mother, daughter, and son), all of whom had dark eyes, hair, and complexions. Matt and his spouse were a little under 30 years of age and the children were preschoolers. Matt is a geologist by train-ing and worked for a natural resources exploration and production company. His spouse worked for a large Fortune 500 company. They lived in a stylish home in a relatively new subdivision. From the outside looking in, it seemed as if they had a good grip on life and were in an enviable position.

My first meaningful conversation with Matt took place at his home. My wife and I went to visit him as a matter of courtesy as representatives of our church. Matt was kind and courteous to us, but he was also a little nervous about having people from the church in his home. We welcomed him to our congregation and tried to encourage him about being involved in the church and developing a personal relationship with Christ. Matt's wife was not home at the time, so he was trying to feed his young son while maintaining a conversation with us. He told us a little bit about his religious background and that of his spouse. Matt had attended a Catholic church with his mother during his younger days, while his wife had sporadically been involved in Protestant churches. Based on the conversation, it seemed that both of them were still searching for truth. However, Matt did display a degree of curiosity and openness regarding spiritual matters. It did not appear that anything truly significant occurred during that visit, but afterwards we did pray for Matt and his family from time to time.

In subsequent months, I occasionally spoke to Matt and his wife, but I did not enter into any significant conversation with either one of them. They always seemed to be on the go, busying themselves with the kids and other endeavors. However, a couple of years or more after our first meeting, I learned that Matt and his wife were having some problems. By the time I heard about the situation, they were already separated from one another.

I learned later that Matt's wife had somewhat surprisingly approached him with the idea of separation and divorce. While he knew that not everything in their marriage was wonderful, he certainly was not contemplating divorce. Unfortunately, it is not uncommon for men to be satisfied with a marriage even when the relationship itself has broken down. Men tend to be satisfied as long as they are achieving things in their work and enjoying other activities. Meanwhile, women may long for relationship. Apparently, this was the case in Matt's marriage.

Matt was devastated by the prospect of breaking up his family. The situation brought Matt to the end of his rope. One night at 4:00 AM, he was searching for answers, and he opened the family Bible. It had been given to them by the builder of their home as a housewarming present, but it mainly just adorned a table in the foyer of their house. However, in Matt's desperation, he began to read the Bible with intensity for the first time. As he did so, he was brought to a point where he began to confess his sins. He said it seemed as if every sin he had ever committed just kept coming to his mind. One after the other he would confess the sin, repent, and ask for forgiveness. As this process transpired, he felt as if weights were literally being taken off his body. After this experience concluded, Matt felt like great burdens had been lifted from him. His marital situation was still adverse, but he knew that something extraordinary had happened between himself and God. He even had the immediate opportunity to share with his wife about the change that had taken place in his life.

Although Matt had been exposed to the gospel of Christ on several occasions prior to his marital difficulties, he had never before come to the point of salvation. Up to this point he had some limited knowledge about God, but he did not have a personal relationship with Christ. Perhaps Matt was like many other churchgoers; he attended church because of tradition, a sense of responsibility to his children, social factors, some level of guilt, or perhaps even subconscious reasons. Maybe he was searching for an answer but had yet to find it. Whatever the reason, **it was not until Matt genuinely confessed his sins and asked Christ to come into his life that he received salvation and became a member of the family of God**. In his desperation, Matt recognized that he could not control life— he needed help. His pride was broken, and he yielded to the wooing of the Holy Spirit.

Some people might speculate that Matt experienced a 'foxhole conversion.' It is said that there are no atheists in foxholes because soldiers make great bargains with God when they anticipate a battle that could mean the end of their lives. I suppose many people turn to God when they are under duress, but their religious experience later dissipates after the stress ends. The measure of whether or not a conversion is genuine is the degree of life transformation that follows the supposed conversion. If the person returns to his or her historical patterns of behavior, there may not have been any real spiritual change. In fact, Jesus said, "Not everyone who says to me, 'Lord, Lord,' will enter the kingdom of heaven, but only he who does the will of my Father who is in heaven" (Matthew 7:21). If the person's life is transformed, that is, they exhibit genuine change in their persona and eventually in their actions, then it is likely that Christ is living in that person. Fortunately, Matt's conversion appeared to be genuine (only God knows with absolute certainty), and he began to receive good counsel from wise Christians.

Despite Matt's encounter with Christ, his marital situation continued to deteriorate. It so happened that a short time later my wife and I were part of a team that was leading a 'Life in the Spirit Seminar' at another church in our community. Matt had a close friend with whom he worked who happened to be a member of this church. His friend strongly encouraged Matt to attend the seminar. The event began on a Friday night. Matt had spent part of that afternoon in an attorney's office dealing with the terms of his divorce proceeding. The evening was mostly filled with periods of worship and teaching, but late in the evening one of the other leaders of the seminar made a statement that he believed was prompted by the Holy Spirit. The statement struck Matt right in the heart. Matt believed the words were specifically meant for his ears. He came to the altar of the sanctuary to pray about the situation, and another team member and I knelt to pray with him. I don't remember exactly what was said in the prayer, but I remember that my heart grieved for Matt. He was obviously distraught, and he needed some encouragement directly from the Lord.

Although Matt was a member of our church, I had not spoken with him about his difficulties until that night at the seminar. Following the seminar, he remained on my heart for several days. My wife and I were just beginning a new ministry we called a 'home group.' We invited people to come to our home one night per week to share in the fellowship of the Holy Spirit and pray. We invited anybody and everybody who seemed to be open to allowing God to work in their lives. A few days after the seminar, I called Matt and invited him to our next home group meeting. Matt later said that he knew instantly when I called that God wanted him to participate in the group.

On the following Thursday night, Matt showed up at our home for the first time to be a part of our group meeting. He was obviously a person who was deeply wounded and in need of both support and prayer. He shared many of the details about his situation, and we attempted to encourage him. Later in the evening, we took time to specifically pray over him and for his family.

Matt became a regular at our group over the following months. Almost every week he would arrive with a despondent countenance. Each week he shared about the events that were continuing to take place in his marital situation. It seemed that every week brought another series of difficulties which made life miserable for Matt. His spouse proceeded with the divorce, despite our prayers that the marriage would be reconciled.

From the outset of Matt's conversion to Christianity, his life was filled with tribulations. This vexing situation caused Matt to yearn to know God more intimately. He devoured the Bible and read many other classic writings about Christianity. It was most interesting to watch Matt change as the weeks and months passed. It was as if his marital problems were an open wound in his soul and the spiritual wisdom he was gaining was life-sustaining medicine. He was simultaneously experiencing one of the most painful circumstances in life and one of the most joyous and rewarding. Matt was in his own crucible. His suffering made him pliable, and the Lord used the situation to work in Matt's life. God was quickly transforming Matt from a lukewarm man of religion into a true disciple of Christ.

Many years have now passed since Matt's conversion. It was most assuredly a genuine work of God. Matt has become an influential Christian. He now helps lead others into salvation and Christian growth. His marriage never recovered and the divorce was finalized. However, the Lord has healed his wounds from the divorce and set Matt on a fresh new course in life. Some years later, Matt met a charming schoolteacher, and after several years of dating, the two married. They are both dedicated to Christ, and they honor Him in their marriage.

As Matt discovered, mere religion will never satisfy the longings of our hearts. Certainly, there are countless thousands of people who are active in churches across the world but are just like Matt. They are faithful attendees and dutiful workers, but they are woefully lost. They have never come to a point of confessing their sins, accepting the atoning work of Jesus, and inviting the Holy Spirit to come and dwell within them.

Unfortunately, many of us are just like Matt before his conversion. We attempt to live life out of our own strength apart from God. Meanwhile, we appease our spiritual longings with the trappings of religion. These artificial approaches to spirituality are simply facades that serve as nice bricks in the walls we build around ourselves. In fact, the strongest, most menacing bricks are often those of religion. When Jesus walked on this earth, He encountered this problem among the Pharisees, who were the religious leaders of Israel. Jesus condemned their religiosity, and said to others, "Unless your righteousness surpasses that of the Pharisees and the teachers of the law, you will certainly not enter the kingdom of heaven" (Matthew 5:20).

Genuine Christianity is a personal relationship with God; it is immeasurably more significant than mere religion. Religion is a man-made substitute for real spiritual relationship. In many respects, religion is man's utmost expression of pride. In relying upon religion, we discount the love and grace of God expressed through the life, death, and resurrection of Jesus. In place of religion, what every human being truly needs and desires, knowingly or not, is an intimate relationship with his or her Creator.

Union with God

The spiritual process that takes place when people come to a point of repentance from their sins and acceptance of Jesus Christ into their lives is the most fascinating, miraculous, and incomprehensible event in all of life. In this most awesome and amazing of processes lies the answers to the critical questions of life! Our best attempts to understand this process will never be complete this side of heaven. Even so, our vigorous study of the process is one of the most meaningful and rewarding of all undertakings.

In order to understand the transformation process, let us return to the diagram of the human condition. When we last reviewed the diagram, we saw that persons who are devoid of Christ are spiritually dead and surrounded by their own unique wall. However, this circumstance takes a dramatic change at the point of salvation. The illustration of the new Christian appears in *Diagram 7-1* on the following page.

At the point of salvation the human condition is altered from the very depths of our beings. That part of our wall that stood as a barrier between God and us is broken by the power of the cross of Christ. Where there was once a lifeless spirit, there suddenly dwells a spirit that is made alive with Christ and which is in union with the Holy Spirit.

Furthermore, since God the Father, God the Son (Jesus), and God the Holy Spirit are one (the Holy Trinity), the new Christian is united with the fullness of God. Our limited minds cannot comprehend how one God can simultaneously be three persons, but this is the case. He is not three different Gods: He is one God; nor is He three different entities: He is one Spirit. The three persons of the Godhead are one, but they retain their distinct identities.[1] Likewise, it is remarkable that when we become Christians we are one with Christ, yet we retain our own distinct being. Of course, unlike the three persons of the Godhead, our union with Him does not make us

Diagram 7-1:

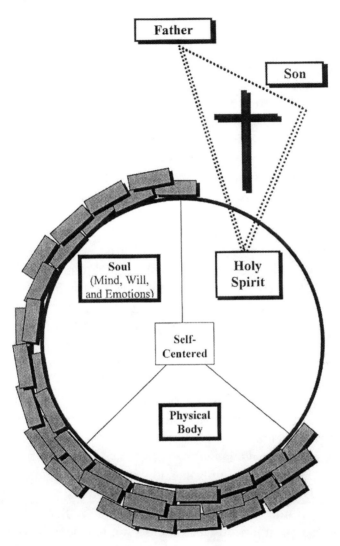

gods. We are merely people who have been created by God, renewed by God, and who will eternally dwell in His presence.

God is omnipotent (all-powerful), omniscient, (all-knowing), and omnipresent (simultaneously present everywhere),[2] yet when He comes to dwell within a human being, He exercises perfect love. In fact, one of the primary scriptures that speaks of God's Spirit living within us is coupled with a discussion of God's love: "Dear friends, since God so loved us, we also ought to love one another. No one has ever seen God; but if we love one another, God lives in us and His love is made complete in us. We know that we live in Him and He in us, because He has given us of His Spirit" (I John 4:11-13).

It is reasonable to presume that the presence of God's Spirit within us would overpower all of our being. We would simply become involuntary vessels through which God's Spirit would make His presence known on this Earth. However, because of God's perfect loving nature, He does not override our soul when He enters our lives. We retain our ability to think, experience emotions, and exercise our will apart from God.

It is not uncommon to encounter people who experienced no emotional catharsis when they accepted Christ. Additionally, they may have undergone little change in their ways of thinking or in their behavior. This type of experience seems to be particularly common among people who accept Christ at a young age. One can only specu-late in this area, but perhaps very young people who come to accept Christ simply have tender, open hearts and appropriately respond to the work of the Holy Spirit in their lives. They may not have built up great walls, harbored strong fears, or developed pretentious pride. Their ways of thinking and outlook on life may be relatively closer to that of God. Consequently, the transformation that takes place at the point of salvation is not a dramatic change of direction but rather a significant step in the ongoing growth process. Such a person is likely to grow gradually (and hopefully steadily) in Christ.

Conversely, persons who accept Christ as adults often, but not always, have dramatic conversion experiences. Such occurrences are particularly pronounced when the person has been involved in a lifestyle that was clearly outside of the perfect will of God. Such persons may harbor years of anguish and may have constructed complex walls. The entrance of the Holy Spirit into such a life is so clearly recognizable that all of life seems instantly different. I have heard testimonies of persons who not only experienced great releases of emotions but also were instantly delivered from bondages such as drug addictions. Persons who go through this type of change often grow very rapidly in their Christian faith. It is as if they are attempting to make up for the years that passed when they were apart from God.

God honors those who fervently respond to the call of His Spirit. He restores the years that were damaged and destroyed when they were estranged from Him. "I will repay you for the years the locusts have eaten" (Joel 2:25). Not only does He restore the lost years, but He also treats us as if we were never apart from Him. As in the parable of the prodigal son,[3] God views us with unconditional love and acceptance. He also sets about accomplishing His great plans in our lives.

An example in our community was a gentleman by the name of Doug Tweed, who was a prominent attorney. Doug had a successful law practice, but his career was unfulfilling. In addition, he was a member of a large Methodist church but only because other members of his family belonged. Doug was rather uninvolved in the church. In reality, he was struggling with stress, emptiness, confusion, and general dissatisfaction in his circumstances. Despite having a beautiful family, his relationships with his wife and children were often tense and distant. Doug confessed his struggles to a former law partner, who invited him to participate in a Walk to Emmaus. Doug did not trust God as the answer, but he did trust his former partner. Even so, Doug accepted the invitation only because of his frustration with life. He attended the retreat despite his misgivings about the outing.

During the weekend, the Spirit of God broke into Doug's life. Most significantly, God convinced Doug of the depth of his problems, particularly the fact that he was losing his wife and children. Doug recognized that God was there—listening and ready to help. He accepted Christ and became a newborn Christian. Doug not only experienced an emotional catharsis, but more importantly, he had a substantial change of mind that altered how he viewed reality. Quickly, his life changed, and he grew rapidly in his relationship with the Lord. He became a spiritual leader in his church and in the surrounding community. After only a few short years as a Christian, Doug felt God was urging him to enter the ministry on a full-time basis. He terminated his work as a lawyer and entered seminary. After graduation, he embarked on an entirely new career as a pastoral servant of Christ. God rapidly transformed this gentleman and set into motion His plans for Doug's life. Today Doug remains a faithful servant of Christ as a senior pastor and professional counselor.

The Beginning Not the End

The point of salvation is really just a point of beginning. Our dead spirits are instantly made alive, but the rest of our personhood must be gradually changed. God desires that from the point of salvation onward all people would learn to yield more and more of their will, thoughts, behaviors—more of their entire beings to Him. In so doing, we are transformed into His image.

Unfortunately, salvation seems to be an ending point for many people. For whatever reason, they fail to see the need for growth. It is possible to accept Christ, invite the Holy Spirit into our lives, and still develop a lifestyle that does not befit a Christian. Even after we come into union with God, He will not force us to submit to His will. However, He works to bring us to recognize our need for greater dependence upon Him for our spiritual sustenance.

I believe it is possible for a person to make a genuine profession of faith but spend many years without truly developing the relationship that was initiated at the point of salvation. If our minds are fully occupied with worldly affairs, we will have little or no ongoing fellowship with God. We can wander in the wilderness just as the Israelites did after their miraculous deliverance from the hands of their Egyptian oppressors.[4] Despite the fact that all of the power of God dwells within us in the form of the Holy Spirit, we may go on attempting to live life in our own strength. This is a grievous condition for both God and the faltering Christian.

Sadly, many people who accept Christ subsequently drift away from their faith. It is not that they completely lose their salvation, but rather they become lukewarm or even cool in their affiliation with God. Often they must reach a point of desperation before they again humble themselves and seek after an intimate relationship with Jesus. The scripture clearly indicates that those who seek God will find Him. "I love those who love me, and those who seek me find me" (Proverbs 8:17). "You will seek me and find me when you seek me with all your heart" (Jeremiah 29:13). If we are estranged from God, it is not because He has forsaken us but rather because we have disregarded our relationship with Him.

External Barriers to Growth

Various factors serve as barriers to growth for Christians. Many of the barriers are internal, but some are external. External barriers might include dysfunctional family environments, negative influences from friends, cultural limitations, inadequate instruction, or false teaching. Except in unusually oppressive circumstances, external barriers to Christian growth may be easier to overcome than internal barriers. Friends who are negative influences can be avoided. Most cultural limitations can be circumvented, except in those countries with extremely oppressive regimes. The Spirit of God can lead us to discover sound teaching. The Apostle Paul indicated that he had learned the secret to contentment whether he was blessed with much or nearly destitute. "I know what it is to be in need, and I know what it is to have plenty. I have learned the secret of being content in any and every situation, whether well fed or hungry, whether living in plenty or in want. I can do everything through Him who gives me strength" (Philippians 4:12-13). In essence, he was saying he could find peace regardless of his external circumstances.

I once heard the public testimony of a man who was a prisoner of war during the Vietnam conflict. The prisoners in his compound were denied all but the most basic necessities of life. They barely had enough food to survive (generally soup consisting primarily of water), resided in very small, crude quarters, had minimal opportunities for exercise, and were allowed no reading materials. Obviously, the sanity of persons confined to these living conditions would be severely challenged. One of the primary things they did to renew their hope and maintain their vitality was to attempt to recall scripture verses they had learned as children. Each time one of the men recalled a portion of a verse he would share it with the others. Each man would memorize the verses the group had reconstructed.

Gradually they were able to reassemble significant portions of the Bible. These men were in some of the worst possible living conditions for humans, but they were able to maintain some degree of peace by focusing on Jesus and His word, rather than focusing on their circumstances. They would not allow their external situation to completely destroy their internal personhood. Obviously, their strategy of seeking the word of God despite their circumstances proved successful, since they were able to persevere, and the former prisoner was able to reflect positively upon the situation years later.

Jesus indicated that the key to finding peace in the midst of difficulties is our faith in Him. He illustrated this principle in the following situation: "He got into the boat and His disciples followed Him. Without warning, a furious storm came up on the lake, so that the waves swept over the boat. But Jesus was sleeping. The disciples went and woke Him, saying, 'Lord, save us! We're going to drown!' He replied, 'You of little faith, why are you so afraid?' Then He got up and rebuked the winds and the waves, and it was completely calm" (Matthew 8:23-26). Jesus admonished the disciples because they succumbed to fear rather than seeking the peace that comes through trust in Him.

Certainly, placing our trust in Jesus does not mean that it is easy to overcome all external difficulties. For example, a spouse who is clearly antagonistic toward Christianity can make life miserable. Nonetheless, God can use such a situation to refine a Christian and turn him or her into a loving gem. Instead of being a barrier to development, the antagonist may be the very tool God uses to facilitate growth.

Unfortunately, the church itself often serves as a barrier to Christian growth. Sometimes the problem results from an overemphasis on one part of ministry; other times the problem is a result of religious strongholds, and on some occasions the obstacle is direct spiritual conflict and deceit. It is common to find churches that place most of their ministry emphasis upon winning the lost to Christ. This is a critical undertaking commanded by scripture. Jesus said, "Go into all the world and preach the good news to all creation. Whoever believes and is baptized will be saved, but whoever does not believe will be condemned" (Mark 16:15-16).

However, we are commanded not only to win the lost but also to make disciples. Jesus also said, "All authority in heaven and on earth has been given to me. Therefore go and make disciples of all nations, baptizing them in the name of the Father and of the Son and of the Holy Spirit, and teaching them to obey everything I have commanded you" (Matthew 28:18-20).

The making of disciples takes time and requires much teaching. Jesus spent three years working diligently to make disciples of the twelve people He had chosen. Unfortunately, many churches and ministries are not adequately equipped to help new Christians grow in their faith and become disciples. So much emphasis is placed on salvation that the process, systems, and organization necessary to make disciples are insufficient. Consequently, many Christians languish in immaturity for long periods of time. What they really need is teaching that is Spirit-inspired and which imparts the wisdom necessary for growth.

The goals and training for persons who have accepted Jesus Christ into their lives are entirely different from those that are appropriate for non-Christians. The primary goal for non-Christians is to help bring them to the point of recognizing their need for forgiveness and their need to be changed. The goal for new Christians is transformation into the very image of Christ. "Whenever anyone turns to the Lord, the veil is taken away. . . . And we, who with unveiled faces all reflect the Lord's glory, are being transformed into His likeness with ever-increasing glory, which comes from the Lord, who is the Spirit" (II Corinthians 3:16,18).

Training for new Christians should focus upon helping them understand who they have become and to develop patterns of thinking and behaving that are dependent upon the Holy Spirit, who now dwells within their being. Unfortunately, some teaching that takes place in churches would be better suited to non-Christians. Instead of teaching individuals to deny their self-orientation and become dependent upon the Spirit, some poor teaching accentuates self-centeredness. For example, a church might emphasize self-improvement programs more than it focuses on developing intimacy with Christ. After exerting tremendous effort to evangelize the masses, we turn right around and fail to provide adequate teaching. We indoctrinate new converts to the ways of religion, but we sometimes emphasize legalistic behavior more than spiritual growth. For the church universal to truly rise to her appointed level of responsibility, she must become a cooperative facilitator of growth, rather than an external barrier.

Internal Barriers and Renewing the Mind

Most of the internal barriers to spiritual growth are in the soul, although it may be possible to have a physical barrier to Christian growth, such as mental instability resulting from physiological causes. However, let us not underestimate the power of the Holy Spirit to facilitate growth even within persons who have physical limitations in their cognitive abilities. For example, it is not uncommon to meet a person with Downs Syndrome who has a vibrant relationship with God. That person may not be able to understand eschatology (who can?!) but may have a personal relationship with God that is quite intimate.

Internal barriers to Christian growth are generally rooted in the mind and will. They include the bricks we have included in our walls, which have resulted from wrong or poor patterns of thinking, blatant self-centeredness (rooted in pride), or spiritual strongholds. Inappropriate thinking may be the residue of sinful thoughts that became patterns in our lives prior to conversion. They may also result from defensive reactions we developed in response to the sinful actions of other persons during our formative years. For example, some abused children later become rather withdrawn, fearful adults who tend to avoid interpersonal encounters. Some of the troublesome thinking these people experience may be part of a spiritual stronghold that is seriously debilitating, and which necessitates supernatural transformation by the Spirit of God.

In order to overcome internal barriers, our minds must be renewed. The admonishment of the scripture is: "Do not conform any longer to the pattern of this world, but be transformed by the renewing of your mind. Then you will be able to test and approve what God's will is—His good, pleasing and perfect will" (Romans 12:2). What you are at this point in life is a function of everything you have thought up to this point. In order for you to become something different, your thoughts must change—they must emulate the thoughts of Jesus.

When sin entered the world, it caused the minds of humans to be open to entirely new ways of thinking. "For God knows that when you eat of it your eyes will be opened, and you will be like God, knowing good and evil" (Genesis 3:5). As both men and women began to comprehend evil, they also began to develop sinful patterns of thinking. For example, the cause of the incident in Genesis chapter four in which Cain killed Abel was evil thinking on the part of Cain. In order for us to be transformed into the image of Christ, we must develop godly thought processes; we must have our minds renewed.

It may be easy to state that our minds must be renewed; it is quite another thing to undertake the process. No one can transform his or her own mind. Certainly, we must be willing participants in the process, but ultimately transformation is the responsibility of God. We must come to a point where we realize we are helpless to live our own lives, and we are in need of not only a savior but also a lord.

It was necessary for the Holy Spirit to bring us to the point where we could recognize our own sinfulness before we could turn to God, ask for forgiveness, and receive salvation. It is also neces- sary for the Holy Spirit to bring us to the point where we realize that we are independently inept at living the Christian life. Only when we realize our deep need for moment-by-moment guidance, direction, and empowering from God can we truly have our minds renewed and be transformed into the image of Christ. For some Christians these two occurrences may come almost simultaneously. For others, there may be many years between the point of salvation and the beginning of genuine transformation.

I have a close friend by the name of Opal Trivette, who is a charming woman in her fifties. As a young child, she was influ- enced by a godly aunt. Consequently, Opal made a genuine profes- sion of faith when she was only five years old. She never strayed far from her Christian roots and made a somewhat normal progression through life. However, Opal's knowledge of biblical principles was limited in her earlier years. She married a gentleman who was not a

Christian and thereby became 'unequally yoked.' [5] Her husband, Jim, was a good provider and became a good father to their two children, but he was verbally profane, occasionally drank too much, and certainly wanted nothing to do with church. Despite his lack of cooperation, Opal took their children to church and attempted to live what she thought was the life of a Christian.

Opal was dedicated to the Lord, but she found it hard to live as she thought she should. There were no major outward sins in her life, but she sometimes harbored anger and hatred; there were some people she just did not like—much less love. She also dabbled in activities that were incompatible with Christianity. Her husband's lifestyle also served to divert her attention away from God's perfect will. Nonetheless, Opal was a rather religious woman; she put on a good performance as a Christian. Her friends in the church and community probably thought Opal had her Christian life in order.

Despite her pious appearance, Opal increasingly began to think that it was impossible to live the Christian life. She recognized and understood the standard by which she was to live but consistently fell short of the mark. She knew quite well that within her mind she conceived and harbored thoughts that were not godly. She also knew that some of her actions were not loving and reflective of Christ. Opal went on pretending to be a perfect little Christian for many years, but in her heart, she knew she was a fake. She knew, as did God, that no matter how hard she tried to be a godly woman, she always failed in some manner.

Opal's condition became very frustrating and sometimes depressing. She wanted something better in life, but she did not know what to do. Fortunately, she did not blame her husband. He was headed in the wrong direction, but she was wise enough to know that her problem was within herself, not a result of his behavior. Sadly, many people who reach a point of frustration similar to that which Opal experienced blame other persons. Often at this point marriages disintegrate. The frustrated person knows something is missing, but they erroneously perceive that the cause of the problem is their spouse. Instead, they need to examine themselves and their relationship with God.

Finally, when Opal was about 32 years old, she reached the end of her rope. She was fully frustrated with the Christian life. Fortunately, however, Opal attended a Bible study where she discovered the power available through the Holy Spirit to live the Christian life. Consequently, Opal turned to God and asked Him to fill her with His Holy Spirit. The Holy Spirit had indwelled Opal since she was five years old, but at age 32 she finally yielded the majority of her will and invited Him to take full control of her life. God had patiently and lovingly waited for 27 years for her to truly seek His Lordship.

Filled With the Holy Spirit

What Opal experienced at age 32 is what many people refer to as being 'filled with the Holy Spirit,' 'baptized in the Holy Spirit,' or some other term which describes an enhanced relationship with the Spirit of God. **This is not a situation where we get more of the Holy Spirit but rather an occurrence where He gets more of us**. The Holy Spirit is resident in the believer from the point of salvation, but He also desires to be president (supreme commander) of our lives. The Holy Spirit fully comes to indwell each person who accepts Jesus as his or her savior. At Pentecost Peter stated, "Repent and be baptized, every one of you, in the name of Jesus Christ for the forgiveness of your sins. And you will receive the gift of the Holy Spirit" (Acts 2:38). Furthermore, the Holy Spirit gives us assurance of salvation. "If anyone acknowledges that Jesus is the Son of God, God lives in him and he in God" (I John 4:15).[6]

Nonetheless, **it is the rare person who yields majority control of his or her life to the Holy Spirit at the point of salvation**. Most of us, like Opal, must come to another crossroad or perhaps a series of crossroads in our Christian lives. Salvation is the point at which we recognize that we need forgiveness for our sins from the one true God. The point at which we are *filled with the Holy Spirit* or, said another way, **the point at which *the Holy Spirit takes majority control of our life,* is the time when we recognize that it is impossible to live the Christian life out of our own strength**. At this point we realize the need to yield to the Holy Spirit in order to receive the power to emulate Christ. This is the point Opal Trivette reached at age 32. She took the step of inviting the Holy Spirit to take charge of her life. Subsequently, Opal was a radically changed person. Her Christian life came to manifest genuine love for all people, she developed a hunger for fulfilling the will of God, and the Lord endued her with power for ministry. Today Opal and her husband (who later accepted Christ and yielded to the Spirit) have a national teaching ministry through which the Lord has touched many lives.

I believe the process of being filled with the Holy Spirit may occur differently for each Christian. For many people it may be a sudden, overwhelming experience—for others it may be a gradual process. Some persons may not be able to identify a specific time following salvation when they were filled with the Holy Spirit. Such people may grow gradually in their relationship with Christ, and they may increasingly become *Spirit-filled* without experiencing any cathartic moment. Such individuals may be like the many people who cannot identify exactly when they became Christians. Instead, they gradually developed a real and flourishing relationship with Christ.

The Spirit-filled life is an ongoing process. That is, we should constantly be filled with the Holy Spirit; we should continuously seek to yield more and more of our will to the Holy Spirit. Furthermore, the filling of the Holy Spirit should be an ever deeper and richer experience. As we grow in our relationship with Jesus, His Spirit assumes greater and greater authority and power in our lives. The result is that we increasingly emulate the life and ministry of Jesus.

Unfortunately, many people stumble and stagger through their Christian lives without yielding to and being filled with the Holy Spirit. This reluctance or unwillingness to surrender to the Spirit explains why the lives of so many Christians are not discernibly different from those of non-Christians. In fact, pollster George Barna found statistics that indicated a number of aberrant (sinful) behaviors were about the same, or in some cases worse, among professing Christians than for non-Christians.[7] Apparently, the Holy Spirit is not that influential in the lives of many followers of Christ because they do not want Him to be so. This condition in many Christians explains why the church is often ineffective in its ministerial endeavors. For example, the renowned evangelist John Wesley was ineffective in his first mission trip to the American colonies in 1736, but later he was a powerful spokesperson through whom God operated. The difference was that John's heart had been "strangely warmed" by the Holy Spirit at his Aldersgate experience in 1738.[8]

The Example of Jesus

Understanding the life and ministry of Jesus may help in comprehending the process of being filled with the Holy Spirit. Jesus, the Son of God, was conceived by the Holy Spirit within Mary. The angel Gabriel said to Mary, "You will be with child and give birth to a son, and you are to give Him the name Jesus. . . . The Holy Spirit will come upon you, and the power of the Most High will overshadow you. So the holy one to be born will be called the Son of God" (Luke 1:31, 35).

Jesus took the form of a human because He was born of a woman. However, in His spirit He was divine because He had been conceived by the Holy Spirit. Unlike humans who have dead spirits at birth, Jesus' spirit was alive because He was in eternal union with God the Father and with the Holy Spirit. Jesus eternally existed as a member of the Holy Trinity, but at the incarnation He also took upon Himself the form and limitations of an earthly human. In speaking about Jesus, theologian J. Rodman Williams said, "Without ceasing to be God through whom all things were made, He concurrently became man by assuming our flesh."[9] Yet because Jesus was in continuous union with the Holy Spirit, He lived a sinless life.[10] Had He been a mere human who was spiritually empty, then Jesus would most surely have sinned. His sinlessness was another proof of His divinity.

Jesus was in eternal union with the Father and the Holy Spirit before, during, and after the incarnation. Nevertheless, His ministry did not begin until He received a special anointing of the Holy Spirit when He was about 30 years old.[11] At that time, Jesus went to the Jordan River where He was baptized by John the Baptist. "As soon as Jesus was baptized, He went up out of the water. At that moment heaven was opened, and He saw the Spirit of God descending like a dove and lighting on Him. And a voice from heaven said, 'This is my Son, whom I love; with Him I am well pleased'" (Matthew 3:16-17). Jesus was immediately led away by the Spirit to be tempted by Satan. After shunning the lures of the tempter, Jesus embarked upon His public ministry with the disciples.[12]

At the point Jesus was baptized by John the Baptist and the Holy Spirit descended upon Him, Jesus did not get more of the Holy Spirit. That was impossible, since Jesus eternally existed in the Holy Trinity; He was eternally unified with the Holy Spirit. Rather, at this point God the Father chose to release through Jesus a greater work of the Spirit, to which the human side of Jesus submitted. He was filled with the Holy Spirit, but it was not an outward work upon Jesus but rather a greater releasing through Him that occurred. The Spirit descending like a dove was an outward representation of the anointing of God.

According to Rev. Dennis Bennett, who wrote *The Holy Spirit And You*, the point of salvation corresponds to the conception of Jesus by the Holy Spirit. The point at which we surrender to the Spirit and receive a greater fullness of the Holy Spirit corresponds to the point when Jesus was baptized and the Spirit descended upon Him.[13] The Holy Spirit comes to fully indwell humans at the point of salvation, but when we surrender to the Spirit, we received a greater release of His work through us.

Still Grace, Not Works

Essentially, there are three basic spiritual conditions. The first is that of a non-Christian—a person who is unregenerate. Such a person is still spiritually dead and has not been renewed by the Holy Spirit. The second condition is that of a Christian who has not truly yielded to the Holy Spirit but attempts to rule his or her own life. This person has accepted Christ as savior but has not yet truly yielded to His guidance and authority. My friend Opal stagnated in this condition between ages 5 and 32. The third condition is that of a person who is filled with the Holy Spirit and is continuously dependent upon the Spirit for spiritual sustenance and direction.

This is not to say that such a person lives a perfect life; rather, he or she always seeks God and depends upon Him for guidance and empowerment.

The most miserable and frustrating of the three conditions is the second. People in this condition suffer through an internal battle of wills. They think and behave just as if God was not present in their lives. Meanwhile, the Holy Spirit is asking them to surrender to His will. Essentially, they are trying to live a Christian life in their own strength. Instead, they need to rely upon the Holy Spirit, who can empower them to truly emulate the life of Christ. Otherwise, there will always be friction, turmoil, and a lack of peace in such a life. Of course, even persons who have mostly yielded to the Holy Spirit may still harbor areas of resistance and experience difficulties in certain parts of their lives.

As previously mentioned, God has two primary desires for each person's life. The first is salvation and the second is that each Christian would be transformed into the image of Christ. We can be assured that the two primary objectives of Satan are directly opposed to these activities. That is, the evil one first attempts to confuse the mind and harden the heart so that people will reject God's free offer of salvation. He deceives us into believing that God is irrelevant and we can manufacture meaning in our lives through human endeavors. If Satan fails to prevent salvation, then he will work to prevent the Christian from growing. What he despises most and what poses his greatest threat are people who are fully yielded to the Spirit of God.

There is a spiritual battle that is taking place in this world, and the primary battleground is in the mind of human beings. Until God renews our minds, the aforementioned barriers can easily impede the growth of Christians for many years. We may strive in vain to live as we perceive Christians should live, but we will inevitably fail. Our efforts at being Christians serve as nothing more than performances. Ultimately, we become fatigued and are unable to maintain the theatrics. We must come to the point where we no longer imitate Christianity out of our own strength, but instead we must actually let Christ live through us.

However, it is at this very point of fully yielding to the Holy

Spirit where Satan seems to be most effective at inhibiting the growth of Christians and at limiting the power and effectiveness of the church worldwide. Since many churches are filled with people and leaders who are stuck in the self-reliant, second condition of spirituality, the churches are no more led by the Holy Spirit and reflective of the life of Christ than many other secular organizations. Satan is effective at blocking spiritual growth at this point because he deceives us into believing that living the Christian life is solely our responsibility. We may have been saved by grace, but we mistakenly believe that we must live by works. We erroneously perceive that God forgave our past sins at the point of salvation, but from then on we had better shape up because God is not going to forgive us over and over. Sadly, many people experience a great release of guilt and shedding of burdens at the point of salvation but then proceed to bear an even greater weight as they attempt to independently live the perfect Christian life.

If you are a Christian, ask yourself what you did to earn or achieve salvation. The only legitimate answer is *nothing*. You merely received by grace the offer that was extended to you by God. You could not earn the gift; you could only receive it. The entire cost of salvation was fully paid by Jesus on your behalf before you were born. God knew you at the cross and bore all of your sins at that point. If you were to go through life without ever accepting Christ, you would have forfeited what was already fully completed on your behalf.

Maybe many Christians never fully understand the grace of God. Perhaps they genuinely believe they must bear the weight of the Christian life. However, this deception is originated in our pride. Somehow we want to believe that there is something we must do to make ourselves presentable to God. In the recesses of our heart what we really want is *control*. We want to keep God on our terms and manufacture human-centered godliness. We may not have been able to save ourselves, but we think we can at least do great things for God. The problem is that God is not impressed by our vain efforts, and He does not need our great works.

What God does want is us! He wants intimate, loving fellowship. He asks us to become living sacrifices. "Therefore, I urge you, brothers, in view of God's mercy, to offer your bodies as living sacrifices, holy and pleasing to God—this is your spiritual act of worship" (Romans 12:1). He does not desire for us to impersonate Christ, but He asks us to become living sacrifices in order that He might live through us. There was absolutely nothing we could do to achieve salvation and likewise, there is nothing we can do to achieve Christ-likeness. As an act of our wills, we receive salvation and by an act of our will we yield to the Holy Spirit and allow Him to bring forth the life of Christ in us.

Unfortunately, many Christians believe that in order to please God, they must read more, pray more, say more, do more, and so on. Many segments of the church encourage this idea. However, this pressure to perform leads to legalism and religiosity. Humans want to systematize and encode religion so we can maintain control over our lives and over other people. This is exactly what occurs in the false religions of the world such as Islam. However, "where the Spirit of the Lord is, there is freedom" (II Corinthians 3:17). Conversely, where there is legalism, there is bondage and oppression. The problem is not that we need greater effort to fulfill specific requirements, but rather we need a new approach to life.

The late W. Edwards Deming became world renowned for his theories about management and productivity.[14] Historically, managers blamed laborers for poor performances and expected them to work harder to provide greater output and greater quality. Deming was keen to point out that most often the workers did not need to work harder, but the systems in which they worked needed to be changed. If managers would provide workers with systems designed to facilitate reaching the desired goals, then workers would respond accordingly. Similarly, God has designed a perfect system for living life both now and eternally. We do not need to work harder at being Christians; we need to get plugged in to His system.

God's System

God's system for life includes yielding our will and allowing Christ to truly reign in us. However, in order for this to occur **we must die to ourselves—die to our self-centeredness, which is**

the major stumbling block. No one voluntarily dies without reservations. Even the last statements of persons who commit suicide often reveal they are in vexing quandaries and suffering enormous stress. We may volunteer to face death to protect the life of another person, but something deep in the recesses of our being wants to live. Unfortunately, it is not only the good in us that wants to live, it is also the evil. We find it very difficult to die to our pride, fears, and self-centeredness. While those who have accepted Christ may have wanted a savior to take away their sins, many do not want a Lord to be in charge of their lives. In other words, an insurance policy on our life is nice, but few want to deed over ownership. Even after we become Christians, many of us still desire to be our own gods; we still want to rule our lives.

However, the Holy Spirit is continuously at work to orchestrate the affairs of our lives to bring us to the point of total dependence upon Him. He waits patiently for our wills to yield. Nevertheless, until we volunteer to die to ourselves, we impede the transformation process. We also forgo participation in the best works of God, which means we also forgo eternal rewards.

Our sin nature was crucified at the cross. "I have been crucified with Christ and I no longer live, but Christ lives in me. The life I live in the body, I live by faith in the Son of God, who loved me and gave himself for me" (Galatians 2:20). **Because our sin nature was crucified with Christ, it no longer has a grip on our lives. We no longer are compelled by our own nature to sin. Nonetheless, the residue of sin is still in our minds. We must go through the process of dying to ourselves in order to have our minds renewed**. However, since it is virtually impossible to voluntarily die to one's self, God must undertake magnificent works to change our beings. His principal tools for bringing about death to ourselves and renewal of our minds are trials and tribulations.

Chapter 8

Trials and Suffering—God's Tools

When sin first entered the world, it was instantly followed by fear and then by the judgment of suffering and death. Both Adam and Eve were immediately ashamed of their sin, and they attempted to hide from God. They began to build walls of self-protection by blaming someone or something other than themselves for their actions. Their fear was genuine because their actions had necessitated the judgment of God:

> To the woman the LORD God said, "I will greatly increase your pains in childbearing; with pain you will give birth to children. Your desire will be for your husband, and he will rule over you."
> To Adam He said, "Because you listened to your wife and ate from the tree about which I commanded you, 'You must not eat of it,' Cursed is the ground because of you; through painful toil you will eat of it all the days of your life. It will produce thorns and thistles for you, and you will eat the plants of the field. By the sweat of your

brow you will eat your food until you return to the ground, since from it you were taken; for dust you are and to dust you will return."

And the LORD God said, **"The man has now become like one of us, knowing good and evil. He must not be allowed to reach out his hand and take also from the tree of life and eat, and live forever."** So the LORD God banished him from the Garden of Eden to work the ground from which he had been taken. After He drove the man out, He placed on the east side of the Garden of Eden cherubim and a flaming sword flashing back and forth to guard the way to the tree of life. (Genesis 3:16-19, 22-24)

It appears the judgment of suffering and death that came upon humankind was the vengeful reaction of an angry God. However, God never undertakes any action on such a shortsighted basis. He does get angry, and He does lament the sinfulness of His creation. However, His responses to our sin are always tempered by His perfect love. Therefore, the question must be asked: *Why did a loving God invoke judgment and consequently, permit human trials and suffering?*

Since trials, tribulations, and suffering are a critical part of the following discussion, let me define the terms as used in this context. For our purposes, *trials* involve the process of testing, trying, or putting to the proof—i.e., a trial of one's faith.[1] *Tribulations* encompass affliction or distress as in an experience that tests one's endurance, patience, or faith.[2] *Suffering* involves pain or distress, which could occur in physical, psychological, or emotional form.[3] Taken together, the three terms encompass the array of possible difficulties and hardships that every human being must face. In the following discussion I use the terms almost interchangeably to refer to the hardships of life. Of course, each person experiences a unique set of trials and tribulations, and his or her suffering is clearly a personal, independent experience.

Does God Have Control?

Some individuals believe there is no God and contend that trials
and suffering are merely functions of an evolutionary process of
survival of the fittest. To these persons there is no ultimate purpose
in tribulations. Such difficulties only possess meaning to the extent
that they affect our current lives and the lives of other people.
However, creation itself speaks of the glory of God; consequently,
these individuals are living in denial of the truth of their existence
and cannot see into the spiritual realm. Furthermore, to simply state
that trials and suffering are mere products of natural processes, and
that they have no purpose, is a terribly insufficient response to
persons who are undergoing immense distress. Persons who truly
desire to seek truth will progress beyond this shallow level of
insight and wisdom. For those who truly seek God will find Him:
"If from there you seek the LORD your God, you will find Him if
you look for Him with all your heart and with all your soul"
(Deuteronomy 4:29).

Another group of people believe God exists, but also believe He
does not have control over the events of the world. In essence, this
philosophy of belief is deism, which became particularly popular in
the 17th and 18th centuries and has remained influential in modern
philosophies. Deists believe God set the world in motion but now is
unable or unwilling to alter the events of life.[4] They may perceive
God as a loving God but one who has His hands tied. For whatever
reasons, they perceive that God is not responsible for suffering, nor
is He able to eliminate it.

An example of this type of reasoning appears in the book *When
Bad Things Happen to Good People* by Rabbi Harold Kushner.
Although Kushner is a Jewish Rabbi, and not specifically identified
as a deist, his reasoning in the book followed deistic logic. Rabbi
Kushner observed his son suffer and eventually die at the age of 14
as a consequence of the disease progeria, which is rapid aging.
Kushner concluded that God was unable to intervene. He said, "I
recognize His limitations. He is limited in what He can do by laws of
nature and by the evolution of human nature and human moral freedom."[5] However, this line of reasoning significantly underestimates

God and His power, for who was it that fashioned the laws of nature and created human moral freedom? According to theologian Peter Kreeft, Rabbi Kushner focuses not on the God of the Bible but on "rationalism, naturalism, and self-justification."[6] In truth, the only limitations that exist for God are those that He chooses to impose.

A third level of argument is that God is involved in the affairs of our lives, but His adversary Satan is so strong that he can block the work of God. Therefore, trials and sufferings result from the actions of Satan, which God cannot preclude. A slight degree of truth exists in this argument, but it too underestimates God. Satan can interfere with the affairs of human beings, but he is not able to thwart God's plans. For example, the book of Daniel reveals a circumstance where an angel of the Lord was delayed, but not prevented, from reaching his desired destination:

> I [Daniel] looked up and there before me was a man dressed in linen, with a belt of the finest gold around his waist. . . .
>
> [He said], "Do not be afraid, Daniel. Since the first day that you set your mind to gain understanding and to humble yourself before your God, your words were heard, and I have come in response to them. But the prince of the Persian kingdom resisted me twenty-one days. Then Michael, one of the chief princes, came to help me, because I was detained there with the king of Persia." (Daniel 10:5, 12-13)

In this case, demonic adversaries impeded the progress of the angel as he attempted to come to Daniel's aid, but they were not able to foil God's intention for this situation.

Another biblical situation that reveals Satan's ability to meddle in human affairs appears in the book of Job. In this case, Satan had to first obtain permission from God before he could even attack Job:

> The LORD said to Satan, "Where have you come from?"

Satan answered the LORD, "From roaming through the earth and going back and forth in it."

Then the LORD said to Satan, "Have you considered my servant Job? There is no one on earth like him; he is blameless and upright, a man who fears God and shuns evil."

"Does Job fear God for nothing?" Satan replied. "Have you not put a hedge around him and his household and everything he has? You have blessed the work of his hands, so that his flocks and herds are spread throughout the land. But stretch out your hand and strike everything he has, and he will surely curse you to your face."

The LORD said to Satan, "Very well, then, everything he has is in your hands, but on the man himself do not lay a finger."

Then Satan went out from the presence of the LORD. (Job 1:7-12)

The Bible nowhere indicates that Satan is equivalent in power to God. Satan is a created being who had a high heavenly position as an angel, but he was and is fully subject to the authority of God. Satan is the "prince of this world" (John 12:31) and "the spirit who is now at work in those who are disobedient" (Ephesians 2:2). However, Satan is subject to the authority of Jesus, who is the "Lord of lords and King of kings" (Revelation 17:14).

Somewhere between deism and the belief that Satan can thwart God's plans are the ideas of Leslie Weatherhead, a British clergyman who gained notoriety during World War II. Weatherhead believed that God's plans change according to the circumstances at hand. In Weatherhead's view, God is far from omnipotent and His will is subject to the circumstances created by humanity. He said, "It was not the intentional will of God, surely, that Jesus should be crucified, but that he should be followed . . . But when Jesus was faced with circumstances brought about by evil and thrust into the dilemma of running away or being crucified, then *in those circumstances* the Cross was his Father's will."[7] In other words, Weatherhead believed that Jesus failed in His primary mission to get people to follow Him and was forced to go to the cross by the circumstances at hand. Jesus' suffering was therefore a consequence of the circumstances contrived by men, rather than the plan of God. However, nothing could be further from the truth. Surely, Jesus' crucifixion was God's plan before He formed the Earth.[8] God was not surprised by sin and evil, but planned to use it as the context in which humans could exercise free will to choose to accept or reject Him. God planned to reconcile humankind to Himself through Jesus long before Jesus set foot on earth. Hundreds of years before Jesus' birth the prophet Isaiah foretold of Jesus' role as a suffering servant and clearly identified the mission as God's will:

> **Yet it was the *Lord's will* to crush Him and cause Him to suffer, and though the LORD makes His life a guilt offering, He will see His offspring and prolong His days, and *the will of the LORD* will prosper in His hand**. After the suffering of His soul, He will see the light [of life] and be satisfied; by His knowledge my righteous servant will justify many, and He will bear their iniquities. (Isaiah 53:10-11, *italics added*)

Likewise, Hebrews 10:5-10 speaks of Christ following God's will in becoming a sin offering for humanity, and Psalms 22 clearly foreshadowed the crucifixion and revealed the planned messianic role of Jesus.[9] Jesus came at just the appointed time.[10] He did not meekly come to the earth hoping people would follow Him. Rather, He knew the course that lay before Him. The crucifixion of Jesus was not God's circumstantial will but rather His perfect will that had the glorious purpose of liberating humanity from bondage to sin. Leslie Weatherhead was so confused about the truth of Christ that he went on to write a book entitled *The Christian Agnostic*, in which he denied the inspiration of the Bible, the sinful fall of humankind, the importance of the virgin birth of Jesus, the necessity of the Holy Spirit, and the atonement of Christ. Weatherhead even embraced reincarnation.[11] Clearly, he was deeply confused not only about God's will but also about the nature of both God and humankind.

Yet another line of argument is that trials and tribulations may be under God's authority, but who would want a relationship with a God who permits such atrocities. This reasoning is really not an argument regarding the issue of suffering but rather a shallow excuse for persons to explain why they do not desire to know God. It is a refusal to honestly delve into the nature and character of God, and it is a superficial response to the difficulties of life.

All of these arguments are insufficient to explain the existence of tribulations, yet humans naturally desire greater insight and understanding into the trials of life. Christianity has traditionally held that God is omnipotent, omniscient, and omnipresent. If He truly is an all-powerful, all-knowing God, then we are left with no choice but to assign responsibility for trials directly to God. That is, even if trials are not the consequence of God's direct or optimum will, they are a consequence of His permissive will. Therefore, the responsibility for all tribulations ultimately rests at God's feet.

If God is fully able to alter any circumstances, the only legitimate answer to the question of 'Why does a loving God permit trials?' is that such tribulations must play a role in accomplishing God's ultimate, eternal purposes. In His infinite wisdom, He chooses to permit trials on a short-term basis in order to achieve His long-term plans for all of humankind. God does not instigate the evil acts of humans. Nonetheless, within the context of the free will He has granted each individual, He is still in absolute control of all of life. Thus, He permits what He could otherwise eliminate because He sees the end from the beginning, and He knows the infinite value of the process. The great difficulty comes in trying to rationally understand God's purposes for any specific circumstance that involves trials and suffering.

The Purposes of Trials and Suffering

God's ultimate order for creation is that it will not include suffering. However, in order to give humans genuine free will, God had to give us the real option of choosing to live apart from Him. As a result, creation is fallen; it reflects God's handiwork, but it is far from the perfection that is reflective of His holiness. Of course, God was not surprised by the sinful nature of humankind because He knew before the creation of the world that sin would pervade all people. He also knew that suffering would enter into creation. Therefore, tribulations and suffering are not beyond God's omnipotence; they are a part of His overall plan for all of creation. Even Satan's fall and his being cast to this Earth are part of God's ultimate plan for all of humankind.

In the end, however, all trials and suffering will end. After Christ's final return, this world will end and a new heaven and a new earth will be created. At that point, there will be no more tears, no more agony, no more suffering:

> Then I saw a new heaven and a new earth, for the first heaven and the first earth had passed away, and there was no longer any sea. I saw the Holy City, the new Jerusalem, coming down out of heaven from God, prepared as a bride beautifully dressed for her husband. And I heard a loud voice from the throne saying, "Now the dwelling of God is with men, and He will live with them. They will be His people, and God himself will be with them and be their God. He will wipe every tear from their eyes. **There will be no more death or mourning or crying or pain, for the old order of things has passed away**." (Revelation 21:1-4)

When perfection comes it will be an overwhelmingly joyous liberation for those who are still bound by this life. In the meantime, it is left to the wise person to seek to understand as much as possible the reasons why God permits trials and suffering.

I have emphasized throughout this book that God's two great desires for all people are that: 1) everyone would receive salvation and 2) every individual would be conformed to the likeness of Christ. These are the two greatest truths that we fail to recognize and admit to ourselves. We fail to acknowledge these realities because our sinful natures are resistant to both of them. First, we resist salvation because we desire to be our own gods. Second, we resist being conformed to Christ's image because it requires us to die to ourselves.

God's decision to permit trials and suffering is inextricably related to His two great goals for all people. Consider the following scriptures from Romans:

> Therefore, since we have been justified through faith, we have peace with God through our Lord Jesus Christ, through whom we have gained access by faith into this grace in which we now stand. And we rejoice in the hope of the glory of God. **Not only so, but we also rejoice in our sufferings, because we know that suffering produces perseverance**; perseverance, character; and character, hope. And hope does not disappoint us, because God has poured out His love into our hearts by the Holy Spirit, whom He has given us. (Romans 5:1-5)

> Now if we are children, then we are heirs—heirs of God and co-heirs with Christ, if indeed **we share in His sufferings in order that we may also share in His glory**.
> I consider that our present sufferings are not worth comparing with the glory that will be revealed in us. The creation waits in eager expectation for the sons of God to be revealed. For the creation was subjected to frustration, not by its own choice, but by the will of the one who subjected it, in hope that the creation itself will be liberated from its bondage to decay and brought into the glorious freedom of the children of God.
> We know that the whole creation has been groaning as in the pains of childbirth right up to the present time. (Romans 8:17-22)

> And we know that in all things God works for the good of those who love Him, who have been called according to His purpose. **For those God foreknew He also predestined to be conformed to the likeness of His Son**, that He might be the firstborn among many brothers. And those He predestined, He also called; those He called, He also justified; those He justified, He also glorified. (Romans 8:28-30)

These scriptures reveal four critical truths that help us understand suffering:

1) **We share in the sufferings of Christ in order that we may share in His glory.**
2) **All of creation remains in its current condition in order that men and women might be liberated from their bondage to sin and enter into freedom as children of God.**
3) **God is working all things to the good of those who love Him in order that we might be conformed to His likeness.**
4) **Suffering produces fruit—it produces perseverance, which yields character.**

These four principles allow us to begin to dig into the eternal purposes of trials and suffering.

The scriptures indicate that suffering and eternal glory are linked to one another. Somehow trials and suffering produce in us fruit that has great eternal value. Tribulations and suffering are also intertwined with the process of liberating persons from their sinful condition. In addition, trials and suffering are among the many tools that God uses to accomplish His goals for our lives. They lead us to accept the sovereignty of God in the affairs of humanity.

Do Not Be Surprised

We should not be surprised when trials come our way. The scriptures clearly indicate that becoming a Christian does not protect us from tribulation and suffering. In fact, trials and suffering can even increase after we become Christians, but facing such difficulties as a Christian is not without purpose. The Bible also clearly indicates that trials and suffering are linked to identifying with Christ and participating in His eternal glory:

> Dear friends, **do not be surprised at the painful trial you are suffering,** as though something strange were

happening to you. But **rejoice that you participate in the sufferings of Christ,** so that you may be overjoyed when His glory is revealed. If you are insulted because of the name of Christ, you are blessed, for the Spirit of glory and of God rests on you. If you suffer, it should not be as a murderer or thief or any other kind of criminal, or even as a meddler. However, **if you suffer as a Christian, do not be ashamed, but praise God that you bear that name.** (I Peter 4:12-16)

Types of Suffering

In order to understand how suffering works to our benefit, we must examine the various types of suffering we may encounter. It is clear that some types of suffering are much easier to bear and much easier to understand than others. However, because God's ways are higher than our ways, it is virtually impossible to fully understand some types of suffering.

Minor, Practical Suffering

The most basic type of suffering is that which results from the minor aches and pains of life. These difficulties may result in intense pain but are generally temporary in nature. In some cases they teach us lessons of life; in other cases they may seem purely arbitrary. Take, for example, some of the pains we experience as children. It could be closing a door on our fingers, running into a piece of furniture, or the agony of a bicycle wreck. These are not enjoyable experiences, but they do tend to teach us to use caution and to protect our bodies. As we get older and our bodies become more vulnerable, these early lessons become all the more important.

It is generally easy to understand the little pains of our lives. They may result from our own faulty decisions or they may simply come with the territory of life. The suffering that results from these difficulties is often confined to superficial parts of our bodies or souls. Rarely do they penetrate deep enough to leave us in serious agony for extended periods of time.

Most of these little pains do teach us something about practical living, but they also serve as subtle reminders that we live in a fallen world. God uses the little bumps and bruises of life to cause our hearts to yearn for a perfect world. In essence, He uses these little difficulties to cause our hearts to hunger for Him. Occasionally, very small, momentary pains have caused me to grieve over the condition of humankind. My heart longs for a world in which there will never again be any suffering. In the meantime, it is worthwhile to allow the little bumps and bruises of life to impart wisdom and understanding.

Self-inflicted Tribulations and Suffering

The bumps and bruises of life are in a class of suffering which is bearable and mostly understandable. Another type of more painful suffering is also somewhat understandable. This type of suffering results from the trials that accompany our own sin. It is obvious that significant portions of the tribulation and suffering in life are the direct result of our own sin. In most cases this suffering is considered reasonable, and it teaches us great lessons. God tends to use this type of suffering as a warning; it serves to help steer us back onto a better course. Bruce Wilkinson refers to these trials and suffering as "discipline or chastening," and notes "discipline is what happens when our loving Father steps in to lift us away from our own destructive and unfruitful pursuits."[12]

Around age 16, I first acquired an unrestricted driver's license and was allowed to drive my parents' cars to various designated locations. Occasionally, I drove our Pontiac station wagon, a veritable 'land yacht.' In comparison to today's automobiles, the cars of that time were very large. This car was a lengthy, rear-wheel-drive model. Although a heavy car, much of its weight was in the front end. As a consequence, the rear end of the vehicle would very easily slide on wet pavement. As you might imagine, the combination of an inexperienced, spirited driver and a car that would easily fishtail was a rather volatile mixture. On one occasion I took the station wagon to an afternoon function at the high school I attended. Sure enough, on this particular day it rained. As I began to leave the parking lot of the school and turn onto the highway, I accelerated too fast, caused the car to fishtail back and forth, and proceeded to drive right over a very steep embankment (first cousin to a cliff). I severely damaged the front end of the car, but fortunately, some trees kept me from rolling down the hillside. I was uninjured, but the worst was yet to come.

First to arrive on the scene were some friends (one of whom had me pose for a picture), but they were quickly followed by a Virginia State Trooper. Needless to say, I was quite afraid of what he was going to do about the situation. Fortunately, he decided the road conditions contributed to the accident, and he did not give me a ticket. I think the only reason was that he did not have a citation designated 'Immature & Foolish Driving.' Next to arrive on the scene was the wreck truck, whose driver just shook his head in disbelief. As if I had not done enough damage, I thought he was going to destroy the rest of the car when he pulled it back onto the road. It survived, but it was not drivable. I don't remember who called him (probably the State Trooper), but the next person to join the fun was my father. Fortunately, he was a rather relaxed and calm person, but by this time the sun had begun to shine brightly and the roads were relatively dry. That made it difficult to explain how I managed to accomplish such a unique driving feat. He responded in a reasonable manner, but he did evidence some degree of disgust.

I survived that fiasco to drive yet another day. However, I certainly learned a tough lesson through the experience. I subsequently had a few more fender benders, but that was the worst accident of my driving career. I learned a degree of caution that continues to pay dividends to this day.

The fishtailing station wagon story is an example of how our sin often results in trials and suffering. Although there were contributing factors, my restless spirit was the primary culprit in this little calamity. The emotional anguish that followed was in direct proportion to my sinful actions. It is clear that even though I was not yet a Christian, God worked in this situation to my good. Even when we are at fault, He still works something positive in our lives.

Not all trials and suffering that follow our own sinful actions are as quick to pass and as easy to learn from as my fishtailing automobile accident. Sometimes our sinful actions have lifelong effects. Some persons have suffered permanent physical disabilities or ailments as a result of their sinful actions. Also, in our culture many young people become sexually active before marriage. Even if a child is not conceived, the premarital activity can adversely affect subsequent marital relations, and if a premarital conception takes place, there will be permanent, long-term consequences. An abortion can end a pregnancy, but the termination cannot eliminate the physical, emotional, and spiritual consequences of premarital pregnancy. Rather, an abortion only creates a different set of consequences that can be emotionally debilitating, unless healed by Christ. Children are a great blessing from God, but when the conception is initiated outside of marriage, many undesirable pains may accompany the pregnancy.

God forgives our sins, but He does not ordinarily take away the consequences of our sin. If we have a repentant heart, He may lessen the severity of the consequences, but oftentimes we must still pay some of the costs. Even so, God does not make us bear the consequences without a reason for doing so. It is imperative that we come to understand that our actions have very real, eternal consequences. Ultimately, our decisions can even lead to eternal separation from God. Therefore, God's decision to allow us to suffer from our sinful actions is also an act of love on His part. He wants us as free individuals to come to recognize and accept the enormous responsibility He has granted us.

One of the increasingly difficult problems in our culture is that we fail to teach children to accept responsibility for their actions. Parents rush quickly to defend their children from punishments, even when it is clear the children are at fault. It is a great disservice to young people to shelter them from the consequences of their behaviors. It is an even greater tragedy when adults fail to accept proper responsibility for their own actions. The proliferation of lawsuits is evidence that we live in an age in which we are quick to blame others for our own faulty actions. Several noteworthy lawsuits have involved situations where persons undertook foolish or negligent behavior but sought to collect awards from third parties who had minimal responsibility. The new American dream is to get rich quick by winning a lawsuit (or winning the lottery). Such a windfall is seen as a quick fix to life's difficulties and an escape from the normal consequences of one's actions.

Instead of spurning responsibility, it is wise for us to accept and bear self-inflicted suffering because it can serve as God's tool. If we attempt to evade the consequences of our actions, we only defer the work of God. He may well have to orchestrate another situation in order to teach us the lesson we failed to learn in the first circumstance. When we accept that our trials are the result of our own actions, we should also find it easier to understand the process. However, all suffering is difficult, even if we can see that God works our mistakes to our ultimate benefit.

Externally Inflicted Tribulations and Suffering

A third type of suffering is that which is caused by someone else's sin. It is generally the result of another person exercising free will in a way that is damaging to us. This type of suffering may be easy to understand, but it is often harder to accept. These types of trials and suffering could result from the harsh words or sinful behaviors of another person. The consequences can be short-term in nature or can have permanent effects. When someone else's sin causes us short-term discomfort, we may find the situation easier to accept as a consequence of a fallen world. However, when someone else's sin causes us long-term suffering, it can become one of life's most severe trials. For example, I have heard or read several accounts of teenagers who were killed in automobile accidents caused by drunk drivers. Obviously, it is easy to understand the origin of the suffering, but the pain is immense, and questions about why God would allow such events can be haunting.

A few years ago a young woman, whom I will call Mary, came to me for counsel regarding her academic record. She had been a student at our school some years earlier, but despite a reasonably good record, she had one terrible semester and dropped out of school. Mary had returned to reenroll and wanted to see if she could have her academic record for that one semester expunged. Our regulations did permit cleansing an academic record for one semester if there were medical reasons causing the academic problems. Since I was the chairperson of the committee that would review the issue, she came to explain the situation to me. In Mary's case, she had been raped during that disastrous semester, and she had become pregnant as a consequence. The rapist had been held accountable for the crime and was incarcerated in a mental institution, but she was left to deal with the emotional and physical consequences.

Mary explained to me that she had been encouraged by almost everyone around her (family, friends, etc.) to abort the pregnancy. However, in her heart she simply could not take that course of action and chose not only to deliver the child but also to retain custody of the little girl. The decision had not been easy, but Mary was glad she had not chosen abortion. After leaving school, she joined the military for a few years where she not only had a successful career but also met and married a young man who formally adopted the little girl. She returned to our school under the G.I. Bill and was determined not to let the tragedy of the rape destroy her life. Instead, Mary had grown through her experience. She chose a course that others thought was unwise, but even some of the naysayers were later appreciative of her decision to continue the pregnancy. Where evil had perpetrated a crime, God brought about love in the lives of many people affected by the event.

I learned of a similar, yet even more devastating, situation a few years ago when I helped lead a Christian seminar held near Washington, D.C. There were several persons who formed a team of teachers for the event. One of the teachers was a lady, whom I will call Ruth Jackson. She was accompanied by her son who was about 12 years old. I had never met her before this occasion. During a morning coffee break between sessions, I developed a casual conversation with Mrs. Jackson. After I greeted her son, I asked if she had other children. She indicated she had six other children, but only five were living. I was hesitant to inquire about the deceased child, but she proceeded to explain that one of her children had been murdered when he was a teenager. Apparently, the young man was mistaken for someone else, or he was the victim of a random, senseless act of violence. He was murdered in a drive-by, gang-style shooting. The young man was a Christian as was his mother, but God had allowed this tragedy in their lives.

I could see the pain in Mrs. Jackson's face as she described the circumstance, but I also saw something else in Mrs. Jackson as the weekend progressed. She was a woman who had a very deep and rich relationship with the Lord, and she exuded wisdom and love. Other people inflicted suffering upon her, but Mrs. Jackson had not allowed it to harden her heart. Rather, she had allowed God to use it to make her more like Christ. Even her young son who accompanied her that weekend possessed maturity that seemed well beyond his years. While this senseless violence had no explanation, Mrs. Jackson had chosen to seek God through the circumstance, and He had worked positively in her heart despite the evil that had been perpetrated. Even though God may permit evil humans to carry out horrendous acts, He is not aloof and unconcerned. He chooses to allow what He could clearly stop for reasons that are beyond our understanding, but He nonetheless brings about good in those situations for those who seek Him.

Large-Scale, Externally Inflicted Suffering

Some of the worst suffering inflicted upon humankind results from decisions made by governments or other sizeable factions of societies that result in large-scale, widespread social problems. Throughout the world, hunger and starvation are often the results of manipulative, ineffective systems that exploit the weakest members of societies for the benefit of those with power. Sometimes those in authority have little regard for the well-being of the citizenry.

War is probably the most hideous example of inflicted suffering resulting from power gone awry. Some wars have started over relatively minor disputes about land or other purported ownership rights. Many regional conflicts have occasionally escalated into massive, worldwide events, such as World War I and World War II. The amount of suffering that takes place during such events is staggering. Not only do many soldiers suffer and die, but also large numbers of civilians are displaced from their homes, faced with possible starvation, and sometimes killed in the course of military actions. Of the estimated 55 million people who died in World War

II, 30 million were civilians.[13]

It is very easy to question God's supposed omnipotence when such events take place. Should not God stop such events before they unfold into massive calamities? Certainly God could intervene. However, when humans exercise free will, shun the moral laws of God, and cooperatively indulge their most sinful desires for power, God allows matters to follow their inevitable course. When nations collectively ignore God, sin inevitably pours out on a large scale among those societies. Furthermore, such sin may spill over to affect other countries, and many people may suffer as a consequence. Still God is intimately involved in the lives of those who seek Him. He may allow them to suffer along with the rest of society, but He will bring about good in their lives even in the face of death. However, God is under no obligation to protect or provide for those who seek after false gods and shun the truth.

Spiritual Battles

Some suffering may be the direct result of attacks by Satan himself or by his demonic forces. The Bible does indicate "our struggle is not against flesh and blood, but against the rulers, against the authorities, against the powers of this dark world and against the spiritual forces of evil in the heavenly realms" (Ephesians 6:12). As we have seen in the Book of Job, Satan does request permission to attack God's people. His attacks are just as intense today as they were in biblical times.

The rationalism of western thinking makes it hard for many people to believe in the existence of a demonic realm. Nevertheless, demonic attacks on humans can and do take place in our day. For this reason it is impossible to explain through purely rational logic much of the evil perpetrated in the world. Such acts have a spiritually evil link and involve conflict in the spiritual realm. As Christians, we can pray for protection from such attacks and trust that God will see us through any conflicts. God can protect us from spiritual battles, but He may choose to allow the struggles to help us grow into spiritual maturity. It is not that God enjoys watching trials and suffering, but He may permit attacks on us in order that He can weave into our beings a deep spiritual principle. Suffering of this type may even seem arbitrary and unjustified, but from God's perspective, it may be important to our position in eternity.

Judgment

Another form of suffering results from God's judgment, which is actually a loving act. God's judgment is always preceded by warning and is purposed to cause us to see our sinful condition and turn from our wicked ways. It is tough love that confronts personal or group sin. Judgment of this type can come in many different forms. God might even use people who are not yet a part of His eternal kingdom to carry out judgment against those who purport to walk with Him.

Judgment might take place only for an individual, or it may encompass an entire nation. For example, the decimation and division of Germany at the end of World War II was probably the judgment of God against the atrocious acts of that nation. If God did not use judgment in such a way, entire groups of people would languish in the poverty of their wickedness. Of course, we should not be quick to assume any given event is a result of God's judgment. Some people rushed to proclaim the September 11, 2001 terrorist attacks on the United States as judgment from God upon the nation. Such comments were hasty; the events could have involved judgment upon the sin of the country, but the attacks could just as easily have been the acts of Satan meant to thwart some positive spiritual events taking place in the land. It will take time and discernment to know the difference.

Some people may see God's judgment upon individuals and nations as unjust. However, God judges not only our actions but also our hearts. Persons who pridefully portray an outwardly righteous life may ignore the warnings of judgment that befall them. Nevertheless, if our hearts are not in right standing with God, we are potentially subject to judgment.

Judgment begins with the house of God because those who know God bear a great responsibility.[14] If we flagrantly violate the will of God and bring disgrace upon His name and His church, we are subject to judgment. It is essential that God's judgment begin with the church, for His followers bear the responsibility of representing Him to the entire world. When God calls Christians to repentance and purification, it may be a prelude to His work of revival in society at large.

There are many more types of tribulations and suffering. I believe all of them can serve purposes in God's eternal plans for individuals, nations, and all of creation. Not that God delights in suffering, but He can take what is intended for evil and make something good from it. The critical need for each individual is to make some sense out of the trials and suffering that we encounter.

Making Sense Out of Suffering

Peter Kreeft completed the best discussion I have ever seen on this topic in his book *Making Sense Out of Suffering*. Kreeft states that the problem revolves around the apparent conflict between four propositions:[15]

1) God exists
2) God is all-powerful
3) God is all-good
4) Evil exists

Since it seems that not all four propositions can be true, we are tempted to deny one of them. According to Kreeft, there are many easy, insufficient answers—such as atheism, deism, or idealism—that deny one of the propositions. However, denying the truth of any of the four propositions may intensify the problem because truth is to be found in reconciling, not denying, the four principles.

Kreeft relied upon the writings of C. S. Lewis to find insight into the apparent conflict. He deduced that the problem is modern humans have largely denied the reality of sin. We view individuals as basically good and the world around us as something to be conquered. In essence, we view our primary problem as external in nature. We seek to determine how we can transform our environment into something that facilitates our happiness. We try to answer the question: How do we overcome the difficulties of life through human ingenuity? However, in adopting this ideology we have invoked a philosophy that prevents us from understanding suffering. We are preempted by our worldview from comprehending suffering because it is inextricably linked to sin. The primary human problem is not external: it is internal. The problem is not the world around us but rather the condition of our hearts. **The ultimate question is: How do we conform the human soul to the expectations of a holy God? Herein lies the meaning to suffering. The tribulations of life transform the soul and spirit of human beings. In so doing, they accomplish the great work of preparing persons for eternity.**

Ultimately the philosophical conflict is between the historical truth of Christianity and the demands of modern humankind to view life in humanistic, rationalistic terms. It is a conflict between God-centered and human-centered philosophies of life. According to Kreeft:[16]

> Modernity finds it very hard to comprehend the biblical (and universal) myth of paradise lost, where suffering and death are seen in terms of sin rather than vice versa. The Christian story therefore also seems incomplete and a failure to the modern mind, for Christ conquered sin, but He did not yet abolish the need for us to suffer and die. A God who did not abolish suffering – worse, a God who abolished sin precisely by suffering—is a scandal to the modern mind, for to that mind such a solution seems to ignore the primary problem. To the Christian mind, it is modernity which ignores the primary problem.
>
> In short, if the most important thing in life is reconciliation with God, union with God, conformity to God, then any price is worth paying to attain that end, if necessary. But if the most important thing in life is conquering suffering and attaining pleasure, comfort, and power by man's conquest of nature, then Jesus is a fool and failure.
>
> When a civilization or an individual puts a second thing, like pleasure or power, first, and makes it an

obsession, an addiction, this blinds the mind's eye to understanding it. And the society that makes the relief of suffering its *summum bonum* [highest good] does not understand the meaning of suffering or of pleasure.

The Work of Trials and Suffering

All people either have or will experience trials and suffering in this world. For some persons the level of tribulations will be greater than for others. The level of trials for each individual varies in accordance with the nature of what God is attempting to accomplish in that person's life and in accordance with his or her responses to the tribulation. A situation that constitutes a severe trial for one person may involve minimal distress for another individual.

When suffering becomes complex and too difficult for us to bear alone, it can be used by God to accomplish some of His greatest work in our lives. Remember that God is always about the business of either bringing us to accept salvation or conforming us to the image of Christ. Complex trials are perfect tools for working in these areas.

In the case of non-Christians, as long as they are able to handle and control the affairs of life, they do not need a savior. Persons who sail through life without great difficulties find it somewhat easy to avoid examining their own sinfulness or dealing with the problem of death. Like the rich young ruler mentioned in chapter four, when everything is comfortable we are satisfied. Although we know that difficulties can and will come, we are somehow able to defer searching for deeper answers. But complex trials and suffering can shatter our perfect worlds and cause us to address the deeper questions of life.

Consider the life of Chuck Colson. He was a former marine and practicing lawyer who became a member of the Nixon White House staff. In his book *Born Again*, he describes the sense of power and pride that accompanied his position.[17] He could instantaneously summon military escorts or requisition top-secret information. His place of work was only a few doors from the Oval Office, the very heart of political power in the United States. His was a very heady position, and he developed a sense of arrogance. However, when the Watergate scandal began to topple the Nixon administration, Colson's artificial world proceeded to unravel. He began to suffer in ways he had never before experienced. Not even a former marine who was politically hardened could deal with all the pressures. In desperation he discussed his situation with Tom Phillips, then President of Raytheon Corporation. Mr. Phillips had converted to Christianity at a Billy Graham crusade in New York City. He shared with Mr. Colson how Christ had changed his life. He also poignantly made Colson come face to face with his own pride. Underneath Chuck Colson's tough exterior was a heart that really wanted to know the truth. His wall broke under the pressure, and he invited Jesus into his life. Mr. Colson went on to serve time in prison for his part in Watergate, but the Lord began a great work in him. Today, Mr. Colson leads a ministry called *Prison Fellowship* and is one of the nation's premiere Christian spokespersons on major social issues.

Some of Chuck Colson's trials and suffering were due to his own sinfulness, but many of them were caused by the actions of others. The complexity of his difficulties weakened his wall. What's more, Mr. Colson's suffering did not end when he became a Christian. Although he played a lesser role in the Watergate affair, he was convicted and sentenced to prison right along with some of the worst offenders. In fact, Mr. Colson ended up spending more time in confinement than some of the persons convicted of more severe offenses. Still, God used this tribulation to form the foundation for Mr. Colson's subsequent ministry.

Trials that take place prior to our point of salvation are designed to invite us to accept Christ. Tribulations that take place after salvation are designed to completely demolish our walls, break our self-centeredness, and turn us into Christ-centered beings. Since many of us want a Savior but not a Lord, tribulations that take place after salvation can sometimes be the most difficult and painful.

Trials of this nature constitute the 'refiner's fire.'[18] They serve to reveal our sin and self-centeredness, compelling us to see our own need for purification. Trials are not needed to deal with superficial, easily identifiable sin. Rather, they serve to reveal sin that is ingrained in our souls. It may not be observable to other parties, and it may not seem as wretched as someone else's actions, but sin is sin. God is not concerned about the depth of our sin. Humans assign an order of magnitude to sin, but God's grace expands to forgive and transform even the worst offenses.[19]

God desires to rid us of all patterns of thinking and modes of behavior that are not of Him. Just as high temperatures are used to bring metal to a molten state and allow the impurities to be removed, God uses trials and suffering to purify our souls. God does not relish the process, but He does cherish the outcome.

Consider what God did in Chuck Colson's life while he was imprisoned. There Mr. Colson had to swallow his pride and dwell among men who were common thieves, despite the fact that he had been a prominent attorney. Not only that, but he learned about genuine Christianity from uneducated men who had been transformed by Christ and filled with the Holy Spirit. Some of these unschooled men became Colson's teachers. A few years earlier he would have looked down upon such people, but in these circumstances he was made to see their wisdom and eternal value. Mr. Colson went from being in one of the world's most powerful roles to being in an environment in which he was stripped of all of his worldly sources of meaning and support. Colson's months in prison were difficult, but they were an absolute necessity if God was going to break him of self-reliance and turn him into a Christ-reliant person. Mr. Colson could have resisted the work of the Holy Spirit during that period, but he did not. Instead, he allowed the Lord to break his will, mold him, and prepare him for important future service in the kingdom of God.

The Effects of Suffering

The chief role of suffering is to reveal the weaknesses of our walls and begin to dislodge our bricks. In the midst of trials and tribulations, our techniques for coping with the world around us often falter. We become too weak to defend ourselves with our traditional methods, and we become very vulnerable. At this point God allows trials and suffering to target our self-centeredness for destruction. In our weakness and vulnerability God is able to transform our souls. The process of transformation is one of dying to our self and being raised to new life in Christ.

In order to understand trials and suffering at a deeper level, let us return to our diagram of the human condition and update it to take account of the effects of tribulations. You will see in *Diagram 8-1* that that two forces are exerting pressure on the self-centeredness of

Diagram 8-1:

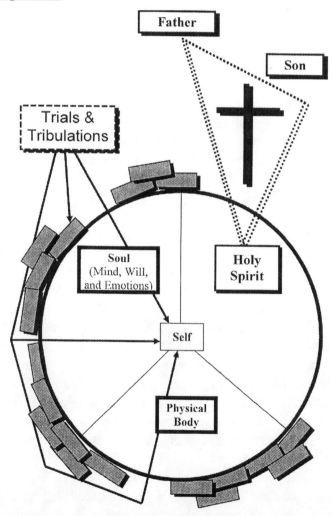

the individual. First, the Holy Spirit is internally encouraging the individual to yield his or her will. In addition, external trials and tribulations are dismantling or circumventing the defensive wall and pressuring the egotism of the person. Essentially, the individual is lodged in a crucible of internal and external conflict from which the only escapes are to: 1) submit to the Holy Spirit or 2) harden one's heart and resist the work of the Spirit. The former is the way of Christ.

Dying to Our Self - The Ultimate Purpose of Trials and Suffering

In order for us to forsake self-centeredness and allow our walls to be demolished, we must deny ourselves and take up our crosses. Essentially, we must die to our self-orientation. Jesus said, "If anyone would come after me, he must deny himself and take up his cross daily and follow me. **For whoever wants to save his life will lose it, but whoever loses his life for me will save it.** What good is it for a man to gain the whole world, and yet lose or forfeit his very self?" (Luke 9:23-25).

The very design of life is such that it is structured to break us of self-centeredness. We are born perfectly self-centered. As infants we are incapable of meeting the needs of others (except perhaps for some emotional needs). Instead, others must dramatically disrupt their lives to meet our most basic needs. The first significant challenge to our self-centeredness usually comes from siblings. The necessity of sharing the love and affection of parents and that of other caregivers threatens the idealistic, self-centered world of small children. Sibling battles in the early years of life can be highly confrontational as children adapt to a world that requires some degree of self-sacrifice. The threats to our self-centeredness become more amplified as we reach teenage years. Adolescents find the post-puberty process of developing relations with members of the opposite sex quite challenging to their perspectives. The sorting process that takes place in modern dating can be highly threatening to self-centeredness and can include painful rejection. For example, spurned young people whose emotions are aroused may find it very difficult to accept that the object of their affection does not share their feelings of love. Nonetheless, they must come to recognize that not every person will fulfill their needs and desires. Despite the fact that the dating process can be tumultuous, most people eventually find a mate and enter into marriage.

Marriage poses a major threat to one's self-centeredness. Opposites often attract one another, and the very things that created the attraction in the dating process can become the things which provide the most conflicts in marriage. For example, extroverts may be attracted to introverts, but after marriage, they may find it hard to communicate. In order for a marriage to succeed, both husband and wife must seek to understand their differences, lay aside self-centered perspectives, and learn to develop a love relationship that is based on self-sacrifice and giving. Much of the explanation for widespread divorce, even within the Christian community, is the refusal by one or both partners to deny their self-centeredness and submit to one another.

The next major stage of life for many people is that of parenting. Perhaps more than any other endeavor, child rearing forces individuals to deny their self-centeredness and sacrifice their personal desires. Of course, many people forsake or inadequately handle their parenting responsibilities. However, those who seek to love their children realize that self-denial and self-sacrifice are absolutely essential. Countless personal endeavors must be set aside to meet the needs of children. Consequently, the role of parenting serves to greatly reduce self-centeredness, except for those who inadequately handle the task.

This process of dying to our self-centeredness is perhaps the most difficult adventure in all of life. It requires us to recognize that we are inept at living not only ordinary life but also the Christian life, and that we must develop entirely new ways of thinking and functioning. We are extremely reluctant to accept this process because it is so revolutionary to our very beings. Therefore, tribulations are required in order to penetrate beyond our superficial points and break the very cornerstones of our walls. If fear is your greatest brick, then it must be broken. If pride is the foundation of your wall, it too must be broken. Christ will not violate your free will; He will not compromise your independence, but He will not be satisfied until your fake barriers have been broken and His life begins to radiate through your being.

Because we naturally resist dying to our self-centeredness, our overall condition may worsen before it begins to reflect the image of Christ. When God orchestrates trials to break certain aspects of our walls, we naturally react with defensiveness. Our walls may temporarily harden and our self-centeredness may become more intense as we resist the pressure. We may experience depression and anxiety, which lead to attitudes and behaviors that are very unlike Christ. **When we reach the point at which trials and suffering are too powerful for us to withstand, we are at a very critical place. It is at this juncture where self-centeredness either dies or becomes accentuated**.

Life is full of real choices. When suffering is acute, the choices we make in our own free will are critical in determining our future. If we submit to God's work, die to our self-centeredness, and yield to the Holy Spirit, then we will become greater reflections of Jesus and more useful tools in the kingdom of God. However, the choice to move forward with God through trials and suffering is not easy. We may clearly recognize the path God has ordained for our life, but it may include obstacles that we consider insurmountable. Consequently, the greatest temptation at this juncture is to abandon God's pathway and run. If we rely on our old ways of thinking, we will perceive that the path is too difficult. We would rather flee the circumstance than die to our old selves.

At one time in my Christian life, I came to a point where I clearly perceived the path that God was preparing before me. It involved an overwhelming personal challenge that forced me to face and deal with what was probably the biggest brick in my wall. In private, I literally screamed out to God: "Anything but this." I had already been through some very difficult trials and somehow expected that I would not have to bear great distress again. I thought I was a broken man who was yielded to God, but not long before this situation developed, I recognized that both fear and pride were still rather strong within me. I knew they were not of God, and I had prayed that God would remove them from my life. He took my prayers seriously and orchestrated the circumstances that would force me to release both hindrances.

At that point, I could have resisted God's will, but because He had already built sufficient faith within me, I chose to move forward with God. It was not an easy decision. The next three years were perhaps the most difficult of my life. Emotionally it was very stressful; I even began to have physical ailments that were obviously a function of stress. During this period I was certainly not a great reflection of Christ. I was often distressed, depressed, and angry. I wanted to run from the situation, but I knew that doing so would mean negating God's optimum will for my life. I did have some degree of hope, and deep in the recesses of my soul, I believed God would never forsake me. The circumstance that caused the trial and anguish never changed, but gradually, I began to change.

During that period, almost everything I had once deemed important no longer seemed to matter. Career or personal achievements became irrelevant, hobbies became meaningless, relationships languished; everything that once yielded meaning fell to the wayside. All that was left was my relationship with God Himself, and sometimes in my heart I was angry with Him. I knew that He was breaking down more of my walls and alleviating more self-centeredness, but it was certainly not an enjoyable experience. I was dying to my self-centeredness and, in exchange, my faith was growing. I persevered through the situation, yet not by my own strength. God's Spirit literally carried me through those years. The only wise thing I did was choose to allow God to carry out His work in me. I fervently believe I could have refused to cooperate with God's plan and forever established a path for my life that was less than God's best for me.

Free will carries with it great responsibility and real opportunities to resist God's will. If we examine any group of Christians to see how extensively God has worked in their lives, we will inevitably find great differences in the spiritual maturity and spiritual effectiveness of people who are similar in chronological and spiritual age. I am convinced the differences are due to the 'yieldedness' of the individuals. The persons who, as an act of their will, choose to submit to God's plan, even when it involves immense suffering, will be the persons who are most useful to God.

God's love is no less for persons who refuse to yield to His Spirit, but He only employs those who desire to be used in His work. Furthermore, He is best able to utilize those people who walk in humility, brokenness, and sensitivity to His Spirit. Individuals who desire to accomplish great things for God but are unwilling to yield their will are inevitably ineffective and potentially damaging to others. They may even bring shame to the name of Christ and to the church in general.

Both the short-term costs and long-term rewards are greater for those who desire to be used to the utmost by God. Jim Elliot was a missionary to the Auca Indians in Ecuador and was eventually murdered by the people he sought to help. Yet before his death, Elliot said: "He is no fool who gives what he cannot keep to gain what he cannot lose." [20] Jim Elliot understood that human life is temporal. What we gain and accomplish in the physical realm only has momentary value. However, when our lives are consumed with Christ and used by Him in His service, then there are eternal rewards that await the faithful servant.

Suffering Builds Character and Yields Rewards

Persons who have experienced some measure of death to their self-centeredness and freedom from bondage realize that dying in this way is good. This is so because nothing eternally good lives within unregenerate human beings. "But now, by dying to what once bound us, we have been released from the law so that we serve in the new way of the Spirit" (Romans 7:6). Therefore, we must recognize that from God's perspective trials and suffering are valuable. They serve as the pruning devices that break our self-centeredness and allow us to produce eternally valuable fruit.

Trials and suffering and the fruit that they produce involve a continuous process. We must daily die to ourselves and daily allow Jesus to live through us in this world. We must desire to know Christ and to experience His life in order that we might share in His glory both now and forevermore.

I want to know Christ and the power of His resurrection and the fellowship of sharing in His sufferings, becoming like Him in His death, and so, somehow, to attain to the resurrection from the dead.

Not that I have already obtained all this, or have already been made perfect, but I press on to take hold of that for which Christ Jesus took hold of me. Brothers, I do not consider myself yet to have taken hold of it. But one thing I do: forgetting what is behind and straining toward what is ahead, I press on toward the goal to win the prize for which God has called me heavenward in Christ Jesus. (Philippians 3:10-14)

Chapter 9

Breaking Spiritual Strongholds

T ribulations not only serve to demolish our self-protective walls
and break our self-centeredness, they also facilitate the process
of breaking spiritual strongholds. Spiritual strongholds reside in the
mind. They are patterns of thinking that are contrary to godly
wisdom. While many thoughts that are incompatible with Christianity are a function of our inherent sinful natures, some patterns of
thinking have a point of beginning that is outside us. The stimulus
for the thinking is demonic. Therefore, spiritual strongholds are
really demonic strongholds in a person's life.

The Apostle Paul referred to spiritual strongholds in chapter ten
of II Corinthians: "For though we live in the world, we do not wage
war as the world does. The weapons we fight with are not the
weapons of the world. On the contrary, they have divine power to
demolish **strongholds. We demolish arguments and every
pretension that sets itself up against the knowledge of God, and
we take captive every thought to make it obedient to Christ**" (II
Corinthians 10:3-5).

Spiritual strongholds are weaknesses in our minds which are in
some form or another influenced by a spirit that is not of God.
According to Neil Anderson, "some strongholds are anchored in

demonic influences and spiritual conflicts from past and present mental assaults which lock their victims in bondage." [1] They are dangerous because they tempt people to participate in sinful and sometimes destructive behavior.

If the word **torment** accurately describes a person's condition, then a spiritual stronghold is likely. Whenever an individual is tormented by thoughts that drive him or her to destructive behaviors, then demons are quite probably the source of the thoughts. Such strongholds might include worry, fear, cravings, and compulsions that impound godly behavior and compel persons to behave in destructive ways. For example, persons who have repetitive thoughts of suicide or ongoing desires to kill others are almost certainly under the influence of demons. The thoughts and feelings that in 1999 drove two young men to murder their classmates at Columbine High School in Littleton, Colorado were most certainly demonic in origin. Jesus is the giver of life, but Satan and his demons seek to kill and destroy—and they drive humans to do likewise. [2]

The spiritual realm is very real; in some ways it is far more real and influential than the physical world we can see and touch. God is spirit, human beings have spirits, and there are good ministering spirits (angels) [3] who carry out roles in this world. Likewise, Satan is a spirit, and there are evil spirits (demons) who also function in this world. They desire to adversely influence our lives and prevent us from walking in full fellowship with God. On several occasions, Christ Himself addressed and dealt with the demonic realm. For example, "the people brought to Jesus all who had various kinds of sickness, and laying His hands on each one, He healed them. Moreover, demons came out of many people, shouting, 'You are the Son of God!' But He rebuked them and would not allow them to speak, because they knew He was the Christ" (Luke 4:40-41). [4]

In our rational, intellectual age it is not popular, even among many Christians, to talk about evil spirits. Persons who enter into such discussions are considered irrational, superstitious, or uneducated. Many people prefer to describe aberrant behavior as merely the function of mental illness. In fact, some psychological problems may be solely due to physiological abnormalities and should be rightly classified as mental illnesses. Nevertheless, mental illness is an insufficient explanation for many of the evil acts perpetrated in society. For example, the concept of mental illness cannot fully explain why, in the fall of 2002, two men terrorized the Washington, D.C. region through sniper attacks that murdered more than ten people. The snipers had apparently committed a string of murders across the country before intensifying their attacks in the Washington, D.C. area.[5] They were cold-blooded but apparently sane murderers who probably had demonic spiritual strongholds that exploded into blatant satanic activity. One indication they were under demonic influence was the tarot card they dropped at one of the killing sites. The card included the words "I am God" written on it.[6] Demons want nothing more than to usurp the authority of the real God.

Mental illness is also an insufficient explanation of the problem of collective evil perpetrated by a group of individuals who have bought into an evil ideology. Some events in life are simply inexplicable apart from understanding the demonic realm. For example, the atrocious and widespread acts of murder and mayhem that accompanied the Nazi regime in Germany during the 1930s and 40s was clearly the result of the influence of demonic beings. To ignore the reality of evil spirits is to play right into the hand of Satan. Furthermore, it is not possible to overcome some difficulties in life until we begin to understand the influence of the demonic realm.

It is somewhat easy for us to conjecture that certain very evil people may have been possessed or influenced by one or more evil spirits. For example, persons who were around Adolf Hitler have publicly stated that he had a certain hypnotic aura about him. He exuded an unusual degree of power and was able to influence large numbers of people to commit horrendous acts. Charles Manson, a person who masterminded various bizarre murder schemes, apparently wielded similar power on a smaller scale. Both of these persons may well have been demonically possessed. Yet, situations in which people are truly possessed are probably few because most people to do not completely yield to demonic influences.[7]

God has the power to override our free will, but as an act of love, He chooses not to undertake such an action. Conversely, demonic spirits desire to override our will but lack the power to do so unless we yield to their influence. Some persons might invite demonic oppression or even possession by participating in occult activities or by being strongly influenced by persons who are themselves involved in the occult. I believe drug use is also an avenue directly into the demonic realm. However, even persons who participate in these most dangerous of activities are not likely to fully yield their will to demonic spirits. Consequently, full demonic possession is probably very rare, even among those who play with fire. Additionally, trials and suffering probably play little, if any, role in helping a person who is truly possessed. In order for such persons to gain freedom, God must divinely intervene.

While demonic possession may be uncommon, many people may experience some form of demonic oppression. Demonic oppression may result from strongholds that exist in a person's family. The Bible indicates that the sins of one generation may be passed on to three or four succeeding generations.[8] Strongholds or oppression may also result from traumas in our lives, or they may be a function of our extensive involvement in sinful behavior.

It is critical to understand just what constitutes demonic oppression and how it works. The spiritual battleground of life is the mind. Demonic oppression primarily occurs in the mind, but it may sometimes affect the body. After a demonic spirit gains a foothold in a person, it is able to influence that person's thoughts. If the evil thought is acted upon repeatedly, the foothold may become a demonic stronghold. Persons who become strongly addicted to various substances find that their thoughts are consumed with acquiring the next 'fix' of the substance. Demonic strongholds can work in a similar fashion but may be more subtle.

Let us consider the simple example of smoking. Many people experiment with cigarette smoking at young ages. Some quickly choose to avoid further contact with tobacco. Other persons begin to smoke on a somewhat regular basis but find it relatively easy to quit. Still other people become addicted to smoking but are able to quit once they break the physical addiction. Nevertheless, some people find it virtually impossible to stop smoking. They may even continue to smoke after they have experienced severe smoking-related ailments. For the first three categories of smokers, there was probably no significant spiritual dimension to the smoking experience. However, those persons who become extremely addicted may well be influenced by a spirit of addiction. That spirit may serve to influence the thoughts of the persons and literally drive them to smoke. They need physical, psychological, and spiritual freedom from the bondage of cigarette smoking. Such freedom can only come through prayer.

> Jesus revealed the importance of prayer in delivering people from spiritual oppression. In one case, Jesus set a little boy free from an evil spirit:
> He rebuked the evil spirit. "You deaf and mute spirit," he said, "I command you, come out of him and never enter him again." The spirit shrieked, convulsed him violently and came out. The boy looked so much like a corpse that many said, "He's dead." But Jesus took him by the hand and lifted him to his feet, and he stood up. After Jesus had gone indoors, his disciples asked him privately, "Why couldn't we drive it out?" He replied, "This kind can come out only by prayer." Mark 9:25-29.

Why some people become subject to spirits and others in similar situations do not is difficult to understand. It is probably a function of spiritual weaknesses that preexisted in the persons. For example, if a person feels rejected by others and undertakes a behavior as a means to gain acceptance on a repeated basis, that person may be inviting a spirit to take advantage of the circumstance. Such influence may be present in persons who become promiscuous and continue such conduct despite their desire to end the behavior. There may even be genetic predispositions to certain sinful behaviors that have been physically passed down through the generations, which make some people more susceptible to demonic oppression. Certain addictions are again good examples. Some people may consume alcoholic beverages all their lives but never become alcoholics. Perhaps they never depend on alcohol as a means to gain acceptance or to accomplish some other hidden agenda. Their consumption habits may be limited to meals and certain social engagements. Such persons may never significantly expose themselves to the possibility of demonic influence. Other persons may initially undertake similar behavior patterns, but their dependence upon alcohol may be driven by various needs for approval, acceptance, or emotional catharsis. They may so thrive on the effects of alcohol that they literally become dependent, not only physically, but also emotionally, psychologically, and spiritually. I have personally known alcoholics who were clearly destroying their minds and bodies. They were aware of the situation but were unable to break free. They needed deliverance from the spiritual bondage.

Probably the majority of sinful endeavors are simply a function of our sin natures or the residue thereof. Nonetheless, some sinful thoughts and actions are directly influenced by demonic spirits. Some of the demonic spirits that seem to be very common in our culture are spirits of fear, lust, immoral sexual behavior, greed, religiosity, racism, and hatred.

Development of Strongholds

Let us consider some of the ways in which demonic oppression may develop in a person's life. First, demonic oppression may result from family strongholds. In my own family it was clearly observable that fear was a factor in the lives of some of my relatives. Some of their fears had developed rationally due to difficulties in their lives, but some of the fears were quite irrational. The fears often resulted from thinking about a particular situation in the most negative of ways and projecting those thoughts into the most dangerous of outcomes. I recognized that some of these tendencies toward fear were also present in me, even after I became a Christian. I asked God to remove these fears from my life, and naturally, He did the one thing that is necessary to conquer fear—He put me right in the middle of the situations that I found most frightening. These circumstances caused much stress and some suffering, but they caused me to examine the sources of the fears and realize that many of my thoughts about these situations were not compatible with God's nature and principles. While there was some gradual improvement in these problem areas, I still struggled until the trials and suffering associated with these thoughts became acute. I then began to intensely seek God's help and engage the prayers of other Christians. Subsequently, I had a unique experience that served as the key to freedom.

After the death of my grandmother, my family members removed her possessions from her home. In so doing, they found a newspaper article that served as the obituary for my great, great grandfather (my grandmother's grandfather). In those days they wrote extensive obituaries that described key aspects of the person's life. This article described his family and the fact that he served in the Confederate army throughout the entire Civil War. It also mentioned that later in life he became a Christian and served faithfully in his local church.

The fact that he served in the Civil War was news to me, and I became very interested in the topic. While I was already an amateur history buff, I began to study the nature of the Civil War with new vigor. I cannot personally be proud of the fact that he defended a government that harbored slavery, but perhaps he was like many other southerners who fought primarily because of a perceived need to defend their land and rights to self-determination. Whatever his motive, my heightened interest in the Civil War was not about the philosophical reasons for the conflict but about the very nature of the military battles. In today's era of technological warfare, soldiers may not even see their enemy. They can literally attack targets with pinpoint accuracy from miles away from the location. However, the Civil War was a gruesome conflict where men stared one another in the eyes as they attempted to kill each other. Sometimes the lines of defense were overrun, and the fighting degenerated into hand-to-hand, life or death struggles. The fear that must have been present just before and during those battles was surely overwhelming. Of course, fear still reigns on modern battlefields, but its intensity may have been different in the context of the close combat of the Civil War. Roughly 20 percent (610,000 men) of all soldiers in the Civil War died, more often from disease than battle wounds.[9] Many more men were captured by the opposition, and numerous soldiers turned in fear and deserted the ranks. Entering the battles, every man knew there was a great probability of dying.

My great, great grandfather, Stephen R. Clear, was a member of the 45th Virginia Infantry. He enlisted shortly after the outbreak of the war and served until he was captured in 1865. During the first few years of the war, his unit was mostly involved in smaller battles (a few thousand combatants) that took place in Southwestern Virginia. Although smaller in scale, the battles were no less vicious and sometimes degenerated into hand-to-hand combat. In 1864, the 45th was reassigned to action in Northern Virginia where it became involved in large-scale battles as a part of the momentous events that led to the end of the war. In July of 1864, the 45th participated in the attempt by General Jubal Early to invade Washington, D.C. and relieve Union pressure on General Lee's forces, which were active further to the south in Richmond and Petersburg. The attack on Washington failed, and the 45th regrouped in the Shenandoah Valley where it became involved in several battles, including the Battle of Winchester, which included more than 50,000 combatants. The last significant action for the 45th Virginia Infantry took place at Waynesboro, Virginia. There my great, great grandfather was captured on March 2, 1865 by cavalry commanded by General George A. Custer. He spent the remaining days of the war as a prisoner in Fort Delaware. Upon his capture, he was one of only about ten percent of the total members of the 45th Virginia Infantry who were still fighting at the end of the war. Many had already died, deserted, resigned, or been captured.[10] Given the casualty statistics from the war, it was a miracle that my great, great grandfather survived four years in a Confederate infantry unit.

During the time period when I was more intensely examining the nature of the Civil War, God revealed a very significant truth to me. I was quietly working at my desk one day and praying within my spirit to the Lord. A most profound thought came to me at this point, which I am convinced was the Spirit of the Lord speaking in my inner being. The thought was that 'the fear which had been so rampant in my family began with my great, great grandfather.' I instantly recognized that the trauma of the Civil War served to subject him to levels of fear that are unimaginable to most people. The repeated exposure to such situations must have made him vulnerable to demonic oppression in this area. A spirit of fear undoubtedly oppressed his life and affected the generations that followed. Some people might wonder how an event that occurred nearly 150 years ago could have such a lasting effect. However, it is understandable when you realize that my grandmother, whom I knew quite well, knew my great, great grandfather, the soldier, on a similar level of closeness. The sins of one generation pass on to the third and fourth generations quite easily through such relationships.

After I received this revelation, I shared it with other Christians who helped me pray that this oppression, which had pervaded the generations of my family, would be broken. While there were no discernible immediate effects, the subsequent prevalence of fear in my life has clearly been significantly reduced. Fear no longer inhibits me from fully living a godly life. Tribulations and suffering caused me to seek relief from the bondage to fear. Thereafter, the Lord orchestrated the processes by which I could discover the entrance point of a spirit of fear, break its stronghold through prayer, and experience freedom that could only be provided by the Spirit of God.

As illustrated by the prior example, episodes of trauma can serve as an entry point for spiritual strongholds. For example, women who are sexually abused might harbor intense hatred of men. Unless God brings healing to the situation, the hatred can fester and become a weakness through which a spirit can develop a stronghold. The spirit might thereafter prompt the woman to behave in ways that are self-degrading. God may allow trials in such a situation to help the person face the traumas of her life, seek healing from the Lord, and find relief from the spiritual strongholds that have developed. Otherwise, the hatred and associated behavior can destroy the individual's life and be passed on from generation to generation.

Sin and Spiritual Infestation

The first sin for a person in a particular area often is rather difficult. Natural inhibitions and rational concerns help us avoid certain sins. However, once a sinful action is undertaken it becomes harder and harder to avoid that sin at later times. Embezzlement is a good example. Many people who embezzle finances of an organization initially take the money with the intent of making repayment. Perhaps they are under financial duress and see the activity as a form of a loan. They may be afraid to undertake the activity, but pressures make the embezzlement scheme appear attractive. The first few embezzlements may be accompanied by an honest intent to repay the money before anyone discovers the situation. Inevitably, however, the need for money snowballs, and it becomes impossible to repay the funds. The embezzler may even move to different cities and jobs in an attempt to stop the behavior, but it is generally repeated.

Persons who become involved in habitual sins also open themselves up to the potential development of spiritual strongholds. Whether the sinful behavior involves money, sexual behavior, alcohol, drugs, gambling, or other repetitive sins, ongoing exposure to such arenas leaves a person very vulnerable to spiritual infestation. Instead of the behavior remaining a mere function of our souls, it may become more deeply rooted and be linked to an oppressing spirit. Again, God will allow tribulations to result from these types of bondages in order to bring persons to a point where they seek and can receive deliverance.

A common spiritual stronghold involves a spirit of religiosity. Humanity's counterfeit for true relationship with God is religion. Religion is simply the series of behaviors we undertake in an attempt to appease God and relieve our own guilt. We may go through the rituals of religion without ever opening our hearts to God and experiencing His love and grace. Satan loves to drive both Christians and non-Christians into bondage to religion. Persons who are victims of this type of spiritual stronghold will likely find it very hard to progress beyond legalism in their spirituality. Even somewhat mature Christians may have some degree of religious strongholds that prevent them from fully understanding and experiencing a rich relationship with Jesus. Trials are perhaps most useful in breaking this type of stronghold. When tribulations are intense, our religious rituals become meaningless, and they are useless in assisting our struggle. At this point, we either seek true relationship with God and have the spiritual strongholds broken, or we retreat into a firmly entrenched (yet miserable) pattern of religiosity.

The Bible indicates that, "for the joy set before Him, Jesus endured the cross" (Hebrews 12:2). The joy that Christ saw was the liberation of humanity from its bondage to sin by the power of His all-sufficient sacrifice on the cross. He could see into eternity, and He could see the glorious plan that is in store for all those who love Him. In order for us to experience this freedom and joy, we must join in Christ's sufferings so that our minds might be renewed and any demonic strongholds in our lives may be broken.

We must realize that Satan does desire to destroy our lives. Therefore, we must develop spiritually strong resources for defeating this mortal enemy. "Be self-controlled and alert. Your enemy the devil prowls around like a roaring lion looking for someone to devour. **Resist him, standing firm in the faith**, because you know that your brothers throughout the world are undergoing the same kind of sufferings. And the God of all grace, who called you to His eternal glory in Christ, **after you have suffered a little while, will Himself restore you and make you strong, firm and steadfast**" (I Peter 5:8-10).

Chapter 10

Jonathan's Ordeal

M ost of the trials and suffering I have experienced in life have been due to my own sinful activities. In fact, the most burdensome, distressing, and anguishing days of my life have come as a direct result of my sin. This type of tribulation is relatively easy to understand, and fortunately, I learned that such trials and suffering served a very positive role in my life.

Not all difficulties are so easy to understand, nor are they easy to accept. Just such a circumstance occurred in my life in the midst of writing this book. It was a sudden, unexpected episode, which truly altered my life, as well as the lives of several other people. Because as Christians we should exercise greater wisdom, we may be less susceptible to trials and suffering that result from our personal actions. However, we are certainly not immune to uncontrollable tribulations. Furthermore, the amount of suffering we have already experienced is not necessarily a deterrent to additional difficulties. I had already gone through what I considered very trying and difficult days (years in some cases) before the circumstance described hereafter developed.

The following account includes both prose and selected email messages I sent to family and friends during the days of trial. They describe the situation as it unfolded and progressed:

Subject: Jonathan Daniel Russell
Date: April 21   3:44 PM

Friends in Christ,

Some of you know more details than others, but I will start from the beginning. On Tuesday (April 15) my wife, Michelle, gave birth to a little boy; we believe the Lord gave us the name Jonathan Daniel for him. He weighed 7 pounds, 5 ounces and was in good health but appeared to have a problem with his intestinal system. Consequently, he was rushed to the Neonatal Intensive Care Unit (NICU). Michelle did not have delivery problems, and she is doing well.

That first day was a roller coaster of hope and concern, but by late evening the physicians had determined that Jonathan had an obstruction in his small intestine and scheduled surgery for the next day. We tried to rest that evening but were summonsed back to the NICU. Jonathan's intestines appeared to have ruptured, and surgery plans were immediately underway. He was not even 24 hours old but had to undergo a major surgery. Fortunately, the intestines had not yet actually ruptured, and the surgeon was able to remove the malformed portion of his bowel that was causing the obstruction. Jonathan was doing fine after the surgery, so we finally got to sleep about 3:00 AM (it was the first time Michelle had slept in three days).

Jonathan has been doing well. He has gained weight, although he is only being fed intravenously. He is exceptionally healthy for a child in the NICU, but I believe he is the only one there who has had surgery (most are premature). He has had a voluntary bowel movement (hooray for dirty diapers!), but his intestines have not yet been able to fully process the digestive waste from his system. This may simply be due to swelling and other effects of the surgery.

Nonetheless, our primary prayer at this point is that his intestines will process his waste without any complications. As soon as this takes place, they will attempt to feed him. Another major prayer concern is that he will tolerate normal feedings.

The doctors have estimated that he will be in the NICU for four or five weeks, but certainly we pray that it will be much less. It is amazing how you instantly love your new baby and how you get very attached in a short period of time. It is very hard for mom and dad to come home each night empty handed.

.There certainly seems to be a spiritual dimension to this situation. We led a 'Walk in the Spirit' seminar in Philadelphia, PA last October. It was a great seminar where the Spirit of the Lord seemed to pour out in abundance. A member of our host family was stricken with a virus that weekend, and we suffered through it a few days later. It was the harshest virus I have ever encountered. My father visited us just after the Philadelphia trip but before we showed symptoms of the virus. He contracted it and ended up spending eight days in the Intensive Care Unit of his local hospital. The virus had caused his intestinal system to temporarily paralyze. Fortunately, he recovered without surgery.

When we were first informed about Jonathan's condition, it was strangely similar to that of my father. Even the methodologies being used to drain his stomach and maintain his nourishment were the same. Unfortunately, Jonathan's situation was worse, and he required surgery to remove the intestinal blockage.

At first the doctors did not think there was any relationship between the two situations. However, after the surgery, the doctor who performed the work indicated that a viral infection could have adversely affected Jonathan's intestinal development. Michelle had the virus when she was three and one-half months pregnant. I recently read that during the third month the intestines are formed in the umbilical cord and move inside the child's body prior to the fourth month. It appears to have been a very vulnerable time. Medically, the relationship is uncertain, but there certainly seems to be a spiritual link.

The Lord has given us 'peace which passes all understanding' in this situation, but we also have sensed that this is a spiritual battle. For this reason, we ask that you pray fervently for this little child. Frankly, we are too drained to wage a spiritual battle by ourselves. We need the prayers of our friends and the entire body of Christ. God bless you and thank you.

Jonathan made some progress following his surgery. He gained weight, had some intestinal function, and became alert and active. Nonetheless, there were various peaks and valleys in his development. Jonathan had a tube going in his mouth down to his stomach that drained digestive waste from his stomach so that his intestines were not overworked. On several occasions, the doctors removed the tube, but it always had to be re-inserted because his stomach would begin to swell.

The primary problem was that Jonathan's intestines could not process waste from his stomach. Since he was born with a blocked bowel caused by an anatomical abnormality, his intestinal system was somewhat inverted. Parts of his small intestine were so inflated they were larger than his large intestine. This problem resulted in waste backing up in his system and prevented Jonathan from consuming normal food.

Days turned into weeks as we waited and prayed for Jonathan's system to improve. He stayed in the NICU and received around the clock attention from many doctors, nurses, and staff specialists. We hoped for a shorter than projected stay in the hospital, but instead Jonathan struggled. The physicians began to talk about an extended stay in the NICU, possibly having to give Jonathan blood transfusions, and even having to consider another surgery. My blood was determined to be compatible and safe, so a pint was taken and prepared for Jonathan just in case he needed it.

God did work goodness into the situation. Jonathan bonded

with a young nurse by the name of Amanda. She was a Christian (as were many of the other nurses) and she took especially good care of Jonathan. We also made friends with another couple who had a child in the NICU. Their infant girl had been born prematurely— she only weighed a little over two pounds. The couple had recently moved to our area, were not married, and he had recently lost his job. We got a number of people from several different churches to bring them food and other assistance. A short time later, the couple called the home of a Methodist minister we had referred to them and indicated they wanted to get married. He took them the money to pay for the license, and they were married that day. Being able to help this couple diverted our attention from Jonathan's troubles and brightened our days.

While we were waiting and praying for Jonathan's intestines to improve, the course of events took another turn. I had some torn cartilage in my right knee that had been that way for about ten years. Some years earlier, an orthopedist examined it but said that surgery could be deferred until it caused more problems. He suggested that the knee locking in place or giving way would be symptoms of such a need. Well, one evening I was preparing to eat dinner and then go to the hospital to visit Jonathan. I simply sat down in a chair and something went crunch in my knee. I immediately lost mobility and could not straighten my leg. The knee joint seemed to be locked in place. I saw an orthopedist the next day, and he determined that I not only had some torn cartilage, but I also had a bone fragment wedged in the joint. Unlike some cartilage surgeries which can be deferred, he recommended that I have surgery as soon as possible. The concern was that the bone fragment would cause additional damage unless it was removed immediately. Therefore, I was scheduled for surgery to take place on the following day.

Meanwhile, Jonathan remained in the NICU. The drainage from his stomach tube was very little for several days, so the doctors removed it again. However, after a few hours Jonathan began to regurgitate bile and other digestive waste. It was very disconcerting. The stomach tube was reinserted and the doctors scheduled Jonathan for some special tests. The analysis of these tests would determine the next course of action. In particular, it would reveal if there was a need for additional surgery.

The testing on Jonathan revealed that he was having additional problems in the upper part of his small intestine. The doctors recommended that he be transferred to a specialty children's hospital because he would probably need additional surgery. The number of hospital options was limited because Jonathan needed a pediatric surgeon who could perform the delicate task of reshaping the small intestine. We set about trying to determine where to move Jonathan, while we were also planning for my knee surgery on the following day.

We made a tentative plan to move Jonathan to Rainbow Babies & Children's Hospital in Cleveland, Ohio. Rainbow is supposed to be one of the best children's hospitals in the country. We were fortunate that we could go there and stay with Michelle's parents, who live in a Cleveland suburb (Strongsville). It had been four weeks since Jonathan was born. Based on the doctor's early estimates, we thought he would be home, not traveling to another hospital. It was a very distressing time. We had greatly anticipated the day that Jonathan would leave the NICU, but we did not fathom that it would be to go to another hospital.

Meanwhile, I did go through knee surgery. The problem was that a bone chunk the size of a silver dollar (with cartilage attached) had broken off from the end of my femur (thighbone). Because of its size, it had to be put back in place with a screw and pins. As a consequence, I was assigned to crutches for six weeks and would then have to undergo another surgery to remove the paraphernalia.

After the knee surgery, we made preparations to go to Ohio. It was tough because Jonathan would be airlifted via a special jet, but none of us could go with him. I don't know if I ever had a heavier heart than the moment when they took Jonathan from the NICU to board the ambulance that would take him to the airport. We so wanted to be by his side. Instead, we had to make the long drive to Cleveland. I was unable to drive because of my knee surgery, so Michelle handled the duties while I tried to pacify our other son, David, who was not quite two years old at the time.

Subject: Jonathan
Date: May 16   12:28 PM

We are all now in Cleveland, Ohio. Jonathan got a first-class trip. He traveled in his incubator condo via air ambulance, accompanied by an EMT, RN, paramedic, and flight crew. He also got ambulance trips to and from the hospitals. Dignitaries don't usually travel this well. His first airplane ticket cost a mere $6,500. Fortunately, our insurance will cover most or all of the cost. We hope Jonathan will settle for coach fares in the future.

We were at the hospital in Tennessee when the transport people arrived, so we did not leave for Ohio until mid-afternoon. Our late departure made it impossible for us to go to see Jonathan until the next morning. Nonetheless, we were assured by the hospital staff that he had arrived safely.

Upon arriving at the hospital the next day, we found Jonathan in a large, new private room. This luxury suite was a dramatic change from the NICU we had been accustomed to for four weeks. Jonathan had apparently requested first-class service upon his arrival. The facility was much more conducive to us having long visits with Jonathan. However, we were concerned about the intensity of nursing care he would receive, since this ward lacked the constant, bedside care provided in a NICU. Nonetheless, we later determined that the ratio of nurses and caregivers to children was almost the same in this ward as it was in our previous NICU. And of course, Jonathan is fully monitored by electronic devices.

A Resident Surgeon soon arrived and gave us a run down on Jonathan's condition. Everything she said, with one exception, was the same as we had heard from our former doctors. The one exception was her discussion of a heart murmur. She indicated that she did not know the exact nature of the murmur or whether it required surgery! This was the absolute first word we had ever heard about a heart murmur. The Resident even said she did not know how they missed that in Tennessee.

Later in the afternoon, a Neonatal Specialist examined Jonathan. She indicated that Jonathan was in good enough overall health not to require 'intensive care.' She plotted Jonathan's growth measurements and found that he was well above average in all categories—not bad for a kid who has never had a normal feeding! She complimented our previous doctors on how well they had managed his intravenous nutrition. As of yesterday, Jonathan had reached 11 pounds. Maybe he has been eating manna when the nurses aren't looking.

Next to arrive on the scene was the cardiologist, who had checked Jonathan's EKG and conducted a physical exam. He declared that Jonathan's heart was perfectly fine. There is some type of murmur, but it is considered very normal. Apparently, many people have various murmurs that are not considered health problems. The doctors in Tennessee had noted the murmur on Jonathan's chart but had not considered it significant enough to even mention to us. By the way, the cardiologist also complimented our previous doctors on Jonathan's growth.

Last to arrive was one of the three pediatric surgeons who are handling Jonathan's care. Jonathan is really here just to be seen by these doctors. They indicated that the early results of a barium study were good. The barium is injected into the intestines, and it then allows the doctors to have a very clear view of the intestines on an x-ray. Some of the barium went all the way through his intestines, which is very positive. Nonetheless, his large intestine is still too small and his small intestine is still too large.

TODAY IS A CRITICAL DAY! The doctors will take a series of x-rays to determine how well the barium is continuing to flow out of Jonathan's intestines. If there appears to be clogging, surgery may be necessary. If the barium continues to flow at a good pace, they may try to gradually work Jonathan's intestines into shape via non-invasive means. Obviously, we pray that no additional surgery will be necessary.

Because of my knee situation, I cannot adequately take care of our son, David, by myself. In Tennessee he often went to the homes of friends or neighbors whenever Michelle went to see Jonathan. In Ohio, we have a good situation because Michelle's mother, Sylvia, (who is great with children) is willing to take care of David whenever Michelle is not available. Would you believe that Sylvia got a Jury Summons in the mail yesterday! I haven't bothered to mention some of the smaller problems, but Michelle got a jury summons one day after Jonathan was born. It was fairly easy to get Michelle out of the duty, but Sylvia may have a harder time. Please pray that she will be released.

Please excuse my verbosity today, but it is an enormous source of encouragement to be able to send these notes and know that people around the world are praying for Jonathan. I got a phone call just today from Sister Margaret, a friend of Michelle's parents, who has 200 nuns praying for Jonathan.

While the situation is still difficult, I am becoming increasingly aware that the King of Kings is going to turn what was meant for evil into good. We all are becoming a little more like Christ through this situation.

Jonathan underwent a series of tests during the following days. He was in good health overall, but the enlarged section of his intestines remained a problem. Consequently, the pediatric surgeons determined that another surgery was going to be necessary. Our surgeon in Tennessee had recommended the move to another hospital because he anticipated that another surgery would be required. Therefore, we were not shocked by the news, but it was still hard to hear. Shortly after we learned of the surgery, Jonathan had to go to have an x-ray. Michelle went with him; she said she just sat in the x-ray area and cried.

Jonathan was tentatively scheduled for surgery on Wednesday, May 21. The full extent of the surgery would not be known until the surgeon actually viewed Jonathan's intestines, but the plan was to taper down the distended section of his small intestine and enlarge the opening at the prior point of surgery. It had been five weeks since his birth and the end was not yet in sight. Jonathan continued to be fed intravenously and still had a 'NG' (nasogastric) tube down his nose that drained his stomach.

Jonathan developed a fever that delayed his operation for one day. He was rescheduled for surgery on Thursday, May 22. The night before I sat down to read a passage from the Bible, and I felt led to go to I Samuel chapter four. The story there is about a battle between the Philistines and Israel. In the battle Israel is defeated, the Ark of the Covenant is captured, and Eli's sons, Hophni and Phinehas, die. It was a very grievous time for Israel. It was certainly not what I wanted to read the night before my son was to have perilous surgery. I wondered if the Lord was forewarning me that Jonathan would not survive. I went to the hospital the next day in almost stunned silence. Fortunately, my speculation was wrong. In the passage I read, judgment fell on Eli's family because of their sin (I Samuel 3:12-14), but the Lord's favor smiled upon Jonathan:

Subject: Some Good News
Date: May 23   12:15 PM

Jonathan was formally scheduled for surgery on Thursday at 1:00 PM. The plan was to: 1) conduct an exploratory surgery of his intestines and make any necessary repairs, 2) install a semi-permanent drain tube in his stomach, 3) implant an intravenous line (broviac) into a vein near his heart, and 4) give him a blood transfusion (using my blood again). At 11:00 AM a nurse was busy cleaning him and preparing him for surgery when the pediatric surgeon walked in the room. We expected a run down of the surgery plans; instead, we got some good news!

Jonathan's morning x-ray showed the dilation of his small intestine was less than in the last view. The enlarged section of his intestine, which has been an ongoing problem, has apparently begun to contract to a more reasonable size. While the intestine is still not close to being normal, at least there was some improvement. As a consequence, the pediatric surgeon canceled the intestinal and stomach portions of the operation!

Jonathan still went to surgery at about 5:30 PM and was put under general anesthesia. However, the installation of the intravenous line in the chest and the blood transfusion were the only procedures that were performed. These activities took about an hour. By late last night, he was alert and doing fine.

Intestinal surgery has not been ruled out. The surgeon simply believed the improvement Jonathan made justified waiting a few more days to see if the small intestine would normalize without intervention. He must continue to progress, otherwise surgery will still be required.

In the last five weeks, we have reached several major junctures. Each time the situation turned in a negative direction. Yesterday's news was the first positive development to take place at a critical period. Frankly, at previous important points it seemed as if God was silent, but yesterday He clearly reminded us that He is in charge!

We were thrilled by the cancellation of the major portion of the surgery, but this has already been a harrowing ride. Consequently, we are guardedly optimistic at this point.

I said a few weeks ago that if I could just get an email message to those folks in South Korea who incessantly pray, Jonathan would stand up and walk out of the hospital. Maybe the prayer request at least reached the Philippines a couple days ago. We continue to communicate with more and more people who are praying for Jonathan. We greatly appreciate this outpouring of God's love.

Although Jonathan's situation and condition did not immediately change, there were encouraging signs. It seemed as if the healing hand of the Lord touched Jonathan the day before his scheduled surgery. After that point, things looked increasingly promising. For example, I was scheduled to give another unit of blood for Jonathan, but the doctors decided it was unnecessary. Jonathan did continue to undergo various tests, and he was fed intravenously via the broviac line in his chest. However, for the first time there was discussion among the doctors about gradually introducing milk to his intestinal system. It was a positive sign that caused us to yearn for the situation to come to a joyous conclusion, although our main task remained that of just persevering.

Michelle and I took shifts at the hospital with Jonathan. She mostly handled the days, and I took the night shift. Meanwhile, our son David had a great time wearing out his grandmother, who got her jury duty postponed until December 19 (Merry Christmas!). We had occasional bouts of fatigue and depression, but mostly we just peacefully walked through each day. The Lord encouraged us through many people. Several of Jonathan's nurses and assistants were Christians. One in particular, Miriam, an African-American Pentecostal, spread cheer wherever she went. We also received email notes, cards, and phone calls from many people in various parts of the world who were praying for Jonathan. It was very heartening. One of the best blessings of the whole ordeal was the feeling of being bathed in the prayers of the saints. Perhaps because of those prayers, I began to develop a sense of dogged determination that we were going to see the situation through to a good conclusion.

Eventually, Jonathan's nose/stomach tube was removed, and for the first time, he did not have problems. As a consequence, on the 50th day of his life, Jonathan received his first official feeding. It was less than an ounce of pedialyte (sugar water). Thereafter, he received a pedialyte feeding every four hours and later worked his way up to breast milk.

We were told early on that it would be very important for Jonathan to breast-feed. The breast milk would be much better for his intestinal development than formula. Consequently, Michelle had been faithfully 'pumping' every three hours, day and night, since he was born so she could maintain her milk supply. Initially, Jonathan was artificially fed via methodologies that imitated breast-feeding. This went fairly well but there were times when he had digestive problems. After a few difficult episodes, Michelle took matters into her own hands. She must have been anointed with wisdom because she skipped over a few stages of the doctor's planned progression and went straight to normal breast-feeding. It was just what the doctor (should have) ordered. Jonathan began feeding much better; he took larger quantities in less time and did not have problems. The breast-feedings went so well that the doctors even disconnected his intravenous feeding line for various intervals and began to talk about moving Jonathan to outpatient status. They indicated that Jonathan could possibly go to the home of Michelle's parents and visit the hospital for regular examinations. Jonathan was still to have an intravenous feeding line, but we were to become his nurses.

To complicate matters, however, I was scheduled to have my second knee surgery just a few days hence. I was supposed to leave Cleveland and have knee surgery on the following Thursday (June 19). I vowed when Jonathan was born to love him as best I could every day. Fortunately, I had been able to be with him in the hospital every single day of his life. I did not want to leave Cleveland without him, but it looked like the only possible route when Jonathan was about to be discharged.

Subject: New Bed & Breakfast
Date: June 14   2:56 PM

Jonathan came to his grandparent's house in Strongsville, Ohio on Thursday. It is his third different bed & breakfast stopover as he attempts to go home for the first time. His nurses were as happy as we were to see him be discharged.

Jonathan's condition continues to improve. He is now taking breast milk at a pace that equals about 70-80% of his total caloric need. His stomach girth also continues to decrease, and he is 'stooling' after almost every feeding. All of these are very good signs.

It is certainly much easier on us now that we do not have to go to the hospital everyday. It was about a 40 minute drive each way through city traffic to go to the hospital. The elimination of the trip alone has reduced our stress. Also, it is much more restful to sleep here and be able to feed Jonathan whenever he is ready.

Jonathan still has an intravenous feeding line in his chest and receives Total Parenteral Nutrition (TPN) for 12 hours during the night. We have been trained to set up his intravenous feeding each evening. It is far more complex than we realized and a little unnerving. We have a home health nurse temporarily assisting us, but this will end soon. Please pray we handle the TPN properly so he does not develop any infections or other problems.

I must go to Tennessee on Tuesday; my knee surgery is Thursday morning (June 19). I received a very pleasant surprise the day Jonathan was discharged. In our final conversation with his surgeon, Dr. Stallion, he indicated there would be no reason why Jonathan could not go to Tennessee on Tuesday. Jonathan is very healthy, and we are simply in a wait and see mode with regard to his feedings. Jonathan will have to come back to Cleveland, but at least we can go home for my surgery as a family, if we so desire. We have not yet decided whether all of us will go to Tennessee on Tuesday. There are various logistics to consider, including the fact that Jonathan is supposed to see Dr. Stallion again on Monday, June 23. Please pray we will have wisdom in this area.

Clearly, we are now at a much better point than just a few weeks ago when Jonathan was scheduled for major surgery. Praise God it was canceled!!! We must still wait until Jonathan is able to tolerate 100% of his nutritional needs from breast milk before we can truly celebrate. Only then will we know that no additional surgery will be necessary. Nonetheless, it is good to enjoy being together as a family for the first time.

Jonathan will be two months old tomorrow (June 15) – Father's Day. My birthday is Monday (June 16). Having Jonathan out of the hospital is a large enough gift to abundantly cover both days!

Thanks again for your support. As I look back over the weeks, I can see many areas in which prayers materially affected the situation. Not only was Jonathan's second major surgery canceled, but also he never developed any of the numerous complications the doctors had warned us could occur. Additionally, we have been able to maintain our sanity, peace, faith, and even our joy. May the Lord bless you!

The entire family headed home on Tuesday, June 17 so I could have surgery on Thursday. We expected to return to Cleveland on the following Sunday, but Dr. Stallion consulted with a local pediatric gastroenterologist and decided Jonathan's feeding care could be handled from Tennessee. We were quite surprised and relieved to learn we could just stay home for a while.

My second knee surgery went well. The screw that had been inserted in my femur was removed and the bone fragment that had broken off remained in place. It appeared to be healing well, but I was ordered to spend five more weeks on crutches and restrict my activity for at least six months.

Jonathan continued to progress. He consistently consumed more than 80% of his caloric need via breast milk. On one day, he even crossed 100%. For a while he still received supplemental intravenous feedings equal to 25% of his need. However, after a few more days he relied solely on natural sustenance. Nonetheless, the doctors wanted to leave the intravenous feeding line in his chest as a precautionary measure.

Despite his improvement, Jonathan's blood analyses did present some cause for concern. He was very jaundiced due to inactivity of his liver, and his blood count was low. These problems were not unusual for someone with his background, but they needed to improve. We did not anticipate additional problems, but the roller coaster ride started yet again.

Jonathan's blood analyses continued to reveal problems with his liver. His bilirubin count was rather high and his liver enzymes were elevated. Jonathan was supposed to have the intravenous line in his chest removed, but that was canceled. Instead, he was scheduled for a series of liver tests that were designed to check for blockages in and around the liver.

Meanwhile, we also received some distressing news about another family member. Michelle's grandmother, Eleanor, suffered a stroke and underwent emergency surgery. She survived the surgery but was in critical condition. Eleanor was 84 years old at the time but she had been relatively healthy and living independently until this occurred. Given all that was going on, it was hard to envision brighter days ahead.

Subject: Jonathan's Liver Tests
Date: July 3   7:58 PM

Jonathan's liver tests did not go well. He had an ultrasound and a 'HIDA nuclear scan.' The scan is designed to detect an atresia (closure) in the ductwork of the liver. It involves the injection of a radioactive isotope in his system. The material is supposed to travel into his liver, then to his gall bladder, and ultimately to his intestines. Jonathan had several x-rays taken today, but they always indicated that the material stayed in his liver. He has another x-ray scheduled for 9:00 AM tomorrow. If the material has not moved by then, the assumption will be that he has some type of blockage associated with the ductwork coming out of the liver.

This situation is rather disconcerting, since it reminds us of his original condition. The original diagnosis was 'Jejunal Atresia' (closure of the small intestine). We thought Jonathan would get his intravenous line removed this week, and we would be at the end of this ordeal. If this situation with his liver does not look better by tomorrow, we may be faced with going back to the hospital for another serious surgery.

I must admit that I am probably more distraught now than at any other time during this entire ordeal. We thought we were at the very end of this situation, but suddenly Jonathan is facing the prospect of a major surgery. We pray that the Spirit of the Lord will intervene!

Subsequent x-rays continued to show that the diagnostic material was stalled in Jonathan's liver. Some of the doctors assumed there was a blockage in the ductwork exiting the liver. However, some of the physicians believed Jonathan's problem was due to the fact that his liver had been dormant while he was intravenously fed, and it had not yet begun to function effectively. They hoped his liver would develop normal function over the next few weeks. Jonathan continued to consume good quantities of breast milk, but he was extremely jaundiced and did not gain weight.

The gastrointestinal specialist decided to administer a drug for three days that would stimulate Jonathan's liver and then repeat the radioactive isotope test. Jonathan's blood analyses improved, which indicated there was some function in the liver. Nonetheless, he again failed the test that checked for blockages. Consequently, the doctors in the various cities conferred to try to determine the next course of action.

Meanwhile, Michelle's grandmother remained in a coma. There was some disagreement among the doctors about her condition. One physician hoped she would come out of the coma in two or three weeks, whereas another doctor was less positive. Michelle's family had to balance the stress of Jonathan's situation at the same time as they dealt with Eleanor's condition. On top of that, yet another family member suffered an injury. Michelle's other grandmother, Rose, fell and broke her leg. Both grandmothers ended up hospitalized in the same facility. Fortunately, the break did not require surgical repair, but Rose faced six weeks without being able to put weight on her leg (which sounded all too similar to my knee situation).

The challenges to our extended family just seemed unending. Next to suffer injuries was my brother-in-law's mother, Eva Kilbourne, who was involved in a serious car wreck. She lived in our immediate area and was much like an aunt to us. In fact, she had just stopped by our house to visit shortly before the accident. An uninsured motorist pulled out in front of her, and Eva slammed into the side of the vehicle. The other driver was unhurt, but Eva suffered a broken wrist, a broken ankle, and another dislocated ankle. The wrist and broken ankle required surgical repair. The doctors ordered Eva restricted to a bed for the next six weeks.

I'm sure all families experience some periods where loved ones suffer physical problems. Over the years, we had occasionally seen some difficult periods. Some of them had even been very serious. Nonetheless, I had never witnessed a time that was so filled with continuous, multiple problems. Our family's situation seemed like the plot of a poorly written soap opera. Nonetheless, God was clearly permitting this time of trial. Apparently, He was accomplishing something very significant, not just in our lives, but in the lives of all who had a vested interest in the circumstances. We tried to trust God and follow His direction, but it was not easy:

Subject: Back to Ohio
Date: July 23   9:16 PM

Jonathan's latest blood analyses again showed improvement. His bilirubin count was down to 7.0; it had been as high as 12.9 (the goal is 1.0). Nonetheless, his liver enzymes remain high and our pediatrician continues to be concerned. She communicated with the pediatric surgeon who handled Jonathan in Ohio, and they prefer that we go back to Cleveland for more testing.

The plan is to put Jonathan on a drug that is designed to stimulate his liver for a period of seven days and then conduct the radioactive isotope test at the hospital in Cleveland. If Jonathan does not pass the test this time, they would then conduct a liver biopsy and dye test. These are surgical procedures. Depending upon the results of these tests, Jonathan could have to undergo surgery to repair or create an adequate bile duct from his liver.

Hopefully, Jonathan can be fully tested in Ohio and get a seal of approval. In our spirits we do not believe Jonathan needs surgery. He seems to be steadily improving. Our neonatal specialist had told us a long time ago about the liver problems that would develop and about the pattern of recovery. He did not assume liver surgery would be required. So far his projections have been exactly right, so we hope Jonathan will completely recover without surgery.

Obviously, this is yet another serious time in Jonathan's life. Please pray for his liver to develop normal function by the time he is examined in Ohio. By the way, yesterday was my last day on crutches. My knee seems to be doing well, but it will be several more weeks before I can walk normally. We're getting closer to the end of this series of trials, but we still need to make some progress. Thank you for continuing to pray for us. God Bless You!

We nervously traveled back to Ohio, concerned that we might be in for another long hospital stay. However, both my wife and I had a strong sense that Jonathan would be okay. We went back to Rainbow Hospital, and they administered the same radioactive isotope test, which Jonathan had failed on two previous occasions. However, this time he PASSED the liver test! The material passed through his liver into the bowel. It clearly indicated he did not have an obstruction of the bile duct, and his liver was improving. A few days later, the pediatric surgeon removed the intravenous line from Jonathan's chest. He was free from any artificial tubing coming out of his body for the first time since minutes after his birth.

We had an official celebration with Michelle's parents in Ohio and then returned home. For the first time, we started to enjoy Jonathan as just a normal baby. It was nice to pick him up and not be concerned with tubes and other paraphernalia associated with his medical treatment. He even began to smile often. After a few weeks, his jaundice was almost gone, and he was steadily growing. He was eventually introduced to solid foods and began going out in public like a normal baby.

Unfortunately, some members of the extended family still suffered through difficulties. Eva Kilbourne, who was involved in a serious car wreck in mid-July, began experiencing complications. The doctors discovered she had a previously undetected subdural hematoma (bleeding into the space between the brain and the skull). Consequently, she underwent brain surgery to stop the bleeding. She recovered but had some lingering health effects from all the injuries. Michelle's grandmother, Eleanor, remained in a semi-comatose state for many months before regaining some function. However, she never returned to her previously healthy condition and required continuous institutional care. As for me, I walked with a limp for some time after the knee surgeries, but eventually regained full function and returned to normal activities. Despite the remaining issues, we were elated about Jonathan's outcome and his prognosis for a healthy life.

Was God Really There?

The ordeal with Jonathan profoundly affected the lives of many people. Obviously, my wife and I were most directly affected, but many family members, friends, and even strangers were touched by Jonathan's struggle. We shed many tears and suffered through various anxious moments. Even so, one thing continually reassured us and gave us both hope and peace. We believed that no matter what the circumstances or outcomes, **God was in control, and He had a purpose in allowing this situation**.

Consider the following quote from Rev. Jack Taylor; he sent the statement to me in the midst of Jonathan's struggle:

> **I continue to pray for you this morning during what appears to be a siege. For all that it might mean, you are not alone. The enemy seems to be laying down firepower as never before, and God seems to be allowing it. GOD IN HIS WISDOM ALLOWS WHAT BY HIS POWER HE COULD PREVENT. Thus, we may be absolutely assured that what is happening will further His Kingdom, further frustrate the enemy, and in the end edify you. THAT IS STUBBORN AND RELENTLESS SOVEREIGNTY.**

There were two primary themes that transcended the days of Jonathan's tribulation. The first was peace that surpassed understanding. This was especially true during the first three or four weeks of the ordeal. I truly experienced peace beyond anything I had ever fathomed in such a challenging situation. I learned at a deeper level what was meant by the following scripture: "Do not be anxious about anything, but in everything, by prayer and petition, with thanksgiving, present your requests to God. **And the peace of God, which transcends all understanding, will guard your hearts and your minds in Christ Jesus"** (Philippians 4:6-7). I did not manifest such a peace from my own strength; it had to come from the Holy Spirit Himself.

The second theme was that of determination. In the early days of the struggle, we were only determined to see each day through and walk as closely with God as possible. We had a quiet determination to love Jonathan as best we could, be attentive to him every single day, and trust God regardless of the circumstances. However, after about five weeks, quiet determination began to be supplanted by dogged tenacity. It was a growing resolve that we would not be defeated by this attack of the enemy, and we would persevere with Jonathan until he could go home healthy. It was not a presumptive, demanding type of attitude. Rather, it was an ever-growing sense of persistent determination. This too must have been the manifest presence of the Spirit of God. By His grace, we were able to both persevere and grow in faith.

Although it was difficult to see Jonathan suffer, I did become very thankful for the many blessings that came from the situation. We were overwhelmingly blessed by family and friends who provided for our daily physical needs in order that we might direct our energies toward Jonathan. I experienced a fresh, new sense of love not only for Jonathan but also for many other people. It also caused me to reassess my priorities, adjust my attitudes, and resolve that I would become a more loving reflection of Christ. There are countless hurting people in the world; it was remarkable how I could more sincerely empathize with their needs while I was suffering alongside Jonathan.

Had Jonathan died, I am sure it would have left a wound in my soul that would never fully heal during this lifetime. Even so, it was not just the joy of his recovery that was important; the process of suffering also had immeasurable value. In the book of James we find the following scripture: "Consider it pure joy, my brothers, whenever you face trials of many kinds, because you know that the testing of your faith develops perseverance. Perseverance must finish its work so that you may be mature and complete, not lacking anything. . . . Blessed is the man who perseveres under trial, because when he has stood the test, he will receive the crown of life that God has promised to those who love Him" (James 1:2-4,12).

I believe God's primary purpose in allowing Jonathan's ordeal was to compel the members of my family, friends, acquaintances, and especially me to become a bit more like Christ. In so doing, we pressed on to maturity as Christians and became better prepared to serve in the kingdom of God. It was not easy; I certainly would not desire to repeat the episode, but it was and is eternally valuable.

Chapter 11

Faith, Hope, and <u>Trust</u>

Trust in the LORD with all your heart and lean not
on your own understanding.
— (Proverbs 3:5)

All of the principles of this book rest on the underlying assumptions that God is always at work in our lives, and He always has a purpose in orchestrating and allowing the circumstances we encounter. I have hypothesized that trials and suffering are not without purpose and that God desires for each of us to die to our self-centeredness. However, when God takes something from us, He generally replaces it with something better. God desires to take self-centeredness from us and replace it with Christ-centeredness.

<u>Dying to Self - Arising in Christ</u>

God does not simply desire to change our focus and get our attention off ourselves. Rather, He desires that we die to ourselves and arise in Christ. In essence, we should experience a personal, spiritual death and resurrection. Our personal goal should be to reach the point where the life of Christ continuously radiates through us. The ultimate goal is not merely that we receive salvation, or that we simply orient our lives toward God. While these are of paramount importance, **the true goal is that Jesus the Christ would become our very life. Without losing our identities as marvelously created human beings, we should develop such unity with God the Father, through God the Holy Spirit, that Jesus the God/Man becomes the very essence of our life!** As the Apostle John said, "He must increase, but I must decrease" (John 3:30, KJV).

The only way Christ can literally live in and through me is by way of the Holy Spirit. I cannot voluntarily reproduce the life of Christ. What I can do is yield to the work of the Holy Spirit in me and allow Him to radiate the image of Christ through me. In yielding our wills we can continuously be filled with the Holy Spirit. Jesus said, "Don't you believe that I am in the Father, and that the Father is in me? The words I say to you are not just my own. Rather, it is the Father, living in me, who is doing His work" (John 14:10). We too can be about the work of the Father by allowing the Holy Spirit to do His work through us.

Unfortunately, most of us resist yielding our wills to the work of the Holy Spirit. This is why trials and suffering are necessary parts of our Christian lives. Trials break down our walls and create the circumstances by which we are encouraged to yield our wills to God. Frankly, without tribulations most of us would remain stranded in the quagmire of self-centeredness. Westernized, modern persons exalt personal happiness and prosperity. Suffering is incongruent and incompatible with these aspirations; it is also intrusive. However, from God's eternal perspective suffering is exceedingly meaningful.

Some might say it is easy for me to talk about meaning and purpose in suffering because Jonathan's situation culminated in a positive outcome. However, I steadfastly believe purpose and meaning would still have been prominent in the situation even if God had chosen to allow his life to end at such an early age. Certainly, positive outcomes are easier to accept, but God is at work in all situations, not just those that appear to be victorious.

Perhaps the most critical day of Jonathan's ordeal was the day when he was scheduled for his second major surgery, but the surgery was canceled at the last minute. On that day a charming lady by the name of Nanci Kulchar came to the hospital room specifically for the purpose of praying with and supporting us. My wife, Michelle, and I did not know Nanci well, but she is a close personal friend of my in-laws. She had been praying for Jonathan and us for several weeks. Nanci wanted to come to the hospital to support us because Michelle's parents had been strong sources of encouragement for Nanci when her husband, Steve, suffered through lung cancer just a year or so earlier.

After Jonathan's major surgery was canceled, we obviously experienced relief and joy. However, Jonathan still had to undergo a lesser surgical procedure later in the day. In the meantime, we spent much of the time talking with Nanci Kulchar about the ramifications of suffering for a Christian. We talked about how suffering either drives people to God or hardens their hearts toward Him. Additionally, we reflected upon the belief that God is much more concerned about the effects of the process He takes us through than about the outcomes. Most people who face a life or death trial focus upon the outcome. God does not fret and worry about outcomes; He is much more concerned about using trials to weave into the tapestry of our lives the fabric of His Spirit. Nanci concurred with this belief, but she nonetheless encouraged us with her conviction that Jonathan was going to recover and be healthy.

It was a most curious experience to have such a conversation with Nanci Kulchar on that particular day. You see, her husband's bout with cancer ended about six months earlier when he died. Both Nanci and Steve were Christians, and they had great faith in God. They had prayed that God would heal him. Yet they came to accept that it was God's will that Steve's earthly life come to an end. While our experience with Jonathan ended with relief and joy, hers ended with grief and pain. However, Nanci still saw meaning and purpose in her husband's struggle. She still grieves and struggles with heartache; she probably always will to some extent. But God did not abandon her—Nanci's eternal hope was not stolen. She is now seeking to walk intimately with God down a road she has never before traveled. Her dependence upon Jesus must be greater now than ever in the past. She now has a unique opportunity to know the Father as only the brokenhearted can know Him. It is not a giddy, happy experience. The experience encompasses peace and a calm sense of joy that are beyond human understanding. The fact is that a loving God will allow a family member to go through the experience of dying, and allow the survivors to experience grief, in order that all parties can become what He has eternally ordained. It is certainly not easy to experience; it is not enjoyable, but it is absolutely purposeful and meaningful! It is the act of a God who loves perfectly.

The Trial Continued

Despite the victories that unfolded in Jonathan's situation, we subsequently experienced the other side of the effects of tribulations. You see, the trial that surrounded Jonathan's ordeal did not end after his liver began to function. Jonathan did begin to experience infancy as a normal child, but other circumstances developed that were equally challenging.

Just about the time Jonathan was settling into a normal lifestyle—and I was beginning to walk normally following my knee surgery—another significant event took place in our family. My father, Robert Murrell Russell, began to experience lower back and side pain, which was diagnosed as kidney stones. He appeared to be passing them without problems, but complications developed, and he underwent a cystoscopic surgery to drain the urinary tract of infection. Upon conducting the surgery, the doctors discovered a malignant tumor in the bladder that was the real source of the problem. They removed as much of the tumor as possible using the cystoscope. The initial treatment plan was to have him undergo surgery that would involve removing his bladder and prostate, which would result in a permanent urostomy (a drain for the kidneys that runs out the abdomen). He was 76 years old but had been active and in reasonably good health during the previous few years. Obviously, the diagnosis of cancer was very disconcerting.

We began to pray for my father just as we had for Jonathan, and we enlisted the prayer support of many friends. However, the entire circumstances surrounding my father's diagnoses and treatment became clouded. First, the oncologists determined that the cancer had already spread (metastasized) to the bone in his hip and to the base of his skull, which seemed rather unusual. This diagnosis caused the doctors to change their treatment plans. Instead of removing his bladder and prostate, they decided to only conduct a surgery that would provide urinary drainage. The bladder tumor had partially obstructed one ureter coming from his kidney to his bladder. Consequently, the surgery involved permanently rerouting both ureters to an opening in his abdomen. After the surgery, he was to undergo chemotherapy and radiation treatment.

The surgery to perform the urostomy went as well as could be hoped for under the circumstances. The biggest concern was that they would find the cancer had spread to other parts of the abdomen, but it had not. The surgeon even began to question whether the cancer had spread to the bone (as previously diagnosed) because he could find no evidence of any other type of metastasis.

Subsequent testing and analyses led the doctors to conclude that in fact the cancer had not spread to the bone as previously diagnosed. The new, revised treatment plan was to allow my father a couple of weeks to recover from the first surgery and go back as soon as possible to remove the bladder. There would be no radiation or chemotherapy treatment. In other words, the original plan to remove his bladder was the correct course of action, and it should have been done during the first surgery.

Regrettably, my father's recovery from the first surgery was very slow. He encountered a variety of complications, including intestinal paralysis and staph infections. Because he was so severely weakened, the doctors decided to give him radiation treatment as a temporary measure and defer his second surgery several more weeks so he could regain strength. Many weeks passed and additional complications, such as a flu-like virus, caused additional delays in the planned second surgery. Finally, he seemed to regain strength and the second surgery was about to be scheduled, but it had been more than four months since the first surgery.

Suddenly, things took a turn for the worst. To almost everyone's surprise, he suddenly experienced a variety of ailments that put him in an intensive care unit. Severe bronchitis was the primary problem, and because he had a very difficult time breathing, he was put on a ventilator. It was deemed a temporary measure to help alleviate fluid in his lungs, which was associated with the bronchitis. However, his condition deteriorated rapidly, and he was airlifted to a specialty hospital for additional treatment. A complete set of tests at the second hospital revealed that the cancer had now metastasized to his lungs and liver. In all the time that had elapsed after the first surgery, the cancer had spread throughout his body. The doctors continued to treat him, but there was little hope at this point. He died about two weeks later with all of his immediate family members at his bedside.

My father's death took place two days (April 13) before Jonathan's first birthday (April 15). It had only been about six months since my father was first diagnosed with cancer. In that week we experienced the full breadth of possible emotions. According to the doctor's estimates, the cancer must have first appeared in my father's body about the time Jonathan was going through the most difficult parts of his ordeal. We were very thankful that Jonathan had survived and made it to his first birthday, but we were deeply saddened by the loss of my father. The preceding year had been a roller coaster of trials, suffering, and emotional swings that left us virtually numb. (Interestingly, after several years have passed we now see that Jonathan is the 'spitting image' of my father in both appearance and demeanor.)

My father was a very kind and loving person. He had become a Christian later in life, but even before that, he was a good father who always treated his children with gentleness and love. As a young man he had been a good athlete and played minor league, professional baseball. (This was the late 1930's, and he eventually quit playing baseball because he did not make very much money doing so—hard to believe in light of today's baseball salaries, even in the minor leagues.) Despite his athleticism, at age 47 he suffered two serious heart attacks that altered his life and mine. Although he recovered and never again experienced heart problems, I was always concerned about his health. The biggest fear I held from age ten onward was that he would die. I could not imagine how I would survive without him. He was not only my mentor but also my best friend, confidant, and the person I turned to for comfort more than any other. In addition, I had wanted my two young sons to know and enjoy their "Grandpa Murrell" for a significant period of time. (He would have also loved my daughter, Abbie, who was born that same year on December 13, six days before what would have been my father's 77th birthday. Abbie is his only female grandchild, but he never knew about her impending birth. We found out just two weeks after he died that we were expecting another child.)

Upon his death I experienced a quandary of emotions. On the one hand, I did not have significant regrets. My father and I had a good relationship for many years that was marked by laughter and camaraderie. While in retrospect I could see ways in which the relationship could have been better, there were not the feelings of remorse that sometimes accompany the death of an estranged loved one. In fact, the last words that we exchanged, just before he was put on a ventilator, were mutual expressions of "I love you."

In contrast, however, I was deeply wounded by his passing. My heart ached from the depths of my soul. I grieved in ways I had never previously imagined. My biggest fear had come true, and I really did not know how I would emotionally survive. On top of those emotions was raging anger. Whenever I dwelt upon the way in which his treatment had been handled, I became furious. Not that I exploded in public, but I privately fumed over the 'blunderous' actions of the doctors who had misdiagnosed his condition and reversed their treatment plans on multiple occasions. I wanted to get revenge by filing a lawsuit against the doctors, but I knew such action would only amplify our distress. Furthermore, I knew the Lord was calling me to have a forgiving heart toward them. Given their human limitations, the doctors had done the best they could under the circumstances. (No, we never filed suit against anyone involved in this circumstance. We were not going to become part of the litigious free-for-all commonplace in our society.)

I knew deep in my heart that I was really most angry with God. Where had He been during this situation? Whereas it seemed He always intervened at critical junctures in Jonathan's circumstances, in this case He seemed to be strangely absent. The ill-fated series of events that surrounded my father's treatment made me really wonder if our prayers had mattered at all. Had God just turned a deaf ear to our pleas? We had been faithful servants of His for many years, but had He been faithful to us in this circumstance?

My sorrow, wounds, and anger soon gave way to depression. I still carried on with the rudimentary requirements of life, but I often just sat motionless and listless. I really wondered what the future would be like. I wondered if I could still trust God. I wondered if I would ever again be a joyful person. I commiserated with the thoughts of Job from the Old Testament:

> Why is life given to a man whose way is hidden, whom God has hedged in? For sighing comes to me instead of food; my groans pour out like water. **What I feared has come upon me; what I dreaded has happened to me**. I have no peace, no quietness; I have no rest, but only turmoil. (Job 3:23-26)

I floundered in my doubts for many months. **During that time I came to a critical juncture. I realized deep in my soul that I had to either go forward with God, trust Him with my future, and trust that He had been faithful in my father's situation—or I was going to harden my heart and probably place a ceiling (limitation) on my spiritual life.** In other words, God was calling me to really die to my self-absorbed perspective; otherwise, I was going to languish in spiritual gloom indefinitely. **Perhaps this was the most critical point of my entire Christian life**. I had intensely witnessed both the blessings of God and the wrenching pangs of life within a short period of time. Like Job, I wanted an audience with God so I could explain why things should have gone differently.[1] However, I knew that I had no grounds upon which to argue, and I knew that real faith requires trust even when we do not enjoy the ramifications of God's decisions to act or not act.

Sometime during that process I sat before God and prayed several things. I prayed that He would give me a heart of forgiveness toward the doctors and others who had failed with regard to my father's treatment. I also prayed that He would forgive me for hardening my heart toward Him and trying to manipulate Him through anger and sulking. Basically I said, "Lord, even though I do not understand this life and the difficulties it encompasses, and I do not fathom what you are doing in me personally, I will trust you—I will go forward with you."

That prayer was a turning point. It was another year or two before I really got back on track with life, but from that point forward, I resolved to trust God no matter what. There were a few milestones along the way—points at which I grieved deeply or let go of wounds. Gradually, I began to experience acceptance, peace, and assurance. Eventually, I even had joy where there had been sorrow. Furthermore, I began to see where God was working in the lives of other members of my extended family through my father's death. It became clear that Jesus had been there all along; He had chosen to allow my father to die at this appointed time, and He was using this situation to bless the lives of other people. I can now see much more clearly that even in the worst of circumstances, God does not forsake us. Rather, He continually sustains us, and He especially upholds us when we cannot see His perspective. I still miss my father greatly, but I realize that my faith has deepened and my trust in God has become stronger through this and other trials. I have become a little more like Christ.

Perfected in Christ

The ultimate purpose of trials and suffering is for them to work toward perfecting us into the image of Christ. Tribulations and suffering help to transform us from one type of being to another. We transgress from being mere physical, emotional, and psychological creatures into spiritually rich beings as well. You [and I] must understand that:

> **You have been given fullness in Christ**, who is the head over every power and authority. In Him you were also circumcised, in the putting off of the sinful nature, not with a circumcision done by the hands but with the circumcision done by Christ, **having been buried with Him in baptism and raised with Him through your faith in the power of God**, who raised Him from the dead. **When you were dead in your sins and in the**

**uncircumcision of your sinful nature, God made you
alive with Christ.** (Colossians 2:10-13)

We were dead in our trespasses prior to conversion, but by
receiving the fullness of Christ we were transformed in the spiritual
realm. The circumcision we received was circumcision of the heart;
our sinful nature was cut away so that it no longer controls our
lives. In essence, we were instantaneously perfected in Christ.
However, what is fully complete in the spiritual realm must still be
worked out in our daily lives. Therefore, **suffering is a form of
psychological circumcision**. It cuts away the residue of sin from
our minds and allows the Holy Spirit to transform our thoughts into
the thoughts of Christ. Our ultimate goal then is to live out on a
daily basis what is already eternally true.

**I do believe all people will face critical junctures in their
spiritual lives**. Of course, the initial critical points regard opportunities for individuals to accept or reject Jesus. No one knows exactly
how this process works, but apparently the Holy Spirit repetitively
woos persons to accept Christ. Eventually, individuals either accept
Jesus or reject Him for the last time. Acceptance of Christ yields
eternal life, whereas rejection of Him produces eternal death.

**Subsequent critical junctures have to do with dying to one's
self and submitting to the Lordship of Jesus**. These decision
points also have long-term ramifications. Those who submit to
God's work in their lives bear greater fruit as they become greater
reflections of the image of Jesus. However, those who harden their
hearts and resist His transformation process forgo the opportunities
to participate in the best of God's plans.

There are very real differences in the spiritual lives of people.
Some age gracefully and become greater and greater emulations
of Jesus. Others become cantankerous, bitter people because they
wage an internal war with the Holy Spirit. Somewhere in between
are those who remain relatively satisfied with spiritual mediocrity.
Although they may have a sense that something is incomplete,
they are only willing to yield a limited amount of control of their
lives to God. Given these differences, it is critical to realize that
the decisions we make in this life have enormous ramifications

both now and forevermore. We do reap what we sow:

> Do not be deceived: God cannot be mocked. A man reaps what he sows. The one who sows to please his sinful nature, from that nature will reap destruction; the one who sows to please the Spirit, from the Spirit will reap eternal life. Let us not become weary in doing good, for at the proper time we will reap a harvest if we do not give up. (Galatians 6:7-9)

Perhaps the greatest purpose of human life is to establish the context of free will in which humans can make unforced decisions to accept or reject God. Evil and suffering play into God's plan because they provide the backdrop against which individuals can freely ascertain the nature of God and submit to all or parts of His eternal plan. Truly wise individuals will recognize that dying to one's self and submitting to the Holy Spirit is the route to greatness in the kingdom of God. It is opposite to the self-exaltation that is prominent throughout much of society. However, it is the pathway of servanthood established by Jesus. He said, "Whoever wants to become great among you must be your servant, and whoever wants to be first must be slave of all. For even the Son of Man did not come to be served, but to serve, and to give His life as a ransom for many" (Mark 10:44-45). Therefore, we should forever live by the truth of the following scripture:

> Since, then, **you have been raised with Christ**, set your hearts on things above, where Christ is seated at the right hand of God. Set your minds on things above, not on earthly things. **For you died, and your life is now hidden with Christ in God. When Christ, *who is <u>your</u> life*, appears, then you also will appear with Him in glory.** (Colossians 3:1-4, *italics added*)

Recognizing that Christ is your life leads to abiding in Him, following His direction, and submitting to His will. It produces the 'Spirit-filled life.'

Chapter 12

The Spirit-Filled Life

I n our day we hear much talk among Christians about the 'Spirit-filled life.' The concept means different things to different people. For many it refers only to supernatural phenomenon. Others speak of prosperity, while some see discipline and rigor. Unfortunately, there exists confusion that sometimes impedes spiritual growth for maturing believers. Consequently, we must legitimately ask: "What is God's perspective on the meaning of the Spirit-filled life?"

First and foremost, the Spirit-filled life is generated by God Himself, not by us. It is God who chooses to initiate the relationship in which the Holy Spirit becomes intertwined with our spirit. Jesus said,

> I will ask the Father, and **He will give you another Counselor to be with you forever—the Spirit of truth**. The world cannot accept Him, because it neither sees Him nor knows Him. But you know Him, for *He lives with you and will be in you*. I will not leave you as orphans; I will come to you. Before long, the world will not see me anymore, but you will see me. Because I live,

you also will live. On that day you will realize that **I am
in my Father, and you are in me, and I am in you.**
(John 14:16-20, *italics added*)

Therefore, at the most fundamental level, the Spirit-filled life is
God living in and through us. We must cooperate with God's plan
by yielding our will, but the burden to produce fruit really rests
upon Jesus.

Second, the Spirit-filled life includes trials and tribulations.
We are not talking about God filling us with spirit in some
emotional sense, but rather the Spirit-filled life involves the person
of the Holy Spirit living through us. In order for the Holy Spirit to
truly live through us, He must remove anything and everything that
is incompatible with His presence. As a consequence, God prunes
those who are growing in Him. Jesus said:

> I am the true vine, and my Father is the gardener. He
> cuts off every branch in me that bears no fruit, **while
> every branch that does bear fruit He prunes so that it
> will be even more fruitful**. You are already clean
> because of the word I have spoken to you. Remain in me,
> and I will remain in you. No branch can bear fruit by
> itself; it must remain in the vine. Neither can you bear
> fruit unless you remain in me.
>
> I am the vine; you are the branches. **If a man
> remains in me and I in him, he will bear much fruit;
> apart from me you can do nothing**. (John 15:1-5)

Third, the Spirit-filled life is a rich, full life. It is not per se a
life of material wealth and grandeur but rather a life that is rich in
relationships, meaning, and purpose. Such is an abundant life.[1] It
involves continuous interaction between our inmost being and the
Holy Spirit. As a consequence, we are repetitively used in the work
of God. God the Father determines the tasks to be undertaken; we
are just the tools of His trade. If we are out of fellowship with the
Spirit, then we can do nothing. However, in fellowship with Him, we
can "do all things through Christ" who strengthens us (Philippians

4:13, KJV). Ultimately, the Spirit-filled life is a growing, anointed relationship that results in the life of Christ being manifested in and through us.

The following illustration represents the Spirit-filled life. It portrays the three-dimensional human being—indwelt by the Holy Spirit and submitted to the Lordship of Jesus. Christ predominates the individual's life to the extent that the person's walls are broken down, and he or she is free to live life to its fullest. God Himself is living in and through the person—affecting everyone and everything:

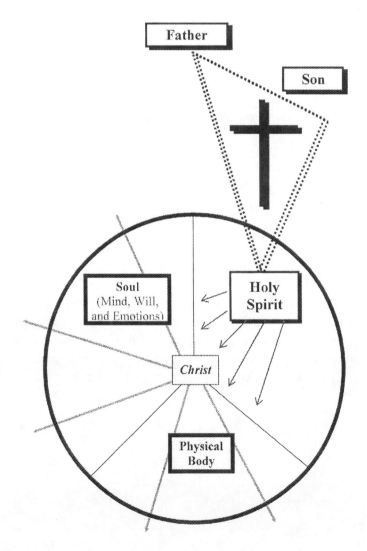

**Nothing could be more significant or more important for us
to comprehend than the complete nature of the Spirit-filled life!**
It encompasses unity with God Himself and submission to His
Spirit to the point that Jesus becomes our very life. It is the opportunity to be the living, physical representative of God. However,
while God is omnipotent, the Spirit-filled life is contingent upon
our propensity to yield our will. God is continuously orchestrating
the circumstances in our lives that will vanquish self-centeredness
and increasingly manifest Christ-centeredness in us. Our responsibility is to *surrender* to His will. The Spirit-filled life is not a
commitment to a self-help program that will manifest good works
and impress God. Rather, it is denial of self and surrendering of our
will, such that we can be the vessels of God's work.

Perhaps you have asked Jesus to forgive you of your sins and
you have received Him as your savior. You have trusted Him for
salvation, but you have been wondering if there was not something
more to Christianity. You really want to experience a more meaningful, fulfilling, and powerful Christian life. In addition, you may
have been struggling with difficulties and wondering if they have
any meaning whatsoever. They may have even caused you to question the reality of your faith. If so, perhaps God desires to become a
bigger part of your life, and He is trying to get more of your attention. Perhaps He is asking you to surrender your will totally to Him.
He is not offering to give you more of Himself; you already have all
of Jesus via the Holy Spirit. Rather, He is asking for more of you:
He wants your will, and He wants to become the very essence of
your life. If this is the case, then you need to seek Him with all your
heart. Privately or in association with other trusted Christians kneel
before God, submit yourself, and ask Him to take total control of
your life. Pray something similar to the following prayer:

> **Jesus, I recognize that you desire to become more prominent in my life. I have continued to try to rely upon my own strengths and abilities, but now I realize that I can do nothing apart from you. I repent of self-reliance and self-centeredness and ask you to take total control of my life. I surrender my will to you. I invite your Holy Spirit to rule and reign in me. I want you to manifest your life in me. From this day forth you can do anything you want to do in and through me. I am yours. Thank you Lord. Amen.**

By praying the above prayer you invite God to take total control of your life. In so doing, you yield to the work of the Holy Spirit. Such a surrender of your will is critical because it has eternal consequences. **For I am convinced we will not be rewarded in heaven for the things we do for God. Rather, we will be rewarded for allowing God to do great things through us**. There is a tremendous difference. In the first case, the burden is upon us, and we want the credit; in the latter case, the burden is upon God, and He gets the glory. It is incomprehensible that an almighty God would choose to humble Himself on a cross so that He could create the bridge that would allow Him to indwell mere humans and replicate His life in them. However, it is the most significant truth known to humanity. **It is the answer to life!!!!!!!**

Letting Christ Live Through Us

If we have come to the point of accepting Christ and have sought to surrender our will to the Lordship of Jesus, then what does it mean to let Christ live through us? I have emphasized that the burden to produce the Christian life is not upon us but upon God Himself. Consequently, the question clearly arises: *What will be the characteristics of a person who is truly emulating the life of Christ?*

First, it is clear that even the most mature, yielded Christian will not reach full perfection until the end of this earthly life. When we are transformed at death, we will enter into a completely new realm. At that point we will enter into eternal perfection where the realized life of Christ is full and complete in us. From a spiritual standpoint, the life of Christ is already within us, but not until after death will we fully comprehend and walk in this completeness. In this life we are striving toward perfection, but we are limited by minds that have indulged in sin and by the finite capacities of human bodies. We should increasingly become like Christ, but our expectations must be realistic. As mere humans, we will still fail, make mistakes, and sin. We must accept ongoing forgiveness and get back on track as soon as possible.

Since absolute perfection will not be realized in this life, it is impossible to specify exactly the qualifications of a person who is walking in the fullness of the Spirit of God. Attempts to do so can degenerate into legalism. In other words, we as Christians are not going to reach a point where we 'arrive.' Frankly, I believe the entire span of life that God gives us after the point of salvation will be filled with continuous spiritual growth. Therefore, when we discuss the characteristics of a Spirit-filled individual, we should not speak so much in terms of specific behaviors but rather in terms of general principles and characteristics.

Furthermore, attempts at qualifying other persons as to their spiritual depth can also be very erroneous. What may appear as spiritual in one person may merely be a human manifestation, not a work of the Spirit. Also, some people who may appear to be struggling with sin may in fact have a rather deep relationship with God. For example, before I became a Christian I was a smoker. I had tried to quit many times but was never very successful. I always regretted that I had ever started smoking, but I could never break free from the addiction. After I became a Christian, I did not immediately stop smoking. Some people may not characterize smoking as a sin, but since it is damaging to one's body, I felt it was wrong for me. It seemed to be incompatible with the idea that our bodies are the "temples of the Holy Spirit."[2] Nevertheless, it took over two years for me to completely quit. If a pious religious gentleman had encountered me smoking during that time period, he may have assumed I was a lukewarm Christian at best. In fact, my relationship with God was very intense, and I was growing rapidly as a Christian. I finally quit smoking and have not returned to the habit, but quitting was an outworking of the Holy Spirit, not a measure of my spiritual prowess.

While we may not be able to specify endpoints, we can identify characteristics and attributes that should become ingrained in our Christian lives. They are not statistical measures by which others can assess our standing. Rather they are attitudes, attributes, or characteristics that we should increasingly exhibit.

We live in an evaluative, comparative culture. We tend to compare everyone and everything to some standard in order to assess quality. We give grades to students, we give performance assessments to employees, we keep track of stats on athletes, and so on. This is such a deeply ingrained part of our society that it can easily and erroneously become part of our Christian life. However, in attempting to identify attributes of Christian living, we should not slip into interpersonal comparative assessment. The question is not: *How do I compare to other Christians?* but rather: *How do I compare to the old me?* The only valid comparisons are *intra*personal in nature. That is, I should periodically take account of my personal spiritual growth in comparison to my former self. Am I growing spiritually? Am I a greater and greater reflection of Christ?

Really, the only ones qualified to assess our spiritual condition are God and ourselves. We know our weaknesses and strengths, as does God. He even knows our hidden thoughts. God sees parts of our beings to which we may be oblivious. Therefore, let us address the issue of spiritual attributes with the purpose of assessing our own personal growth but not for the purpose of classifying the spiritual maturity of other people. The following discussion is by no means exhaustive. Rather, I have selectively focused on seven personal aspects of Spirit-filled living. Chapter 13 follows upon this discussion by focusing upon primary aspects of Spirit-filled ministry. Entire books could be (and have been) written on each of these subjects. The purpose here is not to explore each area in great depth but rather to briefly review important highlights of Spirit-filled life.

1) __Thirst for Righteousness__

The Spirit-filled person will inevitably develop a hunger for knowing God and a thirst for righteousness. Remember Matt (mentioned in chapter seven), who went through a difficult divorce. Almost immediately upon his conversion to Christianity, he developed a deep hunger to know God. He voraciously read the Bible and rapidly developed deep understanding of the scriptures. In addition, he devoured other books that assisted his Christian growth. The Holy Spirit had imparted to him an insatiable desire to know and love God. Such a hunger is clear evidence of the presence of God's Spirit.

I had a similar experience to Matt's when I first came to know Christ many years ago. Immediately upon my conversion, I yearned to know more about God. Furthermore, many of my perspectives on life changed almost immediately. Ideas I had held as true were rapidly replaced by truths that came from God. I did not understand it at the time, but this rapid change could have only been instigated by the work of the Holy Spirit. For example, I had read small portions of the Bible earlier in life in Sunday School classes and a few other settings, but I had no recognition of the inspired nature of scripture. Only after accepting Christ did the Holy Spirit illuminate my mind to the reality that "all Scripture is God-breathed and is useful for teaching, rebuking, correcting and training in righteousness, so that the man of God may be thoroughly equipped for every good work" (II Timothy 3:16-17).

In addition to a hunger to know God, the Spirit also imparts a desire to be like Jesus. Fundamentally, this desire is for holiness and righteousness. Jesus was incarnate holiness: "He committed no sin, and no deceit was found in His mouth" (I Peter 2:22). Prophets foretold of the holiness of Jesus. Isaiah called Him the "Holy One of Israel" (Isaiah 49:7). Even demonic spirits recognized Jesus' holiness. In Mark 1:24 an evil spirit spoke through a possessed man and called Jesus "the Holy One of God."[3] The holiness of Jesus made Him the perfect role model. Because of His holiness, all of Jesus' actions are pure, righteous, and worthy of emulation.

For me, emulating Jesus meant an immediate turning away from sinful behaviors. I was suddenly sensitive to sinful attitudes and actions to which I had previously been oblivious. I swiftly developed a hunger for righteousness. Jesus said, "Blessed are those who hunger and thirst for righteousness, for they will be filled" (Matthew 5:6). The Spirit of God is Holy; that is, He is pure, and He desires to bring about holiness in our lives. Therefore, no one who is indwelt by the Holy Spirit can peacefully go on sinning:

> No one who is born of God will continue to sin, because God's seed remains in him; he cannot go on sinning, because he has been born of God. This is how we know who the children of God are and who the children of the devil are: Anyone who does not do what is right is not a child of God; nor is anyone who does not love his brother. (I John 3:9-10)

This is not to say that Christians can never again sin—quite the contrary. Christians can and do sin, sometimes more than unregenerate people. However, the Holy Spirit will convict Christians of their sin and will not allow them to comfortably indulge their sinful thoughts. Rather, the Holy Spirit gives us power over sin so we can become righteous beings.

Before salvation and the accompanying indwelling of the Holy Spirit, humans are powerless with regard to sin. We were formerly in bondage as slaves to sin, but we are recreated as slaves to righteousness:

> You have been set free from sin and have become slaves to righteousness. . . . When you were slaves to sin, you were free from the control of righteousness. What benefit did you reap at that time from the things you are now ashamed of? Those things result in death! But now that you have been set free from sin and have become slaves to God, the benefit you reap leads to holiness, and the result is eternal life. (Romans 6:18, 20-22)

It is true that our previous sinful behaviors, which we may have enjoyed at the time, subsequently leave us nothing but shame and regret. Many Christians become trapped in the quagmire of regret and unforgiveness of themselves. Refusal to forgive yourself verges on blasphemy since God has already forgiven you, and you are denying the sufficiency of His work on the cross. However, like everything else in the Christian life, God by His power can and will impart a personal sense of transformation to those who desire to receive it. This is where God's grace and forgiveness become most prominent in recreating our lives.

The Holy Spirit teaches us, "with regard to your former way of life, to put off your old self, which is being corrupted by its deceitful desires; to be made new in the attitude of your minds; and to put on the new self, created to be like God in true righteousness and holiness" (Ephesians 4:22-24). Again, it is not a work that we create but rather something that God manifests in us and for us by His Holy Spirit. Such is the joy of the genuine Christian life because it is Jesus who undertakes the transformation process, bears the burden of the work, and completes the task. We must only desire change, be open to His work, and be willing to persevere through the trials that accompany growth. We must cooperate with God's work and resist temptation.[4] This involves taking wise precautions to avoid tempting settings. We are still in control of our will and can override the work of the Spirit if we resist His process. Therefore, as always, we remain personally responsible for our actions.

2) <u>Love and the Fruit of the Spirit</u>

The indwelling presence of the Holy Spirit in an individual will inevitably bring about the "fruit of the Spirit," which are love, joy, peace, patience, kindness, goodness, faithfulness, gentleness, and self-control (Galatians 5:22). While non-Christians may evidence some or all of these interrelated characteristics to some limited extent, the Holy Spirit manifests these attributes in supernatural ways. He takes a moderately loving person and transforms him or her into a person who overflows with love. Likewise, the Spirit can transform a compulsive, unsettled person into one who is self-controlled and peaceful. Again, it is not a comparison between any two persons that matters but rather how the Spirit changes our old sinful life into a new vibrant reflection of Christ.

Love is the foremost fruit of the Spirit; it embodies the other fruit. Colossians 3:12-15 says, "as God's chosen people, holy and dearly loved, clothe yourselves with compassion, kindness, humility, gentleness, and patience. Bear with each other and forgive whatever grievances you may have against one another. Forgive as the Lord forgave you. **And over all these virtues put on love, which binds them all together in perfect unity**." Love is the utmost characteristic of the life of Christ because "God is love" (I John 4:8). God not only loves, but more significantly, His very being is love. It is the same as saying I am human; it is an indivisible reality of my existence.

"The love command is the Magna Carta of the kingdom of God, for it is the love command that best characterizes the ethical instruction of Jesus."[5] The *golden rule* was at the heart of Jesus' teaching. He said that the teachings of the Law and Prophets were summed up in the command to "do to others what you would have them do to you" (Matthew 7:12). While Jesus lived on the earth, He demonstrated love and appreciation of others in many different ways. For example, He fellowshipped with the despised "tax collectors and 'sinners'" (Matthew 9:10-11). In addition, Jesus had compassion upon the crowds of people who followed Him, and He healed their sick.[6] Jesus took time to fellowship with little children, and he miraculously fed the multitudes.[7] He counseled people with love, interceded in prayer for them, and even raised some from the dead.[8] Clearly, love was a pervasive attribute of Jesus' life.

The well-known love chapter of I Corinthians identifies the characteristics of love: "Love is patient, love is kind. It does not envy, it does not boast, it is not proud. It is not rude, it is not self-seeking, it is not easily angered, it keeps no record of wrongs. Love does not delight in evil but rejoices with the truth. It always protects, always trusts, always hopes, always perseveres. Love never fails" (13:4-8). In essence, love manifests itself in practical ways. "If we love one another, God lives in us and His love is made complete in us" (I John 4:12).

Consider the example of Opal Trivette, who was mentioned in chapter seven. Opal accepted Christ at a very young age, but she did not fully yield to the work of the Spirit in her life until age 32. One of the first changes Opal noticed in her life after being filled with the Spirit was an entirely different attitude toward other people. Before that point, Opal had been somewhat judgmental. She disliked some people for no justifiable reason. She would simply size up individuals—sometimes complete strangers—and decide that she did or did not like them. She probably imposed her preconceived notions about human personalities upon the people and, as a consequence, categorized them as likeable or unlikable. However, after Opal's deeper experience with the Spirit, she began to realize that she no longer categorized and shunned people. Instead, where there had previously been cold judgmentalism, there was now a heart of love. Opal developed compassion, empathy, and concern for people she had previously spurned. Such a transformation in her heart was a manifestation of love by a work of the Spirit within her.

Surely, love is the most important characteristic of the Spirit-filled life, although if it is not accompanied by righteousness it can be superficial. The Bible indicates that if I "have not love, I am nothing" (I Corinthians 13:2). Several years ago, I had a student in a couple of my classes who had very recently become a Christian. For this discussion I will give him the name David. He was an athletic young man who had the personality of a leader, but his characteristics were rather unrefined. Before his conversion, David was a strong-willed person who readily conveyed his ideas to others. He could be brash, overbearing, and occasionally obnoxious. Consequently, David's early Christian life reflected his unrefined personality. He tended to be boisterous and demonstrative with regard to his faith.

After accepting Christ, David received teaching about the Spirit-filled life. Unfortunately, David overlooked the basics and emphasized issues regarding the Spirit that would have been better handled by more mature Christians. He went about aggressively (almost forcefully) attempting to convert other people to his view of Christianity. I occasionally overheard him ranting against the behavior of someone else, and David could not stand to lose an argument. On one occasion, David even tried to convince me of my need for a greater relationship with the Holy Spirit. I appreciated his sincerity, but he lacked discernment and wisdom. I observed and prayed for David for about a year, but I was concerned that his witness for Christ on the campus was not very positive. I knew he was 'turning people off' to the Christian message. Finally, near the end of the academic year, I felt the Spirit of the Lord prompting me to talk with David. Essentially, our discussion boiled down to one question—I asked David, "Where is the love?" What was missing in David's Christian witness was the core attribute of love. Fortunately, David received our discussion with humility. He admitted there were problems, and while he tried to be a loving person, he had been more concerned about winning arguments. I suggested to David that he needed to slow down, exercise more caution, and trust God.

David needed to work on his personal relationship with Jesus before he could begin working on other people's lives. As individuals grow closer to Jesus, they inevitably reflect His love. Only in the context of love are we able to minister to the needs of others. Without love Christians are merely clanging gongs who are annoying to others.[9] A person whose love for Christ shows through in his or her actions is a stronger witness than one who boldly speaks yet lacks love.

The genuine love of Christ is self-sacrificial, even to the point of death. Jesus said, "Greater love has no one than this, that he lay down his life for his friends" (John 15:13). We occasionally witness such acts by persons who forgo all concern for themselves in order to save the lives of others. Countless soldiers, firefighters, and police officers have undertaken such acts. Conversely, many people suffer in our time because of the acts of suicide bombers who commit terrorist acts. The terrorists live for a cause, but they die to take the lives of others. Sometimes they even claim to be fulfilling the will of a god, but their actions are the antithesis of God's love. "Love does not delight in evil" (I Corinthians 13:6). Rather, the love of God is manifest not only in loving your neighbor, but also in loving even your enemies.[10]

3) Continual Forgiveness

One of the ways in which love is manifested in the life of a Christian is through forgiveness. Jesus always stood ready to pardon sinners. "For God did not send His Son into the world to condemn the world, but to save the world through Him" (John 3:14-17). Jesus knew the truth about each person He encountered, but forgiveness pervaded His ministry. He extended grace and mercy to the woman caught in adultery.[11] While hanging on the cross, Jesus even prayed that the Father would forgive His executioners.[12]

Forgiveness is a choice, and it is a prerequisite to experiencing the fullness of the Spirit-filled life. Jesus said, "For if you forgive men when they sin against you, your heavenly Father will also forgive you. But if you do not forgive men their sins, your Father will not forgive your sins" (Matthew 6:14-15). This scripture is confusing to some people. It makes them afraid they will lose their salvation if they fail to forgive someone who has wronged them. However, we need to explore the nature of God's forgiveness to better understand this passage.

The offer of forgiveness was extended to present-day humankind even before we were born. Jesus died on the cross to take away the sins of the world, which included past, present, and future sins. Consequently, the offer of forgiveness predated our existence. Salvation is the point at which we repent of our sins and accept the offer of forgiveness. We thereafter embark on a relationship with God. Refusal to absolve other people is sin. It impedes God's work through us and damages our relationship with God.

While our salvation is secured by the work of Christ on the cross, the joy of our salvation can certainly be robbed by unforgiveness. Because the sin of unforgiveness harms relationships, it keeps the forgiveness we received from Christ from being effectual (i.e., operative, effective). In other words, we do not experience the freedom and joy of our own clemency because we harbor anger and resentment against others. In order for our forgiveness to be experiential, we must practice forgiveness of others. Unforgiveness is a form of judgment and condemnation. In essence, when we refuse to forgive, we are reserving the right to seek revenge. In so doing we condemn the relationship we have with the other person. The scripture says, "Do not judge, and you will not be judged. Do not condemn, and you will not be condemned. Forgive, and you will be forgiven" (Luke 6:37).

Unfortunately, many people confuse judgment and forgiveness. Some vow they will never forgive because to do so would release the offending party from responsibility for their actions. Wrongful judgment is to condemn persons as if we are God. This type of judgment pronounces permanent condemnation. For example, if someone embezzles church funds but repents, and yet we still banish him from the church, that would be a form of wrongful judgment. If, on the other hand, we confronted the person with the reality of his sin, offered him forgiveness, and expected him to make restitution, that would be rightful forgiveness accompanied by an expectation that the individual accept responsibility for his actions. Forgiveness does not absolve an offender of personal responsibility. For example, God might pardon a young couple for sexual promiscuity, but if pregnancy occurs, He expects them to take responsibility for the child. In situations that involve crimes, forgiveness is the prerequisite to justice; if we do not extend mercy then we inevitably seek revenge. People motivated by revenge seek only to punish and destroy. However, by forgiving, we can rightfully seek godly justice. Such justice seeks to determine responsibility, apply fair principles of morality, implement restitution, and even restore the offender.

Before I became a Christian, I regularly harbored unforgiveness against many people. If someone wronged me, even in a small way, I tended to bottle up my resentment and hold grudges. I might avoid or refuse to speak to the individual for a long time over a relatively petty issue. When it came to significant issues, I might respond with harsh words or seek revenge through manipulative means. While my actions may have had some negative effects upon others, mostly they hurt me. I harbored damaging emotions and thoughts that ate away at my soul.

Ephesians 4:26 says, "Do not let the sun go down while you are still angry." I have learned (the hard way) what this scripture means. Since becoming a Christian, whenever I have tried to sleep when I was even mildly angry with someone, I have experienced restless, tiresome nights. I have found it necessary to choose to forgive whoever is involved in the situation before I can sleep. In some cases, I must ask the Lord to give me the ability to forgive because it is not possible in my own power. In one recent situation, I was wronged by some people with whom I work. While their intent may not have been malicious, I believe their actions were genuinely wrong. I was deeply hurt and my emotions were raw. I found it very difficult to sleep, even though I had already vowed that I would forgive them. Eventually, I had to get up at 3:00 AM in the morning and write a long letter to the offending parties. I vented my emotions through the letter. Not everything I wrote was good, but it allowed me to release my anger. Later, I reviewed the letter with my wife and submitted it to God. After many revisions in which I deleted the questionable parts, I forwarded it to the offending parties. They received the letter well, and we were able to talk through the situation in a professional manner. The outcome was positive. Had I not addressed the problem, it could have harmed me for a long period of time and damaged my relationship with several of my colleagues.

The prior example illustrates a biblical principle that is helpful in resolving problems. Matthew chapter 18 outlines the appropriate way to deal with interpersonal problems.[13] It indicates that if someone wrongs you, first go to the person directly and address the issue. If he or she refuses to listen to you, then take one or two persons along with you to try to resolve the situation. If this fails, then take the offender before the governing agency that has authority over the situation, such as the church, your employer, or another institution. Far too many lawsuits in our society are a function of the failure to abide by this practice. Rather than address problems directly, we rush to file lawsuits. Such actions are often examples of unforgiveness.

In calling us to be like Jesus, the Spirit will prompt us to pardon those who wound us, even when forgiveness seems impossible. Some people have been victims of extreme persecution, others have been raped, and some have witnessed family members die at the hands of murderers. God calls us to forgive even these extreme actions. We really have no choice because refusal to forgive others is a form of self-condemnation. In so doing, you condemn yourself to a life of torment. Of course, in those situations where forgiveness is virtually impossible, persons must pray for God to forgive the offenders through them. Forgiveness can be a long process, and one must be willing to let God work through him or her over an extended period of time.

When you are no longer tormented by the actions of someone else, you have probably reached a point of forgiveness, but it may take a long time to completely overcome the damaging emotions that accompany serious wounds. In this book there have been many examples of persons who had to overcome very difficult situations through forgiveness. For example, Matt had to pardon his former wife who abruptly divorced him. The young woman who was raped and became pregnant (I called her Mary) had to forgive her offender in order that she might accept and love the child. Of course, in her case forgiveness did not mean absolving the male of responsibility for the act. Rather, forgiveness meant releasing him from her emotions. These are just a couple examples of the necessity of mercy in the Christian life.

4) **The Just Shall Live By Faith**

The Spirit-filled life definitely requires faith. According to Ravi Zacharias, "God has put enough into this world to make faith in Him a most reasonable stance, but He has left enough out to make it impossible to live by reason alone."[14] The Bible indicates that "the just shall live by faith" (Galatians 3:11, KJV) and that, "without faith it is impossible to please God, because anyone who comes to Him must believe that He exists and that He rewards those who earnestly seek Him" (Hebrews 11:6). Faith is the very core of our relationship with God. Salvation and the accompanying righteousness that is imparted to believers "comes through faith in Jesus Christ to all who believe" (Romans 3:22).

Faith really boils down to trust. It is a resolute, yet humble confidence in God that overcomes fear and adversity. It means trusting God regardless of the outcome of any given situation. Job was walking in faith when he said, "though He [God] slay me, yet will I hope in Him," but Job proceeded into arrogant presumption when he next stated, "I will <u>surely</u> defend my ways to His face" (Job 13:15). One must have enough faith to ask God to intervene in a situation, and when He opens doors, one must exercise faith by moving in the directions He ordains. However, we are not to set aside wisdom and discernment. There must be balance in our understanding.

Disbelief is the opposite of faith but so is presumption. For example, some people 'speak faith' regarding their finances and go ahead and spend money they do not have and which God never promised. When God chooses to teach them a lesson by allowing them to work through the mess they created, they inevitably wonder if their faith had been weak. It was not so much weak faith as a lack of discernment. Faith is not assumption or presupposition that fore-tells or claims an outcome before it is known. Real faith is filled with belief but trusts the outcome to God's sovereign will. It also involves obedience to God's will in the face of adversity. Such faith is what Jesus demonstrated in the Garden of Gethsemane when He was contemplating His forthcoming arrest and crucifixion. Jesus said, " 'My soul is overwhelmed with sorrow to the point of death.' . . . He fell with His face to the ground and prayed, 'My Father, if it is possible, may this cup be taken from me. Yet not as I will, but as you will' " (Matthew 26:38-39). The faith demonstrated by Jesus was humble trust in the Father.

Jesus sought to establish trust between Himself and those who followed Him. He said, "Do not let your hearts be troubled. Trust in God; trust also in me" (John 14:1). Not only did Jesus call others to trust in Him, but He also trusted His followers. He gave the disciples the authority and power to carry out aspects of His ministry.[15] Furthermore, Jesus trusted them with the secrets of the kingdom of God.[16] In so doing, He helped their faith grow. Faith grows through experience because we learn to trust in God and His provisions in different situations, some with positive outcomes and others that end in ways we would not prefer.

During Jesus' ministry He identified some who had great faith, such as the Centurion described in Matthew 8:5-13, as well as the

Canaanite woman identified in Matthew 15:21-28.[17] Likewise, Jesus identified some who had little faith, including Peter and the other disciples.[18] The persons who had great faith were identified as such because they believed in Jesus' authority and trusted Him despite the adverse circumstances at hand. They were not presumptive; that is, they did not expect Jesus to act in a way they had predetermined, but rather they exercised enough faith to humbly come before Christ with a request. They had 'mustard seed' faith. As Jesus said, "If you have faith as small as a mustard seed, you can say to this mountain, 'Move from here to there' and it will move. Nothing will be impossible for you" (Matthew 17:20).

Faith is Not Presumption

Presumption is "behavior or language that is boldly arrogant or offensive."[19] With regard to faith it is an expectation that God should act as we demand. In other words, we make Him our puppet, expecting Him to respond whenever and however we ask. The 'word of faith' movement has been a mistaken application of presumption. Those who are active in this movement believe that by exercising enough personal faith and by speaking only positive, faith-filled statements, they will receive that which they declare.

Peter spoke positive words, but he was often wrong and occasionally rebuked by Jesus. His problem was pride. For example, when Jesus 'spoke negatively' by explaining that He must suffer and be killed, "Peter took Him aside and began to rebuke Him. 'Never, Lord!' he said. 'This shall never happen to you!' Jesus turned and said to Peter, 'Get behind me, Satan! You are a stumbling block to me; you do not have in mind the things of God, but the things of men'" (Matthew 16:22-23). Likewise, Peter positively proclaimed that "even if all fall away on account of you, I never will," but that very night he denied he had any relationship with Jesus (Matthew 26:33-34).

The problem with the 'faith/positive confession' movement is that it turns faith into works. People steeped in this ideology believe that by personally generating enough faith they can coerce God to act. Whether it be personal prosperity or physical healing, they believe 'positive confessions' will yield positive outcomes. If their desired outcome does not come about, then the problem is a lack of sufficient conviction. For example, some people with serious medical problems who get worse rather than receive healing are deemed to not have enough faith. To them the outcome is clearly dependent upon their lack of faith, not upon God. Thus, the burden of any outcome is upon the individual and a clear function of their work of manifesting belief. However, real faith perseveres through trials and trusts in God regardless of the outcome of the trial. Berniece Holt continued in her faith and pushed on with life after her husband died. Darrell Golnitz continued as a Lutheran priest even after his son passed away. In our family it took a great deal of trust to persevere through Jonathan's ordeal and even deeper faith to walk with God after my father died. Those are demonstrations of the type of faith that trusts God regardless of outcomes, rather than trying to manipulate Him into providing that which we desire.

Whereas James 2:26 indicates that "faith without works is dead" (KJV), focusing on one's ability to generate faith is really works without faith. The consequence of the faith movement is that many people (those who apparently fail to manifest sufficient faith) are left with guilt and a sense of defeat. Instead of really trusting God, they trusted their teachers and themselves. The result is that God is forced out of the picture. Those who receive positive outcomes to their apparent faith feed their pride because they see themselves as super-faithful Christians. Ultimately, God will orchestrate situations that challenge their artificial faith and force them to come to grips with their sinful pride.

It is true that on more than one occasion Jesus spoke to individuals and indicated that their faith had healed them.[20] Blind Bartimaeus was an example:

> Then they came to Jericho. As Jesus and His disciples, together with a large crowd, were leaving the city, a blind man, Bartimaeus (that is, the Son of Timaeus), was sitting by the roadside begging. When he heard that it was Jesus of Nazareth, he began to shout, "Jesus, Son of

David, have mercy on me!"

Many rebuked him and told him to be quiet, but he shouted all the more, "Son of David, have mercy on me!"

Jesus stopped and said, "Call him."

So they called to the blind man, "Cheer up! On your feet! He's calling you." Throwing his cloak aside, he jumped to his feet and came to Jesus.

"What do you want me to do for you?" Jesus asked him.

The blind man said, "Rabbi, I want to see."

"Go," said Jesus, "your faith has healed you." Immediately he received his sight and followed Jesus along the road. (Mark 10:46-52)

This man did not manifest some type of super faith that forced Jesus to respond to his condition. He simply called to Jesus in humility and believed that Jesus could rectify his situation. His faith did not independently heal him. Rather, his faith was in Jesus, and Jesus healed him.

His Works, Not Ours

Real faith is accompanied by deeds. Paul stated that "a man is justified by faith apart from observing the law" (Romans 3:28). He indicated that faith alone interacts with the Spirit of God to bring us to salvation. However, he did not imply that good works are not an outworking of the Spirit within us. On the contrary, James 2:17 indicates that "faith by itself, if it is not accompanied by action, is dead." According to John Wesley, the founder of Methodism, Paul and James did not speak of the same works—Paul spoke of works preceding faith, whereas James spoke of works subsequent to it.[21] William Barclay said, "Faith and deeds are not opposites; they are, in fact, inseparables. No man will ever be moved to action without faith; and no man's faith is genuine unless it moves him to action."[22] However, we should realize that deeds that have eternal value are manifestations of the Spirit through us, not independent, personal works. As the Spirit directs, those who walk in faith have blessed opportunities to serve. Jesus said, "I tell you the truth, anyone who has faith in me will do what I have been doing. He will do even greater things than these" (John 14:12).

5) God Loves a Cheerful Giver

Faith that manifests itself in works will inevitably be called forth by God in the form of giving. One of the marks of self-centeredness is a desire to excessively accumulate and hoard resources. This behavior is intolerable to God since His very nature is one of self-giving. It is also unhealthy for the individual. Persons who hoard resources become like the Dead Sea, which is located between Israel and Jordan. The Dead Sea is fed mainly by the Jordan River and by several smaller streams. However, the lake has no outlet; the water is carried off solely by evaporation. Despite being fed by fresh water, the Dead Sea is saltier than the ocean because it has no way for water to flow out of its banks. Therefore, it contains no life of any sort except for a few kinds of microbes.[23]

Humans who hoard become like the Dead Sea because with no outlet to express love through giving, their resources become heavy and burdensome. The assets smother life from their owners, making the individuals stagnant pools rather than fresh conduits through which living water can flow. This is why the accumulation of wealth can be such a deceitful and dangerous path. Consequently, one of the works of the Holy Spirit is to make people who are naturally selfish into persons who joyfully and sacrificially give of their resources to others.

Giving of our resources involves more than just our finances. It encompasses using our time and employing our talents to help others. In lesser developed countries it might involve service more than tangible giving because of the general lack of goods, although some of the world's poor are very generous with their limited possessions. In western cultures giving should clearly involve both goods and services. Westernized nations (mostly Europe, North America, and more recently Japan and other parts of the Pacific Rim) contain the vast majority of the world's wealth. Third World (lesser developed) countries contain about 80 percent of the world's population but subsist on less than 20 percent of the world's income.[24]

God actually entrusts some people with wealth in order to benefit others in the world. I know people who give away 20 to 50 percent of their income, although they are typical middle-class Americans. I even heard a story of one successful businessman who reversed the tithe principle and gave away 90 percent of his income. These people demonstrate a genuine concern for others and indicate that not all of the United States' wealth has been squandered. The country has financially sponsored a great deal of the missionary efforts that have taken place in the world. However, **most westerners should seriously consider placing a ceiling on their lifestyle** in order that their abundance might be given for the benefit of others, rather than squandered on an increasingly lavish way of life. The scripture says,

> Remember this: Whoever sows sparingly will also reap sparingly, and whoever sows generously will also reap generously. Each man should give what he has decided in his heart to give, not reluctantly or under compulsion, for God loves a cheerful giver. And God is able to make all grace abound to you, so that in all things at all times, having all that you need, you will abound in every good work. (II Corinthians 9:6-8)

In many respects, persons in developed countries who have modest incomes when compared to their fellow citizens are rich in comparison to the majority of the world. For example, per capita annual income in 2000 in the United States was $26,980 for a population of 278 million, whereas in Bangladesh, a country with over 129 million people, the per capita income was only $240. Other examples from around the world include: 1) India - 1.0 billion population with per capita income of $340; 2) Nicaragua - 5.0 million population with per capita income of $379; 3) Uzbekistan - 24.3 million population with per capita income of $969; and 4) Zimbabwe - 11.7 million population with per capita income of $539.[25] The list of countries whose national income per person is only a few hundred dollars per year could easily go on and on. Meanwhile, a middle income American has income that surpasses that of most of the world's population. Such wealth brings with it responsibility. "From everyone who has been given much, much will be demanded; and from the one who has been entrusted with much, much more will be asked" (Luke 12:48).[26]

Money in and of itself is not the problem. Rather the love of money leads to great difficulties. The scripture indicates that "people who want to get rich fall into temptation and a trap and into many foolish and harmful desires that plunge men into ruin and destruction. **For the love of money is a root of all kinds of evil**. Some people, eager for money, have wandered from the faith and pierced themselves with many griefs" (I Timothy 6:9-10).

The key to handling money in appropriate ways is to first gain wisdom. **Wisdom tempers pride** and allows persons to see money for what it is—merely a tool to provide for the needs of one's family and to provide for the needs of other persons. Money can control us, but wisdom allows us to control money:

> Blessed is the man who finds wisdom, the man who gains understanding, for she is more profitable than silver and yields better returns than gold. She is more precious than rubies; nothing you desire can compare with her. Long life is in her right hand; in her left hand are riches and honor. Her ways are pleasant ways, and all her paths are peace. She is a tree of life to those who embrace her; those who lay hold of her will be blessed. (Proverbs 3:13-18)

The Bible indicates that persons should work and provide for the needs of their families. "If anyone does not provide for his relatives, and especially for his immediate family, he has denied the faith and is worse than an unbeliever" (I Timothy 5:8). There is certainly nothing wrong with working as unto the Lord and receiving financial blessings as a consequence. Working in noble endeavors not only provides for our families, but it also brings honor to God.

The key to godly stewardship of financial resources is to avoid the linkage of pride and money. In Proverbs we find the following teaching: "Keep falsehood and lies far from me; give me neither poverty nor riches, but give me only my daily bread" (Proverbs 30:8). The writer had come to realize that persons who see money only as means to provide for their 'daily bread' had begun to obtain true riches. Furthermore, while one man may be about the business of building his earthly wealth, the wise man is about the business of storing up for himself heavenly treasures. Jesus said, ". . . store up for yourselves treasures in heaven, where moth and rust do not destroy, and where thieves do not break in and steal. For where your treasure is, there your heart will be also" (Matthew 6:20-21). The wise man recognizes that the blessings of this earth are only temporal, but the blessings of God are eternal.

6) An Eternal, Not Temporal Perspective

Fruitful living as a Spirit-filled person requires an eternal perspective. Most of contemporary culture focuses on the temporal, physical issues of life, such as career, possessions, achievements, and pleasure. However, these are fleeting things that only satisfy briefly and leave individuals hungering for more. The scriptures admonish us against storing up treasures on earth.[27] Instead, we are to discern those things that have eternal value. Primarily, they involve relationships with other people. We are to focus first on our relationship with God and, concurrently, concentrate on our relations with the people God has intertwined in our lives. Jesus was asked, "'Teacher, which is the greatest commandment in the Law?' Jesus replied: "'Love the Lord your God with all your heart and with all your soul and with all your mind.' This is the first and greatest commandment. And the second is like it: 'Love your neighbor as yourself.' All the Law and the Prophets hang on these two commandments'" (Matthew 22:36-40).

The Spirit-filled person learns to look at life through God's eyes. His or her perspective is always long-term in nature, and it emphasizes the spiritual over the physical. Developing an eternal perspective means that we accept the reality of death, and we live with the rewards of eternal life in mind. In fact, we are not prepared to live until we are prepared to die. We must recognize that God will allow temporary adversity in order to achieve long-term, eternal value in human lives.

According to the New Testament book of Hebrews, the Old Testament patriarch, Moses, demonstrated the eternal perspective required of a godly person. "By faith Moses, when he had grown up, refused to be known as the son of Pharaoh's daughter. He chose to be mistreated along with the people of God rather than to enjoy the pleasures of sin for a short time. He regarded disgrace for the sake of Christ as of greater value than the treasures of Egypt, because he was looking ahead to his reward" (Hebrews 11:24-26). Moses recognized the dangers of short-term self-indulgence. Rather than choose a path of temporal pleasure, he accepted suffering as a consequence of a perspective that looked beyond the temporal to the eternal.

One of the most significant examples of both faith and an eternal perspective I have ever witnessed occurred in a tragic situation. Two of my most special friends are Greg and Jennifer Lauderback. I first met them when they were still single, but they started dating soon thereafter. They were both relatively new in their Christian faith. Greg was a practicing attorney, and Jennifer worked in an engineering job with a Fortune 500 Company. When they married, they moved into a house on the same street where I lived, and over the years we developed such a close friendship that we walked into each other's homes without knocking. Greg and Jennifer had children in almost the same timing and sequence as did my wife and I. Consequently, we shared many experiences together. We laughed heartily and occasionally shed a few tears.

Eventually, Greg became restless in his career as an attorney and began looking for other opportunities. After a few years of searching his heart and seeking God's will, Greg decided to enroll in seminary. He folded his law practice, moved his family to another state, and embarked on an entirely new career. Upon completing a Master of Divinity (M.Div.) degree, Greg was offered a position as the senior pastor of a Baptist church in Alabama. By the time he accepted the pastoral job, Greg and Jennifer had three small children and a fourth one was born after they relocated to Alabama.

Greg's ministry was moving along reasonably well when their lives were suddenly changed. On a warm Saturday in July, Greg and Jennifer were busy with mundane activities around their home when they realized they could not account for their youngest child, Julia Hope Lauderback. They knew she was in the home somewhere, but they were not quite sure of her precise whereabouts. All parents of more than one child have this experience on numerous occasions. You simply recognize that you are not fully aware of the exact location of all your children and go searching around briefly conducting roll call. Almost always the children are within a few feet, but maybe one is playing in a closet and another is behind a chair. It just takes a few moments to relieve your natural concern for the well-being of your children. However, every parent knows that it is not possible to watch all of your children every second of every day, especially if you have more than two children.

On this Saturday, however, the search for Julia became anxious when after a few minutes she could not be located. Greg and Jennifer looked inside and outside the home, but still they could not find Julia. Finally, they passed by the backyard swimming pool for a second time and Greg found her drowning in the deep end of the pool. He removed her while Jennifer quickly called 911. Jennifer then took Julia and rushed to try to resuscitate her using CPR. Minutes later they were at the local hospital where efforts to revive her were fruitless. In the span of just a few minutes their day went from an ordinary Saturday around the home to the most tragic moment they had ever faced in life. They lost their beautiful baby girl; she was only 15 months old. Somehow the gate on the fence that surrounded the pool had been left open, and Julia escaped out the back door of the house without anybody knowing it. Tragedy ensued.

We learned of the tragedy on Saturday evening and called the Lauderbacks. Greg spoke very little, but his primary statement was: "Robert, we lost our baby today." It was very painful. We proceeded to Alabama the next day to be with our beloved friends. Upon arriving, we found two people who were in stupefying shock. Greg is a tall, handsome man, but on this day he looked deeply wounded and physically withered. He walked very slowly, taking tiny steps like a very old man. He also spoke very slowly, often uttering only a few words before he withdrew into silence. Jennifer is normally a talkative person who often laughs and smiles, but her heart was an open wound; she cried repetitively. In between emotional over-flows, she languished over words of remorse. We mostly just sat and listened because it was impossible to dispel their grief.

The funeral proceedings took a few days and covered two states, since the Lauderbacks brought Julia back to our community for burial. Gradually during those days I noticed a change in both Greg and Jennifer. In the midst of tragedy and incomprehensible anguish, they were choosing to take an eternal perspective. They had reached a crisis point in both their lives and in their faith. Some people encounter such a situation in life and reject or turn away from God. Such individuals deny God's existence or blame Him for being unjust and unloving. Such a response is quite natural. However, persons of deep faith draw closer to God when they can least understand His ways.

Greg and Jennifer had radically altered their lives to follow a path of full-time ministry. Nevertheless, at this point they were faced with the critical question of whether they could really trust God. Unlike Rabbi Kushner (mentioned in chapter eight) who would have said that God did not have control over the events of Julia's life, the Lauderbacks recognized that God is sovereign and all-powerful. Their only possible conclusion was that God had chosen in His infinite wisdom to allow what He could have clearly stopped. God could have easily intervened to prevent the tragedy and avoid the anguish, for it is God who preserves our lives and keeps our feet from slipping.[28]

God creates and sustains life. "In His hand is the life of every creature and the breath of all mankind"(Job 12:10).[29] But why would He allow an innocent child to be taken from her family at such a young age? Perhaps it was a full-fledged attack of Satan, which God permitted, just as He permitted Job to be attacked and Peter to be sifted.[30] We simply do not know why God allowed this event and probably never will in this life. However, we reach the point of true faith when we trust God even though we do not under-stand His ways; such an exercise in faith requires an eternal perspec-tive. That is the outlook the Lauderbacks chose to take in this devastating circumstance. In so doing, they allowed the Spirit of God to comfort their souls and give them the fortitude to persevere through something that could have emotionally destroyed their lives. Their faith was clearly evident in their words and deeds, as well as in their eyes, which are a reflection of the soul.

The Lauderbacks did not grieve as people without faith. They had lost the physical presence of Julia, but their spiritual hope remained secure in Jesus. They recognized that Julia had entered into the perfection of eternity with God. Furthermore, they knew they would see her again. They certainly wished it had been otherwise, but their faith was deep enough to trust God even when their hearts were devastated. The following scripture became a living reality to them:

> Brothers, we do not want you to be ignorant about those who fall asleep, or to **grieve like the rest of men, who have no hope**. We believe that Jesus died and rose again and so we believe that God will bring with Jesus those who have fallen asleep in Him. According to the Lord's own word, we tell you that we who are still alive, who are left till the coming of the Lord, will certainly not precede those who have fallen asleep. For the Lord himself will come down from heaven, with a loud command, with the voice of the archangel and with the trumpet call of God, and **the dead in Christ will rise first. After that, we who are still alive and are left will be caught up together with them in the clouds to meet the Lord in the air. And so we will be with the Lord forever.** Therefore encourage each other with these words. (I Thessalonians 4:13-18)

This is not to say the Lauderbacks did not grieve deeply or that they lightheartedly accepted the loss. On the contrary, they wrestled with broken hearts, feelings of guilt, and diverse emotions, including depression, anger, and overwhelming sadness. Even so, what distinguished their grief from that of others was they chose to look at the situation through God's eyes. They adopted an eternal perspective that yielded hope in the midst of tragedy. They recognized the fundamental truth that even in the most difficult of life's experiences, God's nature is love and He can be trusted regardless of the circumstances.

7) <u>Worship in Spirit and Truth</u>

When the Holy Spirit richly indwells an individual that person will inevitably be drawn to worship God. In addition, the Spirit will lead the person into knowledge of the truth.[31] Jesus said, "a time is coming and has now come when the true worshipers will worship the Father in spirit and truth, for they are the kind of worshipers the Father seeks. God is spirit, and His worshipers must worship in spirit and in truth" (John 4:23-24).

Jesus explicitly said, "I am the way and the truth and the life" (John 14:6). According to theologian J. Rodman Williams, "God is the God of truth. He is the only true God; He is One of complete integrity, dependability, and faithfulness. . . . The true God has been fully revealed in Jesus Christ and nowhere else."[32] The incarnation of Christ brought truth to the forefront of the human experience. Humankind must accept or reject the truth because "the Word became flesh and made His dwelling among us. We have seen His glory, the glory of the one and only, who came from the Father, full of grace and truth" (John 1:14).

Christians have a responsibility to continuously seek after truth, not just rest on their accumulated knowledge. Those who do not earnestly seek God will be "tossed back and forth by the waves and blown here and there by every wind of teaching" (Ephesians 4:14). We cannot slacken into the position of allowing other people to be our source of truth. Rather, we must personally study the truths of scripture and seek to understand the nature of God and His work in the affairs of humanity. II Timothy 2:15 urges us to "study to shew thyself approved unto God, a workman that needeth not to be ashamed, rightly dividing the word of truth" (KJV).

What we perceive as truth affects who and how we worship. Worship is an integral part of human life, and it is essential that we worship only the one true God. Whether we are aware of it or not, all humans worship someone, something, or multiples thereof. Some of us worship material possessions, such as cars, homes, luxury items, or even memorabilia. We sometimes take greater care of these things and pay more attention to them than to the people who are integrally involved in our lives. While some individuals are trapped in materialistic worship, others simply worship people. We might worship our mate, our children, a friend, or any number of popular personalities. For example, I once worked with a woman who kept multiple pictures on her desk of a well-known race car driver. She talked about the driver as if they were old friends, but her only personal encounter with him was when he briefly posed to allow a picture to be taken of them standing together. Whether she knew it or not, this lady literally worshiped this gentleman to the extent that she was infatuated with him, despite the fact that he was married and had no idea of her interest.

We have a tendency to worship things or people because our hearts desire to worship. However, we were created for the purpose of worshiping God. When tempted by Satan, Jesus declared that it is only appropriate to worship God:

> The devil took Him to a very high mountain and showed Him all the kingdoms of the world and their splendor. "All this I will give you," he said, "if you will bow down and worship me."
> Jesus said to him, "Away from me, Satan! For it is written: '**Worship the Lord your God, and serve Him only.**'" (Matthew 4:8-10)

Unfortunately, many people are trapped in some form of deception that keeps them from truly worshiping God in spirit and truth.

Some people wonder why there is so much confusion and disagreement within the church. It is because there are countless areas where the spiritual forces of evil bring deception into the lives of individuals. As a result, individual Christians, as well as their respective churches, wander off into some form of deception. For example, those who emphasize truth without sensitivity to the spirit diverge into *legalism*. Those who focus on spiritual things without regard for truth digress into *relativism*. Of course, those who ignore both spirit and truth simply walk in human pride. Those who worship in both spirit and truth walk in Christ-centered balance and find favor with God. In fact, the Spirit of the Lord has repeatedly impressed upon my heart the following principle: ***Those who seek***

God will find Him, but those who worship Him will know His heart.[33] Therefore, let us "worship the LORD in the splendor of His holiness; tremble before Him, all the earth" (Psalms 96:9).

I attend a unique interdenominational church. The church started a few years ago with only 28 people. In a little over three years attendance skyrocketed to over 1,000 and the church continues to grow. There is an excitement and joy within the church that is unlike anything I have personally witnessed elsewhere. I am periodically asked what has been the cause of our growth. I respond that there appear to be three factors: 1) the teaching in the church is based on biblical truth, 2) the worship is guided by the Spirit, and 3) few barriers exist that keep people away. However, I am quick to add that our church's development has been a genuine work of God. We have never had great systems, programs, or facilities that stimulated the growth. Rather, God has raised up people who want to worship in spirit and truth. We did not follow a formula that left God with no choice but to bless our work. Instead, He created a place where people could seek Him in the context of freedom. When people truly worship in spirit and truth, there is no need for a promotional campaign—God simply draws those who seek Him to such a place of refuge.

Conclusion

The Spirit-filled life encompasses many things. However, this chapter focuses on only seven fundamental characteristics of people who are indwelt by the Spirit of God and seek to yield to the Spirit's direction. Such individuals will inevitably thirst for righteousness, emulate the love of Christ, extend forgiveness to all, walk by faith, give of their resources, maintain an eternal perspective, and worship God in spirit and truth. These are the most basic characteristics that mark a person who has accepted Christ and submitted to God's Spirit. The next chapter discusses some of the means by which the Spirit builds upon these characteristics and empowers us for ministry.

Chapter 13

Spirit-Filled Ministry

Spirit-filled Christians are called to ministry! One of the greatest deceptions that has taken root in the traditional churches in the United States and other western countries has been the idea that ministry is the responsibility of the professional clergy. Somehow many Christians have adopted the idea that since members of the clergy are paid, they should handle all of the ministry work of the church. The implicit assumption is that members of the congregations are to financially support the church, handle a few committee responsibilities, and otherwise selectively consume the services offered by the church. This mindset is a function of the consumer mentality that pervades western civilization. We think the church exists to meet our needs, provide us with uplifting teaching, and make recreational activities available for our children. As a result, the churches often fuel the self-centeredness of individuals and deny them the real joy of ministry, which is giving of themselves to others.

In short, the members of the church laity mimic the rest of American society: they are numbed by entertainment, soft due to a lack of exercise, and fundamentally disillusioned with their role in life. Such persons have a gnawing inner sense that life should be more meaningful, but they do not recognize that ministry is the pathway to fulfillment. They practice religion out of a sense of duty but fail to embrace the excitement of fulfilling the will of God. Meanwhile, members of the clergy are often underpaid, overworked people who either approach exhaustion or leave the ministry altogether. Of course, there are the rare pastors who challenge their flocks to undertake the work of ministry and empower them to do so by teaching them to rely upon the truth of scripture and the guidance of the Holy Spirit. Nevertheless, many Christians long for a more meaningful spiritual life. Whether they realize it or not, they desire to participate in ministry, not just languish as spectators.

My in-laws, Ken and Sylvia Lutke, are excellent examples. Ken and Sylvia grew up in modest economic situations but both managed to complete a college education. Ken attended John Carroll University on a football scholarship, and Sylvia worked her way through Kent State University. The two were married shortly after graduating from college. Ken completed an accounting degree, passed the CPA exam, and eventually started his own accounting firm. His business grew substantially, and by the time Ken reached middle age, he was quite successful. Meanwhile, Sylvia became a teacher and enjoyed working with young children for many years. They raised two children and appeared from the outside to be an 'all-American family.' However, there was something missing. For many years they looked for answers to life in achievements, social activities, and other fleeting endeavors. They were actively involved in their local church but mostly in superficial roles. Ken tried everything from marathon running to social drinking to fill the void in his life.

Sylvia developed a deeper, more serious faith as she progressed through life, but not until Ken was 52 years old did he invite Christ into his life. Ken's life changed immediately, and he rapidly grew in his knowledge of Christ. Soon they started attending a Spirit-filled church. Together they both developed much deeper spiritual lives and desired to serve God in a fresh, new way. God fulfilled their desire by opening the door for them to go on international mission trips. Their first trip was to Cuba, and soon they went to other countries such as Israel, Ukraine, and Mexico. Ken even went on a trip that progressed through Uzbekistan, Kyrgyzstan, and Tajikistan – countries that are surrounded by Russia, China, and Afghanistan. His trip to that region was only about one year before the outbreak of war between the United States and the Taliban/Al Qaeda factions in Afghanistan. Eventually, Ken and Sylvia established a primary link in the Ukraine. Ken helped establish economic programs that fostered the growth of small businesses, and Sylvia was instrumental in establishing a Crisis Pregnancy Center in Kharkov, Ukraine.

What Ken and Sylvia realized in the second half of their lives was that the things that society exalts as answers to life are fleeting and empty. Achievements, wealth, social standing, and success can only provide temporary satisfaction and always leave one searching for more. They are hollow, self-centered endeavors. However, there is a path to fulfillment that leaves one satisfied with his or her role in life. The path is one of selfless service to others as directed by the Holy Spirit. In the Lutkes' case, it meant international mission trips. For others it might simply mean serving those who live just across the street. Over time, it inevitably encompasses diverse opportunities to become involved in the lives of other people.

The Essential Elements: Prayer and Service

Ultimately, Christian ministry boils down to two primary endeavors: 1) Prayer and 2) Service. Prayer is the foundation of the entire Christian life, and it undergirds all ministry. Service to other people is service to and with God. According to Matthew 25:31-40, Jesus indicated that service to the least of God's people is service for Him.[1] It is really God who accomplishes works of value through us, but He allows us to be vessels of service. **Such ministry with God is what brings true joy and satisfaction in life**. The following discussion elaborates on the roles of prayer and service in Christian ministry.

Pray Without Ceasing

Perhaps the utmost action to which Christians are called is prayer. We are beckoned to "pray without ceasing" (I Thessalonians

5:17, KJV). Christians are a chosen group of people who constitute a "royal priesthood" (I Peter 2:9). One of the primary roles of a priest is that of prayer. Prayer is not only a ministry within itself but also a supporting companion for all other ministry. Prayer is the primary means by which we participate in the work of God and receive direction from the Holy Spirit.

Prayer was a significant part of Jesus' life; He was in constant communication with God the Father through prayer. "During His earthly life He offered both requests and supplications, with loud cries and tears, to the one who was able to save Him from death, and He was heard because of His devotion" (Hebrews 5:7). Jesus often went away to a private place to commune with the Father.[2] Sometimes He prayed for very long periods of time. On one occasion, "Jesus went out to a mountainside to pray, and spent the night praying to God" (Luke 6:12). Prayer was the means by which Jesus received, confirmed, and carried out His mission from God.

Part of Jesus' prayer life was intercessory in nature. For example, Jesus interceded for Simon Peter: "Simon, Simon, Satan has asked to sift you as wheat. But I have prayed for you, Simon, that your faith may not fail" (Luke 22:31-32). Jesus continues in intercession today. He "has a permanent priesthood. Therefore He is able to save completely those who come to God through Him, because He always lives to intercede for them" (Hebrews 7:24-25).

Frustration With Our Prayer Lives

Unfortunately, many Christians think their prayer life is inadequate, and consequently, they carry a sense of guilt. The problem may revolve around understanding the difference between a religious endeavor and a normal activity in a *relationship* with Christ. Jesus desires to fellowship with us on an intimate basis, but many Christians do not comprehend how prayer fits into that relationship. For example, one lady stated to me: "For many years I personally had difficulty speaking with, much less listening to, someone whom I didn't regard as my best friend." She was hesitant to pray to God because He seemed aloof and unknowable. Even though she was active in her church at the time and may have had saving faith, she did not have the type of relationship with Christ in which prayer was a comfortable activity.

Some people have trouble praying because they think their spiritual vocabulary is inadequate. These folks may feel inferior, and perhaps their greatest fear is being asked to pray in public. They somehow perceive that pastors and theologians have an inside track to God because they know the right terminology. Of course, God is not impressed with our eloquent words; He is more concerned with the attitude of our hearts.

Other individuals become frustrated with prayer because they see it as a chore that must be completed on a regular basis. They may periodically have lofty goals to pray for a specific, extended time. However, their prayer time may degenerate into repetitive petitioning accompanied by daydreaming. Eventually, they become bored with saying the same old things day after day, and their prayer time becomes shorter and shorter. Sooner or later, they skip a few days here and there until finally they cease the endeavor altogether. When their guilt becomes significant enough, they again establish new goals and repeat the process all over again. Such a course of action can be very frustrating.

I believe prayer should be a more natural part of our Christian lives, and the process should be more encompassing than just a prescribed period of petitioning. It is impossible to meet the command to pray without ceasing if prayer only involves petition. There is a place for imploring God in the course of prayer, but it is not the exclusive focus. Rather, prayer should be an integral part of our relationship with God.

The scriptures indicate that we can have confidence in approaching God because "if we ask anything *according to His will*, He hears us. And if we know that He hears us—whatever we ask—we know that we have what we asked of Him" (I John 5:14-15, *italics added*). **Therefore, the prerequisite to meaningful, effective prayer is discerning God's will, and knowing God's will requires *listening***. The Holy Spirit will inform us about things for which He desires us to pray. Sometimes a person or event might be on our minds repetitively. Such occurrences may well be the Spirit encouraging us to pray for the person or situation. On other occasions, we may suddenly think of an individual and have a sense of urgency about praying for this person. We might sense the need to pray for our children, an old friend, or a political leader in another part of the world. It is awesome to realize that God may call us to affect events throughout the world via prayer.

I find that I am prompted to pray for some people for a time, maybe even years, but the unction to pray eventually dissipates. Sometimes I stop praying for them without having made a conscious decision to stop. Apparently, whatever God was doing in their lives came to fruition, and the need to pray passed. The call to pray for some people might last a few days; for others it might be a long process. For example, after I had knee surgery, a young girl by the name of Madison Seaborn began to pray specifically for my knee. She moved to a city a few hours away, but she continued to pray for me. Many months might pass before I would occasionally talk with her parents. They would ask about my knee and mention that Madison was still praying. I was always appreciative because I had problems for a long time. I had a bit of an unusual injury, and the recovery process was rather slow. It took about three years before the knee began to feel normal. I discovered that Madison stopped praying for my knee sometime during the third year. Madison is a sensitive young woman; I believe she was prompted by the Spirit to pray for me and, at the appropriate time, to stop her intercession.

I do not pray for everything that other people request of me. For example, I knew a young woman (I'll call her Annie) who had been a schoolteacher before having children. She stopped teaching to stay at home and raise her three children during their younger years. After they all started school, Annie began looking for a new teaching job but was unsuccessful. She became very frustrated over the next few years because she could not locate a job. A member of her family asked me to pray that she would get a specific job for which she was about to interview. Having watched the situation, it appeared to me that God wanted her to continue to be at home with her family. He could have easily opened the door for a job for her. Instead, he gave Annie a ministry to her family, in her church, and in the lives of various other people. She was involved in many activities she could not have undertaken if she had a teaching job. Annie was very busy, just not in full-time employment. Had she taken a job, her children may have spent much more time alone. In addition, she would have been fatigued from work and less able to meet her family's needs. Consequently, when I was asked to pray for a job for Annie, I first asked God what He wanted. I did not feel prompted at that time to pray for her to find employment. Several years later, when her oldest son was about to enter college and the other two children were in high school, Annie again looked for a job. This time I felt led to pray that she would find employment. She found a teaching job and enjoyed the undertaking. Even when the family relocated to a new city a couple of years later, she quickly and easily found another teaching job. I believe there had been a season in her life for employment, a season exclusively for family, and again a season for employment. Praying for her was a matter of first discerning God's will for the particular season.

Anytime, Anywhere

In essence, we should be so attuned to the Holy Spirit that we are available for prayer anytime and anywhere. However, praying without ceasing does not mean we should continuously chatter. Jesus said, "When you pray, do not keep on babbling like pagans, for they think they will be heard because of their many words. Do not be like them, for your Father knows what you need before you ask Him" (Matthew 6:7-8). Rather, our hearts and minds should be bent toward continuously listening to the Holy Spirit. In so doing, we exercise the listening side of prayer and make ourselves available 24/7/365 to His call to intercessory prayer. God might call us to pray for many people throughout the day, or He might awaken us in the middle of the night and prompt us to pray for certain individuals. Because of our willingness and sensitivity to the Spirit, the Lord may call upon us at anytime and anywhere.

Prayer has become such a natural part of my life that I find myself praying almost all the time, often without even thinking about it. **I just converse with God throughout the day**. I intercede for other people, I beseech God about the problems that are before me, and I worship God continually. Sometimes I just privately sing worship songs in my heart as I progress through the day. I have a prayerful attitude as I read the Bible or other materials, and I try to listen to uplifting teaching with a prayerful heart. Sometimes my prayers are cries to God for help; other times I simply whisper thoughts of thankfulness and love. Often as I pass persons in the hallway or even as I drive down the interstate highway, I am prompted to pray for both friends and strangers. I like to read the local newspaper each morning as I eat breakfast. Inevitably, I pray about many situations and for many people who appear in the news. I simply commune with God in prayer in a natural way.

Prayer in my relationship with God functions in the same way as my daily communication with my wife. I do not set aside a specific period of time each day to talk with her and then assume I do not need to talk with her the rest of the day. Instead, we communicate throughout the day. Sometimes we have long discussions, other times there are brief interchanges. I feel free to talk with her at almost any time and any place. Likewise, I communicate with God in a variety of ways throughout the day. There might be quiet periods of meditation, times of study, or simply casual conversation. All such exercises in prayer are based on an intimate relationship with God. I cannot fathom how He can simultaneously relate to billions of people, but it is clearly part of His nature to be intimately involved with each of us through His Holy Spirit.

Prayer can take many forms. Paul said, "I will pray with my spirit, but I will also pray with my mind; I will sing with my spirit, but I will also sing with my mind" (I Corinthians 14:15). Praying with his spirit apparently meant praying in tongues since he said, "anyone who speaks in a tongue does not speak to men but to God. Indeed, no one understands him; he utters mysteries with his spirit" (I Corinthians 14:2). While Paul indicates that in a public setting it is better to prophesy, he clearly was thankful that he spoke in tongues.[3] The implication of his statement was to encourage private prayer in tongues, since to do so is edifying to the speaker.[4] It may also allow an individual to pray by means that affect the spiritual realm in ways that we cannot possibly fathom.

The modes and methods of prayer may be as varied as our

personalities. Some personality types prefer structure and order. Such individuals may find their most intimate times of prayer take place in the context of a planned 'quiet time.' Other personality types may find it easier to closely fellowship with God while they are physically active. My wife enjoys taking long, vigorous walks for exercise. She is best able to pray during these periods. With three small children at home, it would be almost impossible for her to sit quietly before God without interruption. Instead, while her body is active in exercise, her spirit is peacefully attuned to God.

Personally, I find many of the times when I am most sensitive to God's Spirit are while I am driving my car. I have a bit of a commute to work, so I tend to actively pray in the mornings and quietly listen in the afternoons. (No, I don't drive with my eyes closed.) In the context of driving, I am able to shut out many distractions and really listen to God speak. In addition, I often listen to worship music in the car and participate right along with the musicians. I truly enjoy driving alone because it gives me such a wonderful time when I can independently pray and worship God.

I believe one of the highest forms of prayer is praise and worship. I define praise and worship in this context as singing and playing music to the Lord. Psalms 33:1-3 says: "Sing joyfully to the LORD, you righteous; it is fitting for the upright to praise Him. Praise the LORD with the harp; make music to Him on the ten-stringed lyre. Sing to Him a new song; play skillfully, and shout for joy." In praising and worshiping God, we acknowledge His sovereignty and seek His presence. The scripture indicates that God inhabits the praises of His people.[5]

It is a humble act to come before God in worship. Consequently, I find the times when God most clearly speaks to me are very often in the context of corporate worship. Somehow, His presence seems more immediate and intense in such circumstances. Perhaps it is because "God opposes the proud but gives grace to the humble. . . . Come near to God and He will come near to you" (James 4:6, 8). In the context of worship the Holy Spirit very clearly speaks to me in a gentle, quiet way. Not that I hear audible voices, but rather He speaks to me and guides me in my inner spirit. Corporate worship facilitates communication with God and prepares our hearts and minds to listen to the voice of the Spirit.

Servant of All

Prayer, especially listening to the direction of the Spirit, prepares us for the ministry of service. Jesus said, "I am the good shepherd. The good shepherd lays down His life for the sheep" (John 10:11). Jesus' death on the cross was His ultimate service to humanity. Jesus calls those who follow Him to follow His example of sacrificial, servant love. He said, "If anyone would come after Me, he must deny himself and take up his cross and follow Me" (Matthew 16:24).

Spiritual Gifts

Service can take many forms and may depend upon the gifts that God has given us. While God will ask us during a lifetime to take on many different roles and responsibilities, He is likely to call us forth in areas that will best use our primary gifts. There are many different kinds of gifts and different types of service, but they are all given for the common good.[6] The gifts are important to the church, but they are byproducts of a life that is filled with the Spirit. They are not prerequisites to Spirit-filled living.

The scripture recognizes at least three different sets of gifts. The lists identify functional gifts, supernatural gifts, and offices or ministries. Note, however, that the lists are not exhaustive. For example, we know that some people have musical gifts to sing or play instruments and thus serve as worship leaders. Nevertheless, the Bible does not specifically list musicianship among the aforementioned lists of spiritual gifts, although such skills are acknowledged elsewhere in scripture.

Personality Types

Romans 12:4-8 identifies the list of 'functional gifts' that appear in the body of Christ:

Just as each of us has one body with many members, and these members do not all have the same function, so in Christ we who are many form one body, and each member belongs to all the others. We have different gifts, according to the grace given us. If a man's gift is **prophesying**, let him use it in proportion to his faith. If it is **serving**, let him serve; if it is **teaching**, let him teach; if it is **encouraging**, let him encourage; if it is **contributing** to the needs of others, let him give generously; if it is **leadership**, let him govern diligently; if it is showing **mercy**, let him do it cheerfully.

The seven functional gifts are characteristics God instills in our personalities. Some aspects of the gifts are probably present at birth, and they may be nurtured through our experiences in life. After we accept Christ, the Spirit of God invigorates and amplifies our gifts to make them even more effective for Christian service. Persons who have not yet accepted Jesus can exercise these gifts to some extent. For example, some people are good teachers or good leaders even though they do not know Christ. Such examples demonstrate that God instills at least some aspects of these characteristics at birth. However, when the Holy Spirit comes to indwell individuals, their personality characteristics are amplified and empowered for ministry.

Dr. George Selig and Dr. Alan Arroyo wrote a book entitled *Loving Our Differences* in which they identified four basic personality types that result from various mixes of the seven functional gifts.[7] Their categories parallel the four personality types identified by the well-known DISC Survey.[8] The personality types and their corresponding DISC types are as follows:

Selig & Arroyo	DISC	Primary Personality Characteristic
Ruler	Dominant	Leadership
Designer	Conscientious	Analytical
Promoter	Influencing	People Oriented
Server	Steadiness	Service Oriented

Leaders, or what Selig and Arroyo call **Rulers**, tend to have the functional gifts of leadership, prophecy, and encouragement. (Note that prophecy as used here is the ability to analytically distinguish truth, not so much foretelling the future.) Persons who have primary gifts of leadership can substantially influence others. At their best, they are decisive, task-oriented visionaries who enjoy challenges. Every part of society needs good rulers. However, bad rulers can be domineering, controlling people who manipulate and hurt others. God calls persons with Ruler personalities to submit to His Lordship. Such leaders can be effective in helping lead others in service that honors God.

Designers are analytical, task oriented, organized people who also tend toward perfectionism. They have the functional gifts of prophecy, teaching, and service. Many of society's analytical jobs, such as engineering, accounting, and medicine are filled by people with Designer personalities. Designers can be artists, good teachers of adults, or people who provide organization and structure to almost any setting. They are essential to Christian service through-out society. As is the case in all of the personality types, Designers can exhibit negative characteristics. Because they are so analytical, they can be slow to make decisions, highly critical of themselves or others, as well as judgmental.

Promoters have the functional gifts of leadership, encourage-ment, and mercy. They tend to be very extroverted individuals who can strike up a conversation with almost anyone. They are relation-ship oriented and attentive to the needs of others. Like Rulers, they can also be leaders, but they lead by motivating people and creating excitement among a group for a project. They are not so task oriented as Rulers. In fact, they can be disorganized people who have a hard time completing projects. Where Designers are the analytical glue that holds groups and societies together, Promoters serve as social glue. God often uses them to minister to others through relationships. On the negative side, Promoters can some-times be manipulated by others because they value relationships more than principles.

Servers tend to be introverted people who like to help others. They have the functional gifts of teaching, service, and mercy.

Servers prefer background duties to those that incur a lot of public attention. They can be excellent teachers, especially of younger children. They can also be very sensitive to the needs of others. On the negative side, Servers can become stressed by change and unable to take charge of a situation when needed. Because they have a hard time saying no, they can sometimes be manipulated by others.

A serious problem that exists among Christians is a failure to recognize the importance of all service gifts. People see noteworthy personality types, such as leaders, and want to be like them rather than accepting who they are and using the gifts God has given them. This is a particular problem for Servers, who often feel like useless people because they do not have gifts that are highly visible in public. Yet God creates more servers than any other personality type, and He does so for good reasons. All societies need more servers than anything else. Each of us needs to recognize the value of our individual gifts, rather than wishing we were someone else.

Jesus embodies the good attributes of all four of the personality types. Therefore, as people grow to be more like Christ their skills and abilities expand. They become more flexible and better able to vary their relational style according to the needs of any given situation. While one's dominant personality characteristics may always maintain a prominent position, it is possible to grow in the positive attributes of each of the other personality types. Furthermore, we should never refuse to undertake tasks because they involve duties that are 'not our gifts.' God may ask us to step out of our comfort zones in order that He might expand and develop our attributes. It is helpful to understand our gifts so that we might understand how God primarily desires to use us in service, but we should not use our personalities as excuses for disobedience or sin.

Supernatural Gifts

The second category of spiritual gifts identified in the Bible is listed in I Corinthians 12:7-11. This passage delineates supernatural gifts, which are purely manifestations of the Holy Spirit through Christians.

Now to each one the manifestation of the Spirit is given for the common good. To one there is given through the Spirit the message of **wisdom**, to another the message of **knowledge** by means of the same Spirit, to another **faith** by the same Spirit, to another gifts of **healing** by that one Spirit, to another **miraculous powers**, to another **prophecy**, to another **distinguishing between spirits**, to another **speaking in different kinds of tongues,** and to still another the **interpretation of tongues**. All these are the work of one and the same Spirit, and He gives them to each one, just as He determines.

Like the functional gifts, these gifts are also important to effective service as a part of the body of Christ. Immediately after listing the above gifts, the Apostle Paul wrote a treatise that emphasized the importance of having every gift operational in the church. However, he emphasized that the gifts are given according to how the Spirit wills, and not everyone functions in every capacity. In fact, in I Corinthians 12:29-30 Paul states, "Are all apostles? Are all prophets? Are all teachers? Do all work miracles? Do all have gifts of healing?" The clear implication of his statement is that while such gifts should be active within the body of believers, no individual should expect to fulfill all of these roles.

Collectively, the supernatural gifts are quite important to the effective ministry of the church. For example, God might gift leaders with wisdom or faith to enable them to carry out responsibilities that would otherwise seem impossible. The miraculous gifts can also serve as important witnesses of the presence of God. For example, several members of a mission team I served on in Mexico felt led to gather around a local, elderly man and pray for healing for him. The man appeared to be a hard-hearted person, but something changed during the prayer, and he began to cry. Persons who knew him said it was the first time they had ever seen him cry. During the following days, the man realized that he was in fact healed of an intestinal disorder that had plagued him for years. His healing spoke as a loud witness to others about God's power. God is sovereign; He sometimes chooses to miraculously intervene in the lives of people. Other times He chooses to allow the natural course of events to unfold. Our responsibility as Christians is simply to have enough boldness to ask for His touch and sufficient faith to trust Him regardless of the outcome.

All of the supernatural gifts are given for some form of ministry. God sometimes gives individuals 'words of knowledge' in order that they might pray for the very thing He intends to accomplish. The word gifts (prophecy, tongues, and interpretation of tongues) are often used to deliver words of encouragement and direction to believers. In writing I Corinthians, Paul indicated that prophecy is important for the edification of the church. However, he limited speaking in tongues to public settings where there was an interpreter, in which case the combination of a message delivered in tongues accompanied by an interpretation has the same effect as prophecy.[9] The gift of discerning of spirits enables individuals to have insight into the spiritual causes of behaviors or events. With such insight, they are equipped to pray or counsel in ways that could not otherwise be understood. In short, all of the supernatural gifts can play an important role in the ministry of the church.

Of course, some people purport to speak or work by the Spirit, but they are really imitating or counterfeiting the genuine work of God. Many people have supposedly prophesied on behalf of God, but their prophecies proved to be false. Such abuses are inevitable, but the discerning Christian should not dismiss the genuine work of God because of the false activities of some people. Unfortunately, some segments of the church have lacked discipline or sound theology with regard to the supernatural gifts. For example, those who argue that individuals must speak in tongues in order to be saved or to demonstrate they are Spirit-filled are simply ignoring important parts of scripture that indicate otherwise. While the gifts are valid, they must be discussed with wisdom and exercised with the discipline that is a fruit of the Spirit.

Some people have tried to entirely dismiss the supernatural gifts or pick and choose among them. They argue that some or all of the supernatural gifts are no longer functioning today. However, the preponderance of scriptural evidence indicates that the supernatural gifts are normal manifestations of the Holy Spirit. Furthermore, countless individuals have witnessed the reality, validity, and importance of the gifts in contemporary ministry.

Dr. Jack Deere was a professor at a seminary that taught that supernatural gifts are not for today. According to this cessationist theology, supernatural gifts, such as healing and speaking in tongues, ceased to function when the written New Testament of the Bible was completed and the last of the original disciples died. Deere adopted the cessationist philosophy and abided by its doctrine. However, the Holy Spirit broke into his life in a fresh way and opened his heart and mind to the truth. Dr. Deere witnessed powerful works of the Spirit in ministry, and consequently, he changed his entire perspective. He later wrote a wonderful book entitled *Surprised by the Power of the Spirit* in which he admitted his former theology was born out of prejudice, lack of experience, and a bias toward scripture born out of tradition and the teachings of others.[10] His perspective was transformed by the Spirit as he witnessed the reality that God still performs miracles, and He still speaks to His children today.

<u>Offices/Ministries</u>

The third category of gifts is listed in I Corinthians 12:28 and in Ephesians 4:

> And in the church God has appointed first of all **apostles**, second **prophets**, third **teachers**, then **workers of miracles**, also those having gifts of **healing**, those able to **help others,** those with gifts of **administration**, and those speaking in different kinds of **tongues**. (I Corinthians 12:28)

> It was He who gave some to be **apostles**, some to be **prophets**, some to be **evangelists**, and some to be **pastors** and **teachers**, to prepare God's people for works of service, so that the body of Christ may be built up. (Ephesians 4:11-12)

Some of the gifts listed in these passages are repeats of those listed elsewhere, but the gifts exclusively delineated in these passages are offices or ministries that are to be fulfilled within the church. Apostles, prophets, evangelists, pastors, and teachers are leaders within the church that have profound responsibilities to direct others in the wisdom and knowledge of Christ. Note that the scripture says the purpose of these offices is **"to prepare God's people for works of service"** (Ephesians 4:12). The spiritual gifts are not established to exalt the work of humans. Rather, they are given to provide leadership so the church can undertake effective and powerful ministry.

In the I Corinthians 12:28 passage some of the supernatural gifts (miracles, healing, and tongues) are intermingled with the leadership gifts and with the gift of helping others. This listing indicates that no gifts are of greater or lesser significance, but all are important. Clearly, the unassuming ministry of helping others is just as important as the conspicuous ministry of teaching. Furthermore, the miraculous gifts are as important to service in the body of Christ as are the seemingly mundane gifts or the highly visible gifts. All of the gifts are indispensable to the proper functioning of the church.

I have heard some teach that 'every person has at least one spiritual gift.' Their premise may be valid, but I think this type of teaching tends to cause people to look for their one and only gift. They assume they have only one ability that will be effective in ministry. However, we are to be continually growing in knowledge, faith, and love.[11] Therefore, as we mature God may work through us in ever-increasing ways, including the manifestation of additional gifts for use in ever-expanding service.

Additionally, we should recognize that we do not own specific spiritual gifts that we can manifest at any moment. God gives the gifts, and He controls their genuine function. For example, one might attempt to use the gift of teaching that God has instilled in them, but if the teaching is not of the Lord, there will be no anointing upon the work, and no real fruit will come forth. Conversely, those who walk closely with God know when He is urging them to act in a certain fashion. I have some good friends through whom prophetic and miraculous gifts have been manifested. However, they are not 'loose cannons' who go about haphazardly purporting to carry out the work of God. Quite the contrary, they are discerning, wise people who act when prompted by God but refrain from showmanship and other prideful exploits.

Unnecessary Confusion

Unfortunately, some unnecessary confusion and controversy exists within the church regarding spiritual gifts, mostly concerning supernatural gifts. Such problems are the result of human folly, not God's intention. Division and strife are outworkings of the sin nature of human beings, whereas the Holy Spirit creates unity. Regrettably, too much of Christendom is committed to God but not surrendered to His Holy Spirit. It is unnatural for humans to yield control of their lives; therefore, surrendering to the Spirit is oftentimes contrary to ingrained tendencies. As a consequence, Christian leadership often settles for religious practices and bureaucratic methodologies to manifest the appearances of spirituality. Instead, they should seek and encourage face-to-face (really spirit-to-Spirit) contact with God.

In regard to spiritual gifts and functions, leaders should provide training and seek opportunities to allow group members to exercise their gifts. Unfortunately, fear may inhibit people from exploring that with which they are not familiar. Also, the sin of pride is often manifested in the forms of power and control in organizations. As a consequence, group members may be under great pressure (explicit or implicit) to conform to standards of behavior that are approved by the leadership. Gifts or functions that are not well understood or which threaten the authority of leaders tend to be shunned. The result is group conformity.

The Holy Spirit promotes unity, but He does not necessarily intend to create conformity. Rather, the Holy Spirit generates diversity for the ultimate purpose of fostering "complementarity."[12] Complementarity involves the recognition of interdependence and eternal equality but differing attributes and skills among individuals. Complementarity is a part of God's grand design and has applicability to every institution. It recognizes that God made us complements of others—not clones!

Because it is the Holy Spirit who establishes unity, all Christians, and particularly all Christian leaders, should recognize the preeminent role of the Spirit. Unity among humans is not easily achieved because of the propensity of each individual to sin. Consequently, groups or organizations that do not earnestly rely upon the Spirit can expect internal conflict. However, unity does not mean conformity. The same Spirit who unifies also diversifies. Christians must honor freedom so that diverse gifts can be manifested.

Service Beyond the Church Walls

Understanding spiritual gifts is part of understanding the work of service as a Christian. However, we need to understand that the majority of our time is spent outside the confines of a formal church setting. Therefore, the majority of our service should take place beyond the church walls. God can and will employ our gifts in roles that extend into many segments of society. We might be called to be leaders or administrators at work, to serve as a helper in a volunteer setting, or to teach children in a public school. Even more significantly, we may need to employ our gifts in simply meeting the needs of our families.

Because our service roles extend to all of society, we should work as unto the Lord in all things. Colossians 3:23-24 indicates that in "whatever you do, work at it with all your heart, as working for the Lord, not for men, since you know that you will receive an inheritance from the Lord as a reward. It is the Lord Christ you are serving." So long as it is an honorable endeavor, every aspect of work that we undertake is service to God. (Obviously, immoral and illegal activities are dishonoring to God, not service to Him.) According to Chuck Colson, "In the ancient world, the Greeks and Romans looked upon manual work as a curse, something for lower classes and slaves. But Christianity changed all that. Christians viewed work as a high calling—a calling to be co-workers with God in unfolding the rich potential of

His creation."[13] There are simply no limits to the ways in which God may call us to serve Him.

Unique Ministry

Part of our service might come in the form of a unique ministry to one person. For example, one Wednesday evening a few years ago my brother-in-law, Dwight Kilbourne, and I were traveling from the church he pastored to his home. We came upon what appeared to be an automobile accident but quickly realized that a pedestrian had been struck by a car. The accident had just happened and no emergency personnel were yet on the scene. We felt led to stop and lend whatever assistance we could.

The scene was ghastly. Witnesses said the injured man had left a convenience store in haste and run into four lanes of traffic that was moving at a fast pace. The man was obviously drunk and had darted right in front of a young female driver who could not avoid him. She clipped his legs, which sent his head directly into her windshield. The glass was collapsed to the point that it rested on the steering wheel of her car. She had undoubtedly slammed on the brakes to come to a stop, which threw him forward about 20 feet onto the pavement. He was lying there motionless with a stream of blood running down the road away from his body. He appeared to be dead.

As Dwight and I got out of our car and approached the scene, I felt led to stop and pray not only for the injured man but also for the young driver. She had exited her car and was in the parking lot of the convenience store where she was hysterical. This was a very busy section of highway, so I also prayed for the safety of those who were attempting to help. Meanwhile, Dwight noticed another teenager from his church who had stopped. He grabbed the young man, and the two of them approached the injured gentleman. They knelt down to pray; Dwight simply laid one hand upon the injured man as he literally prayed for his life. Soon the emergency personnel arrived. They quickly checked the man but made no attempt to provide medical treatment. Instead, they hastily scooped him onto a stretcher and left the scene. Their actions made me assume he was already dead. We stayed and continued to pray until the police officers had asked sufficient questions and begun to clear the scene. As we were leaving, we talked about how God had apparently put us there immediately after the incident so we could pray for the parties involved.

The next day Dwight did some follow-up work with the local police department and, to our surprise, found that the man had been taken to a local hospital and was still alive. He had extensive injuries, but he was hanging on. Dwight decided to go visit him in the hospital and pray with him. Soon the man's prognosis turned positive, and after extensive treatment, he was eventually released from the hospital. Because of two severely broken legs, he had to use a walker to get around, but otherwise he recovered reasonably well. Dwight discovered that the man was a Vietnam veteran who had no family to speak of and was staying at the local Veteran's Administration (VA) Hospital trying to overcome his personal problems. He had left the VA Hospital and gone on a drinking binge the night of the accident.

Dwight visited the man several times while he was in the hospital, and when he was about to be released, Dwight invited him to come to his church. The first Sunday after leaving the hospital the man showed up. He became a regular attendee of the church and appeared to develop a genuine relationship with Christ. He continued rehabilitation at the VA Hospital and seemed to get his life in order. He still struggled with some aspects of life, but at least he was headed in a new direction. The accident could have terminated the man's life, but instead God used it to turn his life around. Dwight was used explicitly by God as a vessel through which the Lord spoke to the man's heart. While this example was extreme, such opportunities for service are commonplace for the Christian who is attuned to God's Spirit.

The Example of Servant Leadership

Much of Christian service comes in rather simple forms. It involves meeting the physical, emotional, and spiritual needs of others. Such service involves discerning the will of God and then being obedient to His will. It involves following the example of Jesus:

Who, being in very nature God, did not consider equality
with God something to be grasped, but made himself
nothing, **taking the very nature of a servant**, being
made in human likeness. And being found in appearance
as a man, **He humbled himself and became obedient to
death**—even death on a cross! (Philippians 2:6-8)

The example of Jesus was one of **servant leadership**. He
possessed all authority in heaven and on earth, yet He was the
world's utmost servant. Henri Nouwen said Jesus' leadership is that
"in which power is constantly abandoned in favor of love. It is true
spiritual leadership." [14] Jesus willingly surrendered His position of
power to serve humankind humbly and sacrificially through death
on the cross.

God has predestined that all who call on His name should be
conformed to the likeness of His Son. Part of that process should
incorporate servant leadership. However, according to Paul Cedar,
"servant leadership is not easy; nor is it natural." [15] It is contrary to
the self-centered tendencies of every human being. Humility and
sacrifice mark Jesus' path, but ultimately, it is the paradoxical route
to greatness in the kingdom of God. "For he who is least among you
all—he is the greatest" (Luke 9:48).

Consequently, Christians should seek to emulate Jesus above all
others. Emulation must involve service. Jesus said, "Whoever
serves me must follow me; and where I am, my servant also will be.
My Father will honor the one who serves me" (John 12:26).
Furthermore, "the greatest among you will be your servant. For
whoever exalts himself will be humbled, and whoever humbles
himself will be exalted" (Matthew 23:11-12). The person who
aspires to genuine servant leadership seeks to follow the footsteps
of Christ. At the Last Supper Jesus showed the full extent of His
love for the disciples by washing their feet. [16] Furthermore, He
explicitly instructed them to follow His example: "Now that I, your
Lord and Teacher, have washed your feet, you also should wash one
another's feet. **I have set you an example that you should do as I
have done for you**. I tell you the truth, no servant is greater than his
master, nor is a messenger greater than the one who sent him. Now

that you know these things, you will be blessed if you do them" (John 13:14-17).

The most notable example of servant leadership I have ever witnessed came in the life of Coach Fred Selfe. Fred was a mountain of a man. He had been an all-American offensive lineman during his collegiate football career. He had arms the size of many people's legs and legs that resembled tree trunks. Despite his size, he was agile and extremely quick. In addition, he had a big, booming voice and a razor-sharp mind. After earning a graduate degree, Fred became a coach and teacher at the college where I work. He coached football, baseball, track, and during part of his career, he served as the athletic director of the college. Fred was extremely loyal to the institution; he spent 29 years working there. He coached, befriended, and mentored hundreds of young men and women.

I had the pleasure of knowing Fred for 25 years. We were friends who respected one another, although we were hard-nosed combatants on the racquetball court. There was one thing I always knew about Fred: if I ever needed help in any way, he would be there. In fact, I was cautious in what I said around Fred because if I mentioned any need he would immediately seek to solve the problem. In addition to his many acts of service to students and staff, Fred helped community members build houses, move furniture, cut firewood, etc. Anybody who was on the campus for any length of time soon learned that Fred was the number one servant at the school.

Because of his imposing stature and forceful demeanor, some people were initially intimidated by Fred. However, once they got to know him, they realized that Fred had a heart as big as his body. He could be tough whenever needed, and he did not tolerate foolishness. There was simply nothing weak about Fred—he naturally commanded respect. Yet Fred's forceful personality did not prohibit him from loving people through service.

I am not sure when Fred became a Christian, but I watched him grow in his faith over the years. Clearly, his desire to serve Christ became a bigger part of his life with each passing day. The president of our college said of Fred: "He was one of a kind because of his example—his personal example, his humility, and his attention to detail. These are all qualities that are in short supply in today's society. He always put other people first. . . . He always deflected the credit to someone else, and I think daily lived out his Christian faith. . . . He understood that leadership is primarily about your personal example. . . . He was a unique individual for our times."

A few years ago, Fred was diagnosed with kidney cancer and had to have one kidney removed. Despite his health problems, Fred's servant attitude continued. In 2001, our school's football team had the unfortunate circumstance of having one player seriously injured. The player, Danny Carter, suffered a neck injury that left him partially paralyzed. The one person from our school who ministered to Danny more than any other was Coach Selfe. Fred took it upon himself to become Danny's personal physical therapist. Fred worked several days per week to help Danny regain some movement and muscle strength.

Unfortunately, in the spring of 2002 cancer again returned to Fred's body. This time he had a tumor removed from his leg, but the cancer had already metastasized to his lungs. By the late fall of 2002, Fred was experiencing serious health complications. I talked to him just before Christmas. Although he was scheduled to go to Duke University for special treatment, we both knew that his prognosis was not good. He told me that he had experienced a good life—filled with many blessings, and if the Lord determined that this was the end of his earthly life, it was okay. Fred had accepted the Lord's sovereignty and trusted His grace. I prayed with Fred, and before I left, I made sure to tell him that I loved him. Unexpectedly, it was the last time I would speak to Fred before his death.

Fred's memorial service at the college chapel attracted the largest crowd I had ever seen amassed in the huge facility. Extra chairs lined the aisles and an overflow room was set up downstairs. Several people spoke at the ceremony—all of them noted Fred's service, and some mentioned how profoundly Fred reflected the life of Christ in his deeds. One of Fred's former football players told a story that perfectly demonstrated Fred's nature. The former player said that one day he was walking across campus and noticed an unusual man. The man had tattered clothes, looked unclean and disheveled, and had the appearance of a homeless person. The young man thought that some authority figure (like a security officer or administrator) would probably see the person and have him removed from the campus. Later the student-athlete arrived in the sports complex of the school and again saw the disheveled gentleman in the hallway. About that time, Coach Selfe came out of his office, and he too saw the man. The student thought Fred would certainly handle the situation and have the man escorted away. Instead, he witnessed Fred approach the man, call him by name, and put his arm around him. The student also overheard Fred ask if the man needed any more firewood. Coach Selfe was not about to banish the man from campus; Fred was going to help him. Apparently, the man lived alone in substandard conditions. Fred had previously taken firewood to him so he could heat his modest home. The man was on campus specifically to see Fred and get additional assistance.

That was just Fred—anyone who had a need was Fred's target of service. Fred trained and coached many young men in sports, but more than that, he taught them about integrity and character. Above all, Fred taught all of us about service and love! Our basketball coach, who worked daily with Fred, said, "I have never met anyone who lived the servant's life as he did. His capacity to give was unique, well beyond what could be even unreasonably expected of anyone." In reflecting on his life, several people indicated that his name should have been Fred Self*less*. He would not have liked the recognition, but Fred Self*less* was a 'Hall of Fame' servant leader.

Chapter 14

Living Reflections of Christ

⌒ ⌖ ⌖ ⌒

In this book we have addressed several critical issues of life. We have sought genuine, yet uncomplicated answers. Such a process begins with facing the reality of death and recognizing the nature of human sin. Unfortunately, many of us avoid facing the complex issues in life. Because of fear and pride, we build walls around ourselves and live as if our earthly lives are infinite. However, such a perspective leads to an isolated, self-centered life. Real answers to life begin by recognizing that we are three-dimensional beings who must nourish not only our bodies and minds but also our spirits. The critical, most meaningful issues are really spiritual in nature. God is continuously wooing us by His Spirit into an intimate relationship with Him. The critical juncture in life comes when we are faced with the life or death decision to accept or reject the offer of salvation that comes from Jesus the Christ via the Holy Spirit.

Acceptance of Jesus is the beginning of the transformation process that yields answers to life's important questions. At this point the Holy Spirit comes to dwell within us and begins the transformation process. Ultimately, the desire of God is that all of us would become conformed to the likeness of Christ, which is only possible through a magnificent work of the Spirit. God orchestrates circumstances in our lives that invite us to yield our will to that of the Father. In so doing, we allow the Holy Spirit to manifest the life of Christ through us. The transformation process may include many tribulations, which are necessary to break spiritual strongholds and make us dependent upon the Spirit. Ultimately, we become God's hands, feet, and heart in accomplishing His will in this world.

I know many people who are living, breathing reflections of Christ, some of whom have already been mentioned in this book. In closing, I want to focus on three people who have lived very different lives, yet are vibrant examples of the work of Christ in humanity. They are Spirit-filled people who are running or have run the race and fought the good fight.[1] One has already received his reward, while the other two await their day at the throne of Christ when they will also receive a great eternal reward. The first person, Robert Waag, is a gentleman who is approaching middle age and has seen the power of God in his life. The second individual is a young lady of more than 90 years who glows with the love of Christ. The last person is a very young man, Jake Aquino, whose life has had a significant impact upon many people.

Robert Waag

Robert (a/k/a – Bob) Waag was born in North Olmstead, Ohio, a suburb of Cleveland. Bob was the second oldest of the four Waag kids; he had an older sister, as well as a younger brother and a younger sister. He attended public school in Ohio and periodically attended a Lutheran church. However, his family's church attendance was mostly a social endeavor, rather than a heart-motivated activity. Unfortunately, Bob's father had problems with alcohol. He was both emotionally and physically abusive to some of his family members.

Most of Bob's childhood was spent in Ohio where, in addition to the normal activities of a youngster, he also worked alongside his dad in the family business. When Bob was a senior in high school, his father left for Florida, but the family remained behind. Not until a year later did the entire family move to Florida. Unfortunately, within another year or so Bob's parents split up again. This time the marriage ended in divorce, and Bob's relationship with his father became even more strained and complex.

Bob's family situation had been very difficult for him. Bob and his older sister seemed to take the brunt of their father's abuse. Consequently, Bob harbored some difficult emotions and turned to drugs and alcohol for relief. He also started working as a bartender. His appearance and lifestyle reflected a rebellious attitude and the heart of a wounded person. While serving as a bartender, Bob met and eventually married a young woman. The marriage lasted only about a year and ended in divorce. Bob was a broken, hurting, and angry young man.

About this time, Bob received some disconcerting news. His uncle, Larry Rybka, who had also moved to Florida, had been diagnosed with colon cancer and given a small chance of survival. Growing up in Ohio, Bob had been part of a close-knit extended family. It was common for grandparents, uncles, aunts, and cousins to share many life experiences. One of the family members Bob most respected was his uncle. Consequently, when Larry was diagnosed with cancer, Bob felt compelled to go to see him. Although they lived about one hour away from each other, Bob went to visit his uncle every weekend. During this process Bob started attending church with the Rybka family. One day during the time Larry was undergoing chemotherapy, he sat down and had a long talk with Bob. Larry told his personal testimony to his nephew. He explained that his own mother had been an alcoholic, and he had experienced troubles as a young man, but he had accepted Christ into his life and undergone a life transformation. Uncle Larry invited Bob to do the same, and he agreed. After having lived a purposeless and destructive life until the age of 25, Bob recognized his need for salvation and invited Christ into his life on December 16, 1989. Uncle Larry had been praying for Bob to come to Christ for 25 years. What a joy it was to see his prayers fulfilled.

Bob did wonder why he had never before heard the message of Christ from the Rybka family. They explained that they had often asked him questions about his spirituality, and he seemed to have appropriate answers. Bob may have known the right religious responses, but in reality his eyes, heart, and mind had been blind to the gospel of Christ. Like many other people who attend church,

Bob had heard the words associated with the message of Christ, but he had never understood and internalized them. Not until this broken point in his life did he submit to the wooing of the Holy Spirit, understand the gospel message through the illumination of the Spirit, and accept Jesus into his life.

After receiving Christ, Bob experienced a rapid personal change. He immediately stopped drinking and using drugs (and never returned to such use). Bob even changed his outward appearance. He began to hunger and thirst for righteousness, and he wanted to get his life on a positive course. About six months later, with the help of his uncle and other family members, Bob enrolled in the Word of Life Bible Institute (WOLBI) in Schroon Lake, New York. Given Bob's past, the college's administration placed various restrictions upon him, and some of the staff weren't too sure Bob would make it in their school's environment. Bob did tend to see himself as a second-class Christian because his past was more checkered than that of most of his Bible school classmates. However, Bob's conversion was real, and he persevered through the full two-year program at WOLBI.

During Bob's second year he met Marisa Zuniga Hernandez, with whom he became friends. One of the restrictions on Bob was that he could not date while at Word of Life. Consequently, he only maintained a friendship with Marisa; they never so much as held hands. Marisa was from Matamoros, Mexico, a city of well over 350,000 inhabitants, but she was a United States citizen because she was born during a brief three-month period that her mother lived in Brownsville, Texas. Marisa was the youngest of 16 children. She lived in an area where the poorest of the poor Mexicans reside. Marisa grew up in a shack house that had no running water, no electricity, and no indoor plumbing. Five and six kids slept in one bed, and Marisa never knew what it meant to have a new dress while she was growing up. Nevertheless, at age 11, Marisa accepted Christ, and when she was 16, members of a Berean Bible Church from Columbus, Indiana met Marisa while on a mission trip to Mexico. They offered to bring her to the United States for a high school education. She agreed to go and entered public high school in Columbus without knowing English. She struggled her first year and barely made passing grades because of the language barrier. Yet Marisa was intelligent, and she soon began to master the English language. She ultimately became nearly as fluent in English as she was in her native Spanish. Marisa completed all four years of her high school education, and because of her success, the church offered to send her to a Bible college. Marisa received a scholarship to go to the Word of Life Bible Institute, and well . . . divine providence ensued.

Bob and Marisa's friendship first flourished but later cooled while at Word of Life because Bob could not see a future in the relationship. He wanted to be in full-time ministry and had told God he would go anywhere in the world. Therefore, he assumed God had plans for him to travel. Going permanently to Mexico, which was Marisa's planned course of action, was not part of Bob's expectations. Bob needed to undertake an internship to complete his Bible school training, so he left Word of Life and was introduced by his uncle to the director of Adventures in Missions (AIM). AIM agreed to provide Bob with an internship and decided to send him to—where else—Reynosa, Mexico, which is not far from Matamoros. While there he not only participated in missions work, but he also learned much about the life that Marisa had experienced as a child. He could envision her life through observing the children he saw in Reynosa. In spite of being separated from Marisa by physical distance (she remained at WOLBI in New York), Bob's heart grew closer to her. Finally, he was praying about the situation one day and believed the Lord spoke to him in a quiet way and told Him that Marisa was to be his wife. Despite not having talked to Marisa in nearly seven months, Bob wrote her a special letter that expressed his feelings of love. Meanwhile, unbeknownst to Bob, Marisa could not get him off her mind. She asked God to give her a sign with regard to this man. The next day the letter arrived.

After completing his internship, Bob returned to New York to go through graduation at WOLBI. The day before graduation he met with Marisa and talked with her for several hours. Eventually, he stopped 'beating around the bush' and asked her to marry him. Stunned, she did not respond. He asked again—still no response. The third time he asked for a yes or no answer—she said yes!

Somehow word about their engagement spread rapidly through the campus, and some members of the administration came to Bob to inform him he could not graduate because he must have been dating and in so doing, had violated the conditions of his enrollment. However, the administration's assumption was false, so the next day they relented and allowed Bob to graduate. After graduation Marisa returned to Indiana for a while and then went home to Matamoros, where she returned to her former living conditions. Meanwhile, Bob went back to Florida where he tried to make some money so he could move to Matamoros and get married. In the midst of this period, AIM approached Bob and invited him to undertake a full-time missionary job in—you guessed it—Matamoros, Mexico.

Bob left immediately for Mexico but had to accept rather meager conditions. He slept on a cot in a church office and had none of the creature comforts of the typical American lifestyle. He had some financial support from AIM, but after a few months, it was his responsibility to raise his own support. As timed progressed Bob developed an understanding of the culture and learned the language of northern Mexico. (By the way, before going to Mexico he knew no Spanish. The only Spanish course he had ever taken was in the ninth grade, and he flunked the course! God does have a splendid sense of humor.) Most of Bob's missionary endeavors involved working with groups from the United States who came to Mexico to build homes for the poorest members of society. The houses mostly amounted to one-room wooden structures, but they were far superior to the shacks the people previously occupied. One of the first houses Bob personally constructed was for Marisa's mother.

Bob and Marisa's relationship continued to grow, and they were married in March of 1993. They did not have much money, so they rented a house for $100 a month; the house had previously been used as a chicken coup. They did manage to save a little money and later bought a piece of land in a modest neighborhood. Bob eventually built a wooden house that measured 16 feet by 24 feet (384 sq. ft.). It had no running water but was certainly better than the housing Marisa had previously known. They lived in the house for the next five years during which time Marisa bore two sons, Andrew and Joshua Thomas (known as "JT").

Bob fit in well in the Mexican culture; despite having been born in Ohio, his Italian heritage gave him a dark look that actually appears rather Mexican. Furthermore, after a couple of years of living in Matamoros, Bob became quite fluent in Spanish. The average observer would not easily identify Bob as a non-native Mexican.

Bob and Marisa's ministry as missionaries for AIM blossomed over the next few years. They continued to work with incoming groups to build homes, and they also branched out into other endeavors. Bob did some teaching in various settings, including short-term programs in several other countries, such as Ecuador, Costa Rica, Peru, and the Dominican Republic. The two of them also began teaching 'Homebuilders' courses for families. The fact that both Bob and Marisa were bi-lingual gave them many extra opportunities to minister in various settings. Even their two young sons became proficient in both languages and served as adequate interpreters.

In the last few years, Bob and Marisa have experienced personal growth as they have come into a deeper understanding of the role of the Holy Spirit in their lives. Consequently, they have developed a hunger for even more ministry opportunities. The Lord has fulfilled that hunger by leading them into church planting. They have started small 'house churches' that meet in individuals' homes. The primary church they lead started out meeting in the front yard of the Waags' home. (Bob built by himself a larger cinderblock and concrete structure that replaced their former small home. It is nice by Mexican standards but still modest by American norms.) Eventually, the home church rented a former nightclub and transformed it into an excellent meeting place for the church. The church took on the name Castillo Del Ray (The King's Castle), and Bob serves as the senior pastor. There are Castillo Del Ray churches in other cities in Mexico, but Castillo Del Ray is not a denomination, just a few churches with similar visions. Bob's ten previous years of experience in missions work seemed to have been a proving ground where God was refining him and preparing him for this new pastoral role. The Waags' church focuses on building relationships, making disciples, and worshiping in spirit and truth. Some of the members of the church are former drug addicts who Bob helped gain freedom by sending them to a rehabilitation center. While the

Castillo Del Ray church of Matamoros is still in its formative stages, it is apparent that the Lord is raising it up to minister to the city and surrounding community. Bob and Marisa are happily married, their ministry is rich and vibrant, and their lives are full. They truly enjoy their family and the opportunities that God has put before them. They are people who know their purpose and seek to surrender to the work of the Spirit in their lives.

The story of the Waags is a great demonstration of the work of God in transforming lives. God took the son of an alcoholic, who was himself heading down a very destructive path, and transformed him into a person who overflows with love. God forgave him of his past failures, including his divorce, and wiped his slate clean. While early on Bob may have viewed himself as a second-class Christian, God saw him as pure. His sins were taken away as far as the east is from the west.[2] Now Bob is well respected in Matamoros, and many people's lives have been changed through his ministry. Likewise, God raised up Marisa from very difficult economic circumstances and created in her a special heart. She is a very warm and loving person who has a real heart for children. While both Bob and Marisa faced many difficulties in their earlier years, it is clear that God had a providential plan. He transformed them, intertwined their lives, and set them on a journey that blesses everyone who crosses their path. They are living examples of the principles of this book. By the power of the Holy Spirit living in them, they are fulfilling great works that God has ordained for them. In so doing, they are experiencing a rich and abundant life. It may not be rich in material goods, but they are storing up for themselves great treasures in heaven by being enormous vessels of God's love to the people of Matamoros, Mexico. Only God can take broken, downtrodden lives and remake them into pure gold. Such is the case with the Waags.

Louise Gibson

Another wonderful example of Spirit-filled living is Louise Gibson, who was born in 1910. I first met Louise quite a few years ago at a Christian conference in Virginia Beach, Virginia. She was there with her husband, Jim, to whom she had been married for more than 50 years. As it turned out, we were from the same city, but we had never previously met. Our meeting at the conference was the start of a relationship that continues to this day.

Jim and Louise were a truly marvelous couple. They both had gentle, kind demeanors, and they could engage almost anyone in conversation. They were also people who loved to worship God in song and deed. Louise became a Christian at the tender age of nine, and when she was in her thirties she asked the Holy Spirit to take greater control of her life. She has since steadily grown in her relationship with Christ and in her ministry to others. Jim accepted Christ sometime well before they were married in 1931, and he too grew to reflect the likeness of Jesus. They both knew the Bible thoroughly and had proven themselves worthy of the title Christian. They were Spirit-filled people who sought to honor God in all they did.

The Gibsons and I stayed in fairly close contact over the years. We periodically went to special church services together, and occasionally, I went over to their house for dinner. Despite being in their late eighties at the time, the Gibsons were energetic people. They would intermittently take long automobile trips (hundreds of miles) with Jim as the driver. He always handled the trips well. In addition, they were very active in ministering to the people in their church and community. Out of concern for Louise, a person once suggested that she should slow down. Louise scoffed at the idea, saying she did not have time to slow down; she had to go "visit the old people," which she really did. Louise commonly visited various persons who were confined to nursing homes. On one of her more recent visits, someone there recognized that Louise, who had reached 92, was older than any of the residents.

Very simply, the Gibsons were people who exuded love. Whenever I was with them the focus of their conversation was on other people, never on their own problems. They did not focus on their aging bodies but rather on the joy of walking with God each day. In fact, every morning Louise prays that the Lord will help her to be a blessing to everyone she encounters during the forthcoming day.

A few years after I met Louise and Jim, my last living grandmother died. It was quite a loss to me, since she had been a loving, benevolent member of our family. Upon hearing of my loss, Louise volunteered to be my surrogate grandmother (as did another loving lady with characteristics similar to Louise). I accepted her offer, and she has taken it quite seriously. Louise regularly calls to check on my family. Every time she calls she offers encouragement and love. Inevitably, I hang up the phone with a big smile on my face. Sometimes we stop by Louise's house with our three children. She always finds little trinkets to give them as gifts. Like me, my children always leave her house with joy in their hearts and smiles on their faces.

Not everything in Louise's later life has been easy and joyous. Early one morning in 1996, her husband got up from bed and went into the bathroom. Louise later found him there deceased. He had collapsed and died from a heart attack. Of course, Louise was deeply wounded; they had been married for more than 64 years. Losing a life-long soul mate is one of life's most difficult experiences. Louise grieved deeply, but she lost neither her hope nor her joyous personality. Yet her path in life became even more difficult a couple of years later when she had to undergo open-heart, triple-bypass surgery. Louise said her grief over Jim's death had caused her heart problems. Because of her advanced age, the physicians and others doubted that Louise would survive the surgery. She not only survived; she rebounded to good health. Although it seemed like Louise's life was spiraling downward, she did not see it that way. She maintained her faith, and love radiated from her just as it always had.

A year or so after having surgery Louise had to go back into the hospital because she was experiencing more heart problems. I went to visit her, and she informed me that her heart was having some timing problems and the doctors wanted to install a pacemaker. She briefly mentioned the problem and proceeded to ask about my family and me. We discussed my children and many other related issues. I probably spent close to an hour with Louise, and the entire time her focus was on me or on some of the other people who came into her hospital room. She was confined to the bed, but she might as well have been standing at the door as a greeter. She blessed every medical aide or visitor who walked into the room. It was simply not Louise's manner to lie there and focus on her problems;

she just wanted to love those who came to visit.

When Louise was well into her eighties (but before her husband's death), she was invited to go on a women's Walk to Emmaus. This was the women's version of the same retreat that Darrell Golnitz (mentioned in chapter two) attended after his son's death. It is a three-day spiritual retreat that involves more sitting than walking. The walk is physically demanding, however, because it involves a full schedule and limited time for sleep. The walk focuses on study, prayer, fellowship, and fun. Most people Louise's age would have shied away from such an endeavor but not her. She went and was her normal loving self. At the end of each walk the participants are given the opportunity to make a public statement before several hundred people about how the walk had affected them personally. Many of the statements are very moving, and the listeners often respond with applause. However, in Louise's case something different happened—something I had never seen before, nor since.

When Louise arose from her seat and approached the speaker's podium, all of the other participants in the walk spontaneously leaped to their feet and erupted in applause and cheers. When Louise stood up the effect on the crowd was as if she had just set a world record in the 100 meter sprint. The crowd simply went wild. It was obvious to any observer that Louise had so showered the other women with love that they could only respond with unbridled thankfulness. She had been the physical representation of Christ to those younger women throughout the weekend, and they knew it. Of course, wherever Louise goes she has the same effect. She is so surrendered to the Holy Spirit that He is able to manifest the life of Christ through her in a vibrant and wonderful way.

The fruit of the Spirit is obvious in Louise's life. She is a faith-filled woman who is a servant to all those who meet her. When she reaches 100 years of age in the not too distant future, the entire city will probably spontaneously erupt in celebration. If the Lord chooses to take her into heaven before her 100th birthday, then I am sure there will be one giant party there. Louise embodies everything that has been presented in this book. She is one of the best examples of a Spirit-filled person that I know. We should all seek to emulate her example of faith, hope, and love—most of all love.

Jake Aquino

Jake Ikaika Aquino was born on May 27, 1990 in Charleston, South Carolina, where his father was stationed with the United States Navy. Jake was the first-born son of José and Penny Aquino. His middle name, Ikaika, means strength in the Hawaiian language of his father's family. Jake had a normal childhood, but he was unique. He had an unusually sweet personality, and he was always concerned for other people. He simply did not demonstrate the self-centeredness that is typical of most small children. When Jake was two years old, his father completed his four-year tour of duty in the Navy, and the family settled in Kingsport, Tennessee. A couple of years later, Jake's little brother, Nathan, joined the family. José had a good job with a large company, and the family members were simply enjoying life.

Jake's parents were both Christians and made it their goal to instruct their children in the ways of God. Consequently, Jake attended church regularly where he heard the message of Christ. Perhaps many little children have no significant interest in God because they are not yet capable of comprehending His existence or of being accountable before Him. However, Jake was different; he was quite interested—he asked many questions and developed a genuine concern for his personal salvation. Jake seemed unusually mature for his age and earnestly wanted to know the truth. One evening Jake emerged from his bedroom and informed his parents that he had accepted Christ into his heart. Apparently, Jake had simply spent some time alone contemplating what he knew about God. At some point, he just decided to pray and ask Jesus to come into his life. I am sure many children make comments about God that are well intentioned but lacking in real substance. However, Jake's encounter with Christ was genuine. His parents witnessed a noticeable change in his character immediately thereafter. Like Opal Trivette (mentioned in chapter seven), Jake had made a genuine confession of faith at merely six years of age. He was a typical first grade student in many ways, but his interest in God and his loving demeanor distinguished Jake from the crowd.

In January of 1997, about a month after Jake accepted Christ, he began experiencing unusual pain that could have been associated with various ailments. Consequently, Penny took Jake to see their pediatrician, Dr. Joe Ley. Dr. Ley sent Jake to a nearby hospital where he went through a variety of tests. A consulting physician concluded Jake had an appendicitis and wanted to immediately take him to surgery. Dr. Ley did not concur and kept looking for answers to the problems. All the while Jake was undergoing testing, he was his typical loving self. In fact, he was very concerned for another little boy in the hospital who Jake could hear crying from the room next door. Jake persistently prayed for the little boy, and he eventually calmed down. Some nurses indicated it was the first time the child had stopped crying since he entered the hospital.

Finally, Dr. Ley came to the family to describe the diagnosis of Jake's condition. Dr. Ley himself was pale as he revealed that Jake had neuroblastoma, a cancer that arises from the nervous system.[3] The cancer had already advanced to stage four, the worst phase of the disease. Jake had a large tumor on his adrenal gland, and the cancer had already metastasized to his bone marrow. Essentially, Jake's body was ravaged with cancer. His prognosis was very poor. José and Penny were devastated by the news, but their first response was to pray. They immediately felt the strong presence of God. Word of the diagnosis rapidly spread throughout the community, and the first night in the hospital a throng of people came to comfort Aquinos.

Because of the severity of Jake's condition, he began chemotherapy the very next day after the diagnosis. The goal was to shrink the primary tumor and arrest the cancer cells in his body. The chemotherapy treatment would continue for nearly six months. During Jake's first chemotherapy treatment, Dr. Ley stopped by for a visit with him. According to Dr. Ley, Jake "was sick but so full of life and confidence that he would get better. He would not let people be sad and would make jokes to keep people and especially his mom encouraged." Not even severe health difficulties could stop Jake from being his normal, loving self.

In June of 1997, Jake had surgery to remove the adrenal gland tumor, and a month later, he went to Cincinnati, Ohio for a bone marrow transplant. The family remained in Cincinnati for three months as Jake underwent treatment. Penny quit her part-time job so she could be with Jake, and fortunately, José's employer allowed him to take paid personal time from work. The aggressive treatment was rough on Jake. He even lost most of his hearing capability as a side effect of the bone marrow transplant.

After the treatment in Cincinnati, the Aquinos returned home and prayed the cancer would be overcome. The word about Jake continued to spread, and thousands of people prayed for the little boy and his family. Several Christians who met regularly in our home at the time were often moved to tears when we prayed for Jake. There were numerous people who had abounding faith and believed that God could deliver Jake from the ravages of this disease.

Nonetheless, Jake underwent a scan in November that indicated cancer cells were still existent in his body. Consequently, he went back to Cincinnati for additional treatments. Because of the advanced stage of Jake's disease, he was eligible for various experimental treatments. The chosen treatment in this case involved antibody therapy that attacked the cancer cells. It was an all-day, arduous treatment that was extremely painful. While Jake was going through this treatment, his church fasted and prayed for him. The treatment was amazingly successful. Subsequent scans revealed that all cancer cells had left his body, except for a couple spots on his hips, which were treated with radiation.

The success of the last round of treatment was phenomenal. For the next two years Jake continued to be checked, but his scans were always clear. The fact that he had survived so long and the cancer was in remission was far beyond reasonable expectations given the advanced nature of his disease. Surely the prayers of many people and the faith of this little boy had given him the ability to persevere.

Jake returned to school and was a living testimony of Christ wherever he went. He naturally beamed with a big smile, and his outlook on life was so positive that he simply radiated the presence of Jesus to all who met him. On a couple of occasions, stories about Jake appeared in the local newspaper. His trial and perseverance were simply an overwhelming testimony to his faith. Likewise, his parents began to experience joy and relief once again. I happened to see José at the local park one day, and he had a big smile on his face as he described the fact that Jake's last scan had been clear.

In December of 1999, the Aquino family was busy working around their home to prepare for Christmas. José was on the roof putting up Christmas lights when the phone rang. Penny answered the call; on the line was a team of doctors who were obviously talking through a speakerphone. They informed Penny that the last scan had revealed a return of the cancer. She burst into tears. When Jake got the news, he dropped to the ground and screamed.

Jake immediately started chemotherapy again at a local hospital. A few months later, he went to San Francisco for an experimental, total-body radiation treatment. In this treatment he was totally isolated for one week and given continuous intravenous radiation treatment. Jake returned to San Francisco three times for the radiation. The treatment did seem to have some positive effects. Jake was able to return to school, but in a few months more cancer appeared. This time he went to Birmingham, Alabama for an experimental antibody treatment that was again very painful. Jake made it through Christmas that year without problems, and the family still persevered in faith and hope.

In the early spring of 2001, some local friends of the family—mostly people from Jake's school—organized a special prayer service for Jake. Approximately 400 people showed up for the service. There were several songs and prayers, after which Jake was invited to come forward to the altar area of the church. Someone read the scripture from James 5:14, which states, "Is any one of you sick? He should call the elders of the church to pray over him and anoint him with oil in the name of the Lord." The leader invited everyone to come forward, gather around Jake, and lay hands on him in prayer as he anointed Jake with oil. What actually happened was most interesting. Many of the children who were present that evening spontaneously gathered around Jake. He was engulfed in a river of children as everyone prayed for Jake. I remember thinking that surely if God was going to heal Jake, it would take place during that event.

However, in April of 2001 scans revealed that tumors had returned to Jake's body, and cancer had spread to his bone marrow and to other spots in his body. The host of doctors who had treated Jake had reached the end of their alternatives. There were more experimental treatments available, but Jake and his parents decided to stop undergoing any additional treatment. Jake was intricately involved in the decision. Apparently, he had courageously accepted the fact that, short of a divine miracle, he would die. The family did go to St. Jude's Children's Research Hospital in Memphis, Tennessee but only for chemotherapy treatment that would control pain. Thereafter, the local Hospice organization became involved. Jake received the maximum dosages of pain medications during the next few months, but he continued to bless many other people.

Eventually, Jake said, "Mom, you know I'm not going to get better." He had accepted his impending death. Soon thereafter, his family, who had prayed incessantly for Jake, realized they too had to let go. On one occasion while Penny was praying to God, she released Jake into Jesus' hands. Late one evening Jake tried to get up and walk, but he was unable to do so. His father grabbed Jake, hugged him, and said, "It's OK." Jake laid his head back on the couch and passed into eternity. It was 12:03 AM on Sunday, November 18, 2001. Jake died at only 11 years of age.

Jake had struggled for five years with cancer. Throughout the ordeal he had demonstrated deep, abiding faith. Every person who encountered Jake was blessed by his presence. Furthermore, Jake had been a true evangelist of the gospel of Christ. Jake did not hesitate to put doctors, nurses, and anyone else who visited him on the spot. He would inquire about the condition of their heart and about their relationship with Christ. In some of the hospitals the medical personnel even warned each other that they had better answer with the name Jesus when they went into that little boy's room, for he would surely interrogate them about their faith. Some Christians are ashamed to publicly speak of their faith but not Jake. It was not that Jake had a presumptuous belief that God would heal him. Rather, Jake professed his faith while recognizing that in His sovereignty God could choose to heal his body or allow him to depart from this world at an early age.

Once Jake stood up in his church and witnessed about his faith. He declared that he wanted healing, but if it did not come, he could accept it. His faith influenced and inspired many people. Jake especially affected one person who had gone through a divorce and was disgruntled with God. She realized that she could not hang on to her own dissatisfaction with the course of her life when this little boy could demonstrate such resolute faith in the face of much more difficult circumstances.

Jake not only exercised the gift of evangelism, but he had simple, joyous faith. Before Jake had been diagnosed with cancer, the family owned pet finches. Because of the chemotherapy and Jake's weakened state, the family had to give the birds away to help protect his health. Later, after the cancer went into remission, Jake again asked for a bird. However, his parents thought it would be best for health reasons not to get one. So, Jake decided he would pray that God would bring him a bird. One day Jake's grandfather was outside and noticed a strange looking bird. As he approached the bird, he realized it was a cockatiel, which had obviously been a pet. The bird literally walked right onto his hand, and he took it inside to Jake. Jake responded with, "See, I told you God would give me a bird." You see, when Jake prayed he did so with specificity, and when he had finished praying, he believed God would answer his prayers. Jake did not badger God; he just prayed and trusted. The bird, which he named Jack, was clearly a specific answer to Jake's prayer, and the bird became a special friend. In fact, one day the bird escaped the home as Jake was leaving for school and followed him to the bus stop. Recapturing a bird is often difficult, if not impossible, but in this case the bird returned with Jake to their home. The bird remained as Jake's faithful pet throughout the remainder of Jake's life.

When Jake's illness was first diagnosed, the family lived in a trailer. Jake prayed for a house, and during the two years the cancer was in remission, they started building the home. When Jake was again diagnosed with cancer and went to San Francisco for treatment, members of local churches banded together to help finish the house. Jake got to move in and live there for almost two years.

I indicated in chapter 12 that Spirit-filled people exhibit love, faith, an eternal perspective, and a heart of worship. Jake tremendously displayed these attributes. For example, on one trip to Alabama for treatment Jake sang and worshiped God all along the journey. Jake was simply a person through whom God was clearly evident.

Because of his hearing loss, Jake's school system assigned an oral interpreter to work with him as he tried to continue in school. The interpreter, Mrs. Linda Conkin, wrote these words regarding Jake:

> It only took a few days to fall in love with this absolutely wonderful, special, unique young man whose priority in life seemed to be his concern that all of the people he came in contact with knew Jesus Christ. There was no shame or embarrassment in Jake's love for the Lord. He taught me love, patience, perseverance, and so many things about life that I thought I knew. He made me realize that I knew very little about these things. When he was in pain, he was concerned about others. He always had a beautiful smile on his face and a skip when he walked. He shared secrets with me that made me feel like the most important person in the world. He would look at me and say, "We're best buddies, aren't we Mrs. Linda?" I will never forget one evening when my husband and I were taking Jake out to eat; he asked me if I had gone to church on Sunday. I replied that I had been a little lazy and stayed home. Jake did not hesitate to say, "Mrs. Linda, Jesus is counting on you." Wow! Did that have an impact. I will never forget his words to me that day. He would lovingly scold me if he felt it necessary, and so many times I felt like the child. . . .
>
> I know that today Jake is surely looking down on us and saying, "Jesus is counting on you." Our loss was heaven's gain, and sometimes I think I hear him skipping along up there with a great big smile on his face.

For whatever reason, God chose not to heal Jake, but it was not because of a lack of prayer, faith, or desire. Literally thousands of people from around the world prayed for Jake. The fact that he lived five years after being diagnosed with stage four neuroblastoma was itself a miracle. Nonetheless, in His wisdom Jesus appointed Jake's life to be only 11 years.

Despite the brevity of his life, Jake Aquino's impact was more pronounced and more widespread than that of most people who live 70 or more years. Jake had one special saying that he often expressed. He said, "Remember me and smile." Those who knew Jake probably shed tears when they think of him now, but anyone who dwells upon Jake's life inevitably develops a broad smile. His joy was infectious, and even though he has departed this life, his memory in the hearts and minds of thousands of people still reflects the very image of Christ.

Jake escaped the pain of cancer and received a new, eternal body. Yet his family was left to pick up the pieces of their lives that had been shattered during the previous five years. During those years their lives had continued to progress in some ways. The third Aquino son, Joseph, was born in 1999, and Penny received word that she was pregnant with their fourth child just days after she learned of the reoccurrence of cancer in Jake. The family experienced a flood of emotions that ran the full gamut of possibilities. The fourth little guy arrived in 2001, just a couple of months before Jake's death. Jake named him Gabriel. At the point of Jake's death, his next younger brother, Nathan, was eight years of age, and Joseph was two years old.

After Jake's death, the family dealt with the range of emotions that accompany such an event. In addition to sorrow, they dealt with anger, depression, guilt, and many other difficult emotions. They faced the critical point of either trusting God in spite of the outcome or hardening their hearts toward God. Fortunately, José and Penny did not have shallow faith; rather, theirs was deep abiding reliance upon God. In spite of their anguish, they still trusted God and His sovereignty. Their perspective on life had been vastly changed, and their daily outlook is continually touched by eternity and their knowledge that someday they will see Jake again. Meanwhile questions remain. One evening about three months after Jake died, Penny sat down and wrote the following words as she wrestled with her grief:

Dear Jake,

How do I begin? I have so much to tell you—so many remembrances—remembrances of your smile and laughter, your thoughtfulness, and your love—remembrances of happy times, funny times, and sad times—sometimes too many remembrances—sometimes not enough time to remember. It seems when darkness comes and night falls they come rushing faster and faster in torrents, some are filled with sunshine, some are filled with rain. All are filled with pain—pain of the years of sickness, frustration, and never quite reaching the pinnacle of where we wanted to be. We laughed, we cried, we whined, we begged, we pleaded, but we always did something. We never quit or gave up. As I'm sitting here tonight with the remembrances haunting my mind, I try to think of where you are—what you're feeling—what you're doing. Are you happy? Do you think of us? Are you allowed to remember us? There are so many unanswered questions that I know cannot be answered until God Himself tells us. . . .

I try to tell myself all things work together for the good of those who love the Lord. At this point in time, I cannot see the good, but I know God is looking farther out there than I can see, and He has a perfect plan. I know all your whys have been answered, and you are at perfect peace and rest. Your smile has to be so bright as it lights up every room in your mansion and puts the sparkle in every jewel in your crown. How I long for your smile to lighten my heart again. . . .

For now, just stand at the gate and watch for us to enter. Welcome us with your smile and a great big hug, for tomorrow is coming, and we will meet again. I love you my son, and I'll see you in the morning.

With all my love,
Mommy

Jake and the entire Aquino family are evidence of the type of faith that perseveres through trials and recognizes that answers to life are found in trusting God when we cannot understand His ways. The anguish that sometimes accompanies life is very real. It is no trite thing to walk with God in the midst of great trials. However, there is resounding joy in knowing that there is a God who is in charge of our lives and who can be trusted to see us through even the most difficult of life's circumstances. The Aquinos have walked—and continue to walk—through one of the most challenging hardships life could offer. Yet their faith has grown deeper, and their eternal hope is even greater. Jake and the entire family have been the living presence of Jesus to countless individuals. Only when we enter heaven will we grasp the extraordinary nature of the eternal reward they have garnered.

<u>Conclusion</u>

My prayer is that all of us can grow to reflect Christ in the same way that Bob Waag, Louise Gibson, and especially Jake Aquino have done. However, the Spirit-filled life has limitations so long as we remain in earthly bodies. We will always be working toward perfection, all the while knowing it can only be fully obtained at the end of this life. We will long for a better home because "our citizenship is in heaven. And we eagerly await a Savior from there, the Lord Jesus Christ, who, by the power that enables Him to bring everything under His control, will transform our lowly bodies so that they will be like His glorious body" (Philippians 3:20-21).

Someday Jesus will return, and He will create a new heaven and a new earth. In the meantime, we are to be alert servants of Christ. In fulfilling our responsibilities as Spirit-filled Christians, we will face opposition from the spiritual forces of evil. We must resist them, submit to God, and live in the power of the Holy Spirit. We should be vigilant to seek truth and serve only Christ. The scriptures indicate that we should "not believe every spirit, but test the spirits to see whether they are from God, because many false prophets have gone out into the world" (I John 4:1). We must focus our hearts and minds on discerning God's will.

We also must recognize that where sin abounds grace abounds all the more. It might be easy for some of us to sit in judgment and say that certain persons should not enter into heaven. However, God offers salvation to all who repent, humble themselves, and come to Him seeking forgiveness. My high school friend, Eddie (mentioned in chapter three), may have committed an atrocious act of murder, but he is not beyond the grace of God. In fact, Moses was guilty of murder, and King David was guilty of adultery and conspiracy to commit murder.[4]

It is not the supposed righteousness of our acts which attracts God's attention, nor is it the unrighteousness of our acts which causes Him to reject us. Rather, our own hardened, prideful hearts stand between God and us. Unfortunately, when asked what determines the difference between whether or not a person enters into heaven, many (perhaps most) people respond that our actions are the determining factors. The idea is that if we live a reasonably upright life, we will find heaven. If we commit horrible crimes and damage other people, we will be eternally condemned. Unfortunately, this perception is born in pride. It is conceived in the idea that humankind is capable of being moral, upstanding, and righteous. Such thinking and behavior is simply beyond our capability. Isaiah 64:6 says, "All of us have become like one who is unclean, and all our righteous acts are like filthy rags."

Until we accept Christ, we are only capable of temporarily controlling or altering the modes of behavior that will come from our own sinful natures. We are incapable of avoiding sin. While we can influence the outworkings of the sin nature, we cannot completely eliminate it; that requires a divine work of the Holy Spirit in the inmost being of each person. However, those who yield to the Spirit can be truly transformed into the likeness of Jesus.

The Bible is replete with declarations that there are rewards for those who obey Christ. For example: "the Son of Man is going to come in His Father's glory with His angels, and then He will reward each person according to what he has done" (Matthew 16:27). Jesus also said, "Behold, I am coming soon! My reward is with me, and I will give to everyone according to what he has done" (Revelation 22:12). Unfortunately, many people miss the eternal rewards of a life submitted to Christ. Instead, their lives are consumed with self-centered endeavors that rob them of real meaning and ultimately lead to destructive thoughts and behaviors. Jesus said, "wide is the gate and broad is the road that leads to destruction, and many enter through it. But small is the gate and narrow the road that leads to life, and only a few find it" (Matthew 7:13-14).

The End

In chapter one (Give Me an Answer!), I posed the question: *What is the meaning and purpose of life?* Is it the unbridled pursuit of human achievement, success, and material possessions—or is life a spiritual journey? What I have tried to define and illustrate throughout the remainder of this book is this: ***The meaning and purpose of life is primarily spiritual; it is to know God, love Him with all our hearts, and serve Him forever***. The process of coming to know God and living in Him is a mystery. How can we love Him whom we have not seen? Nevertheless, the evidence of creation and of countless transformed lives is that God is real, and He wants to fellowship with us on an intimate basis. "Those who obey His commands live in Him, and He in them. And this is how we know that He lives in us: We know it by the Spirit He gave us" (I John 3:24).

We can make the enormous mistake of focusing only on our physical, earthly lives, but real life is found by denying our self-orientation and submitting to the Lordship of Jesus. It is an eternally dangerous thing to wallow in human pride and ignore the truth of God. Unfortunately, "the man without the Spirit does not accept the things that come from the Spirit of God, for they are foolishness to him, and he cannot understand them, because they are spiritually discerned" (I Corinthians 2:14).

If you have read this entire book and you are still confused, doubting, or standing in objection to Christ, then I ask you to do one thing. Ask God to impart to you the ability to understand that which can only be revealed by the power of the Holy Spirit. Only the Spirit can illuminate your mind and heart so that you can understand the truth of Christ.

If you do not recall anything else from this book, please

remember these thoughts: **The responsibility to provide salvation rests upon Jesus, the burden to produce the life of Christ in us is shouldered by the Holy Spirit, and the director of our Christian lives is God the Father Almighty**. Our responsibility is to yield . . . yield . . . yield; He bears everything else! Therefore:

Come, let us bow down in worship,
let us kneel before the LORD our Maker; for He is our God
and we are the people of His pasture, the flock under His care.
Today, if you hear His voice, do not harden your hearts . . .
(Psalms 95:6-8)

Soli Deo Gloria!
Amen.

Chapter Notes

Introduction

[1] Billy Graham, *Storm Warning* (Dallas, Texas: Word Publishing, 1992), 25.

[2] Telemarking: "A downhill turn performed on cross-country skis in which the knees are bent, the inside heel is lifted, and the weight is on the outside ski, which is advanced ahead of the other and angled inward until the turn is complete." *The American Heritage Dictionary of the English Language*, 3rd ed., s.v. "telemark," (Houghton Mifflin Company, 1992).

Chapter 1 – Give Me an Answer!

[1] Josh McDowell, *The Disconnected Generation: Saving our Youth from Self-Destruction* (Nashville, Tennessee: Word Publishing, 2000).

[2] Gene Koretz, "Economic Trends: Yes, Workers are Grumpier," *Business Week*, 13 November 2000, 42. See also: Robert O'Neill, "Americans Unhappier With Work," *The Associated Press*, 26 August, 2002 (AOL News – online at www.aol.com).

[3] Matthew D. Bramlett and William D. Mosher, "First Marriage Dissolution, Divorce, and Remarriage: United States," *Advance Data from Vital and Health Statistics,* no. 323 (Hyattsville,

Maryland: National Center for Health Statistics, online at www.cdc.gov/nchs/data/ad/ad323.pdf, 2001).

[4] *The American Heritage Dictionary of the English Language*, 3rd ed., s.v. "theism, atheism, and agnosticism" (Houghton Mifflin Company, 1992).

[5] David B. Barrett, George T. Kurian, and Todd M. Johnson, "Table 1-1, mid-2000 Adherents," *World Christian Encyclopedia: A Comparative Survey of Churches and Religions in the Modern World – Volume 1*, 2nd ed. (New York: Oxford University Press, 2001), 4.

[6] Raymond Hammer, "The Eternal Teaching: Hinduism," in *Eerdmans' Handbook to The World Religions* (Grand Rapids, Michigan: Wm. B. Eerdmans Publishing Co., 1982), 170-172.

[7] Richard Cavendish, "Hinduism," in *The Great Religions,* (New York: ARCO Publishing, Inc., 1980), 13-55.

[8] John A. Hutchison, "Hinduism," in *Paths of Faith*, 3rd ed. (New York: McGraw-Hill Book Company, 1981), 141.

[9] Ibid., 144.

[10] Huston Smith, "Hinduism," in *The World's Religions* (New York: HarperSanFrancisco, a division of HarperCollins Publishers, 1991), 12-81.

[11] Hutchison, "Buddha and Early Buddhism," in *Paths of Faith*, 100-135.

[12] Richard Drummond, "The Buddha's Teaching," in *Eerdmans' Handbook to The World Religions* (Grand Rapids, Michigan: Wm. B. Eerdmans Publishing Co., 1982), 231.

[13] Cavendish, "Buddhism," in *The Great Religions*, 58.

[14] Drummond, "The Enlightened One: Buddhism," in *Eerdmans' Handbook to The World Religions*, 231.

[15] Hutchison, "Buddha and Early Buddhism," in *Paths of Faith*, 107.

[16] Smith, "Islam," in *The World's Religions*, 222.

[17] Ibid., 223.

[18] Michael Nazir-Ali, "Genesis," in *Islam: A Christian Perspective* (Philadelphia: Westminster Press, 1983), 11-29.

[19] Frederick Mathewson Denny, *An Introduction to Islam* (New York: MacMillan Publishing Company, 1985), 71-78.

[20] Hutchison, "Islam," in *Paths of Faith*, 400-405.

[21] Ibid., 404.

[22] See: Flavius Josephus, *Antiquities of the Jews* (94 A.D. - approximate date), William Whiston, trans., in *Bible Explorer Version 2.0 Deluxe* (San Jose, California: Epiphany Software, 1999).

[23] Smith, "Islam," in *The World's Religions*, 236.

[24] Eric W. Gritsch, "Luther Posts the 95 Theses," *Christian History* 9, (28) no. 4, (1990): 35-36.

Chapter 2 – The Reality of Death

[1] Anne Wyman, "Life or Death: Who Decides?" *Boston Globe*, 25 April 1983, cited in John Jefferson Davis, *Evangelical Ethics: Issues Facing the Church Today*, 2nd ed. (Phillipsburg, New Jersey: Presbyterian and Reformed Publishing Company, 1993), 159.

2 Jack B. McConnell, MD, "Keynote Presentation" (Hilton Head, South Carolina: 18th Annual Symposium on Christian Faith and Economic Values, 2 November 1995).

Chapter 3 – Our Ailment

1 "Then God said, 'Let us make man in our image, in our likeness, and let them rule over the fish of the sea and the birds of the air, over the livestock, over all the earth, and over all the creatures that move along the ground.' So God created man in his own image, in the image of God he created him; male and female he created them" (Genesis 1:26-27).

2 As described by Martin Luther, *The Bondage of the Will*, trans. James I. Packer and O. R. Johnston (Grand Rapids, Michigan: Revell - A Division of Baker Book House, 1993), 273-318.

3 Newspapers reported on the events and circumstances of this situation. However, to help protect the anonymity of the person and his family, the actual citations are withheld from this publication.

Chapter 4 – Pride – the Primary Barrier to Truth

1 "I have great confidence in you; I take great pride in you. I am greatly encouraged; in all our troubles my joy knows no bounds" (II Corinthians 7:4).

"As for Titus, he is my partner and fellow worker among you; as for our brothers, they are representatives of the churches and an honor to Christ. Therefore show these men the proof of your love and the reason for our pride in you, so that the churches can see it" (II Corinthians 8:23-24).

"Each one should test his own actions. Then he can take pride in himself, without comparing himself to somebody else, for each one should carry his own load" (Galatians 6:5).

2 Henry Fairlie, *The Seven Deadly Sins Today* (Washington, D.C.: New Republic Books, 1978), 39.

3 See Muhammad Ali with Richard Durham, *The Greatest: My Own Story* (New York: Random House, 1975).

4 "God, who knows the heart, showed that he accepted them by giving the Holy Spirit to them, just as he did to us" (Acts 15:8). "If we had forgotten the name of our God or spread out our hands to a foreign god, would not God have discovered it, since he knows the secrets of the heart?" (Psalms 44:20-21).

5 Donald Capps, *Deadly Sins and Saving Virtues* (Philadelphia: Fortress Press, 1987).

6 David Halberstam, *Playing for Keeps: Michael Jordan and the World he Made* (New York: Random House, 1999), 323.

7 Charles Barkley played in the National Basketball Association (NBA) from 1984 to 2000. In the 1992-93 season, Barkley was named most valuable player (MVP) of the NBA, and led the Phoenix Suns to the NBA championship tournament, where they lost to the Chicago Bulls. He was named as an All-Star on multiple occasions during his career, and in 1996, Barkley was named as one of the 50 Greatest Players in NBA history. See: NBA.com, "Charles Barkley" (NBA Media Ventures, LLC: online at http://www.nba.com/playerfile/charles_barkley/index.html, 25 September, 2002).

8 Russell Miller, *The House of Getty* (New York: Henry Holt and Company, 1985).

9 Robert Lenzner, *The Great Getty: The Life and Loves of J. Paul Getty – Richest Man in the World* (New York: Crown Publishers, Inc., 1985), 4.

10 Miller, *The House of Getty*, 1.

Chapter 5 — The Triune Human Being

[1] Charles R. Solomon, *Handbook to Happiness* (Wheaton, Illinois: Tyndale House Publishers, Inc., 1989), 29.

[2] The following scriptures also support the distinction between the body, soul, and spirit:

"Therefore I will not keep silent; I will speak out in the anguish of my spirit, I will complain in the bitterness of my soul" (Job 7:11).

"My soul yearns for you [God] in the night; in the morning my spirit longs for you" (Isaiah 26:9).

"Be merciful to me, O LORD, for I am in distress; my eyes grow weak with sorrow, my soul and my body with grief" (Psalms 31:9).

"O God, you are my God, earnestly I seek you; my soul thirsts for you, my body longs for you, in a dry and weary land where there is no water" (Psalms 63:1).

"Watch and pray so that you will not fall into temptation. The spirit is willing, but the body is weak" (Matt 26:41; Mark 14:38).

"An unmarried woman or virgin is concerned about the Lord's affairs: Her aim is to be devoted to the Lord in both body and spirit" (I Corinthians 7:34).

"Since we have these promises, dear friends, let us purify ourselves from everything that contaminates body and spirit, perfecting holiness out of reverence for God" (II Corinthians 7:1).

[3] The discussion of the triune nature of man is adapted (and modified) from the work of Dr. Charles R. Solomon, *Handbook to Happiness*, with particular emphasis upon chapter 2.

[4] Mark D. Alicke, Richard H. Smith, and M. L. Klotz, "Judgments of Physical Attractiveness: The Role of Faces and Bodies," *Personality & Social Psychology Bulletin* 12 (4): 381-389

(December 1986).
John E. Stewart, "Appearance and Punishment: The Attraction-Leniency Effect in the Courtroom," *Journal of Social Psychology* 125 (3): 373-378 (June 1985).
Joel Wapnick, Jolan Kovacs Mazza, and Alice Ann Darrow, "Effects of Performer Attractiveness, Stage Behavior, and Dress on Evaluation of Children's Piano Performances, *Journal of Research in Music Education* 48 (4): 323-336 (Winter 2000).

5 George Eldon Ladd, *A Theology of the New Testament*, revised ed. (Grand Rapids Michigan: William B. Eerdmans Publishing Company, 1974, 1993), 505.

6 Ladd, *A Theology of the New Testament,* 506.

7 "Jesus stood and said in a loud voice, 'If anyone is thirsty, let him come to me and drink. Whoever believes in me, as the Scripture has said, streams of living water will flow from within him.' By this he meant the Spirit, whom those who believed in him were later to receive" (John 7:37-39).

8 "Now Abel kept flocks, and Cain worked the soil. In the course of time Cain brought some of the fruits of the soil as an offering to the LORD. But Abel brought fat portions from some of the firstborn of his flock. The LORD looked with favor on Abel and his offering, but on Cain and his offering he did not look with favor. So Cain was very angry, and his face was downcast. Then the LORD said to Cain, 'Why are you angry? Why is your face downcast? If you do what is right, will you not be accepted? But if you do not do what is right, sin is crouching at your door; it desires to have you, but you must master it.' Now Cain said to his brother Abel, 'Let's go out to the field.' And while they were in the field, Cain attacked his brother Abel and killed him. Then the LORD said to Cain, 'Where is your brother Abel?' 'I don't know,' he replied. 'Am I my brother's keeper?' The LORD said, 'What have you done? Listen! Your brother's blood cries out to

me from the ground. Now you are under a curse and driven from the ground, which opened its mouth to receive your brother's blood from your hand. When you work the ground, it will no longer yield its crops for you. You will be a restless wanderer on the earth'" (Genesis 4:3-12).

[9] Solomon, *Handbook to Happiness,* 39.

[10] Eileen M. Stuart, Ann Webster, and Carol L. Wells-Federman, "Managing Stress" in Herbert Benson & Eileen M. Stuart, eds., *The Wellness Book: The Comprehensive Guide to Maintaining Health and Treating Stress-Related Illness* (Secaucus, New Jersey: Birch Lane Press - Carol Publishing Group, 1992), 177-188.

Chapter 6 – Fear and the Development of Walls

[1] Various authors cited hereafter materially influenced the statements regarding rejection. Readers who are particularly interested in this subject are encouraged to read these works:
Dan B. Allender, *The Wounded Heart - Hope for Adult Victims of Childhood Sexual Abuse* (Colorado Springs, Colorado: NavPress, 1990).
David A. Seamands, *Healing for Damaged Emotions - Recovering from the Memories That Cause Our Pain* (Wheaton, Illinois: Victor Books, 1981).
Charles R. Solomon, *the ins and out of REJECTION* (Littleton, Colorado: Heritage House Publications, 1976).
Jeff VanVonderen, *Tired of Trying to Measure Up* (Minneapolis, Minnesota: Bethany House Publishers, 1989).
Sandra D. Wilson, *Released from Shame - Recovery for Adult Children of Dysfunctional Families* (Downers Grove, Illinois: InterVarsity Press, 1990).

[2] Anytime there is a significant number of students in a class, the resulting grades will tend to follow a normal distribution.
A normal distribution is defined by the mean and standard

deviation of the population. A graph of a normal distribution looks like a 'bell-shaped curve.' Approximately 68.2 % of the data in a normal distribution lie within one standard deviation on each side of the mean. Approximately 95.4% lie within two standard deviations and 99.7% within three standard deviations. From: Charles Henry Brase and Corrinne Pellillio Brase, *Understandable Statistics: Concepts and Methods*, 6th ed. (Boston: Houghton Mifflin Company, 1999), 280-283.

[3] Thomas H. Holmes & Associates, "Vulnerability of Stress Scale," University of Washington School of Medicine – cited in Ron Blue, *Master Your Money: A Step-by-Step Plan for Financial Freedom* (Nashville, Tennessee: Thomas Nelson Publishers, 1991), 66-67.

[4] "The LORD, the compassionate and gracious God, slow to anger, abounding in love and faithfulness, maintaining love to thousands, and forgiving wickedness, rebellion and sin" (Exodus 34:6-7). See also Numbers 14:18 and Psalms 86:15.

[5] 'Jesus the Christ' refers to Jesus the Messiah. Modern usage often shortens the phrase to Jesus Christ as if it refers to a first and last name. Instead, Christ refers to the nature and role of Jesus.
"Christ, meaning 'anointed one,' is the Greek equivalent of the Hebrew word *Messiah*."
The New International Dictionary of the Bible, pictorial ed., s.v. "Christ, Jesus," J. D. Douglas and Merrill C. Tenney, eds. (Grand Rapids, Michigan: Regency Reference Library - Zondervan Publishing House, 1987), 207.

[6] Irving L. Janis, *Victims of groupthink: Psychological Studies of Policy Decisions and Fiascos* (Boston: Houghton Mifflin, 1972). Irving L. Janis, *Groupthink: Psychological Studies of Policy Decisions and Fiascos* (Boston: Houghton Mifflin, 1982). See also: Annette R. Flippen, "Understanding Groupthink From a Self-Regulatory Perspective" *Small Group Research* 30 (2): 139-165 (April 1999).

7 ". . . deal with each man according to all he does, since you know his heart (for you alone know the hearts of all men)" (I Kings 8:39 and II Chronicles 6:30).

8 "Since the children have flesh and blood, He too shared in their humanity so that by His death He might destroy him who holds the power of death—that is, the devil—and free those who all their lives were held in slavery by their fear of death" (Hebrews 2:14-15).

Chapter 7 — The Transformation Process

1 For a more expansive explanation of this subject see: J. Rodman Williams, "Chapter 4 – The Holy Trinity," *Renewal Theology: God, the World and Redemption* (Grand Rapids, Michigan: Academie Books of Zondervan Publishing House, 1988).

2 Williams, *Renewal Theology: God, the World and Redemption,* 70-79.

3 Luke 15:11-32 describes the parable of a prodigal son who had wandered from his family roots and squandered his wealth. He eventually repented of his sin and returned to his father's home to ask forgiveness. His father was filled with compassion for him and treated him as if he had never wandered away.

4 See the biblical books of Exodus, Numbers, and Deuteronomy for a description of the wanderings of the nation of Israel.

5 II Corinthians 6:14 admonishes Christians not to marry unbelievers: "Do not be yoked together with unbelievers. For what do righteousness and wickedness have in common? Or what fellowship can light have with darkness?"

6 See also Acts 15:8, Romans 8:15-17, Galatians 4:4-7, and Ephesians 1:13-14, all of which refer to the gift of the Holy Spirit

in relationship to salvation.

7 Barna Research Online, *"Christians are More Likely to Experience Divorce than are Non-Christians"* (Ventura, California: Barna Research Group, Ltd., online at www.barna.org, 21 December, 1999).
George Barna, *Morality and the Church* – video recording (Ventura, California: Barna Research Group, Ltd., 2002).

8 Robert G. Tuttle, Jr., *John Wesley: His Life and Theology* (Grand Rapids, Michigan: Francis Asbury Press of Zondervan Publishing House, 1978), 195.

9 Williams, *Renewal Theology: God, the World and Redemption*, 305.

10 "Therefore, since we have a great high priest who has gone through the heavens, Jesus the Son of God, let us hold firmly to the faith we profess. For we do not have a high priest who is unable to sympathize with our weaknesses, but we have one who has been tempted in every way, just as we are—yet was without sin" (Hebrews 4:14-15).

11 "Now Jesus himself was about thirty years old when he began his ministry" (Luke 3:23).

12 See Matthew 4, Mark 1, and Luke 4.

13 Dennis and Rita Bennett, "Chapter 3 – What Do the Scriptures Say?" *The Holy Spirit And You* (South Plainfield, New Jersey: Bridge Publishing, Inc., 1971).

14 See: W. Edwards Deming, *Out of the Crisis* (Cambridge, Massachusetts: Massachusetts Institute of Technology, Center for Advanced Engineering Study, 1986).
See also: Mary Walton, *The Deming Management Method* (New York: Perigee Books - The Putnam Publishing Group, 1986).

Chapter 8 — Trials, Tribulations, & Suffering—God's Tools

[1] *The American Heritage Dictionary of the English Language*, 3rd ed., s.v. "trials," (Houghton Mifflin Company, 1992).

[2] Ibid., s.v. "tribulations."

[3] Ibid., s.v. "suffering."

[4] Williams, *Renewal Theology: God, the World and Redemption*, 146.

[5] Harold S. Kushner, *When Bad Things Happen to Good People* (New York: Schocken Books, 1981), 134.

[6] Peter Kreeft, *Making Sense Out of Suffering* (Ann Arbor, Michigan: Servant Books, 1986), 49.

[7] Leslie D. Weatherhead, *The Will of God* (Nashville, Tennessee: Abingdon Press, 1944), 20-21.

[8] "So do not be ashamed to testify about our Lord, or ashamed of me his prisoner. But join with me in suffering for the gospel, by the power of God, who has saved us and called us to a holy life— not because of anything we have done but because of His own purpose and grace. This grace was given us in Christ Jesus before the beginning of time, but it has now been revealed through the appearing of our Savior, Christ Jesus, who has destroyed death and has brought life and immortality to light through the gospel" (II Timothy 1:8-10).

[9] "Therefore, when Christ came into the world, he said: "Sacrifice and offering you did not desire, but a body you prepared for me; with burnt offerings and sin offerings you were not pleased. Then I said, 'Here I am—it is written about me in the scroll— I have come to do your will, O God.'" First he said, 'Sacrifices and offerings, burnt offerings and sin offerings you did not desire, nor

were you pleased with them' (although the law required them to be made). Then he said, 'Here I am, I have come to do your will.' He sets aside the first to establish the second. And by that will, we have been made holy through the sacrifice of the body of Jesus Christ once for all" (Hebrews 10:5-10).

"My God, my God, why have you forsaken me? Why are you so far from saving me, so far from the words of my groaning? . . . But I am a worm and not a man, scorned by men and despised by the people. All who see me mock me; they hurl insults, shaking their heads: 'He trusts in the LORD; let the LORD rescue him. Let him deliver him, since he delights in him.' . . . Dogs have surrounded me; a band of evil men has encircled me, they have pierced my hands and my feet. I can count all my bones; people stare and gloat over me. They divide my garments among them and cast lots for my clothing" (Psalms 22:1, 6-8, 16-18).

[10] "You see, at just the right time, when we were still powerless, Christ died for the ungodly" (Romans 5:6).

[11] Leslie D. Weatherhead, *The Christian Agnostic* (New York: Abingdon Press, 1965).

[12] Bruce Wilkinson, *Secrets of the Vine: Breaking Through to Abundance* (Sisters, Oregon: Multnomah Publishers, Inc., 2001), 36.

[13] *Microsoft Encarta Encyclopedia 2000*, s.v. "World War II."

[14] "For it is time for judgment to begin with the family of God; and if it begins with us, what will the outcome be for those who do not obey the gospel of God? And, 'If it is hard for the righteous to be saved, what will become of the ungodly and the sinner?' So then, those who suffer according to God's will should commit themselves to their faithful Creator and continue to do good" (I Peter 4:17-19).

[15] Kreeft, *Making Sense Out of Suffering*, 29.

[16] Kreeft, *Making Sense Out of Suffering*, 169-170.

[17] Charles W. Colson, *Born Again* (Old Tappan, New Jersey: Chosen Books, Fleming H. Revell Company, 1976).

[18] "'See, I will send my messenger, who will prepare the way before me. Then suddenly the Lord you are seeking will come to his temple; the messenger of the covenant, whom you desire, will come,' says the LORD Almighty. But who can endure the day of his coming? Who can stand when he appears? For he will be like a <u>refiner's fire</u> or a launderer's soap. He will sit as a refiner and purifier of silver; he will purify the Levites and refine them like gold and silver. Then the LORD will have men who will bring offerings in righteousness, and the offerings of Judah and Jerusalem will be acceptable to the LORD, as in days gone by, as in former years" (Malachi 3:1-4).

[19] "The law was added so that the trespass might increase. But where sin increased, grace increased all the more, so that, just as sin reigned in death, so also grace might reign through righteousness to bring eternal life through Jesus Christ our Lord" (Romans 5:20-21).

[20] Elisabeth Elliot, *Shadow of the Almighty: The Life & Testament of Jim Elliot*, (New York: Harper & Brothers, Publishers, 1958), 19.

Chapter 9 – Breaking Spiritual Strongholds

[1] Neil T. Anderson, *The Bondage Breaker: Overcoming Negative Thoughts, Irrational Feelings, Habitual Sins* (Eugene, Oregon: Harvest House Publishers, 1993), 54.

[2] "The thief [Satan] comes only to steal and kill and destroy; I [Jesus] have come that they may have life, and have it to the full

(John 10:10).

3 "Are not all angels ministering spirits sent to serve those who will inherit salvation?" (Hebrews 1:14).

4 The following scriptures are also relevant:
"When evening came, many who were demon-possessed were brought to him, and he drove out the spirits with a word and healed all the sick" (Matthew 8:16).
"When he arrived at the other side in the region of the Gadarenes, two demon-possessed men coming from the tombs met him. They were so violent that no one could pass that way. 'What do you want with us, Son of God?' they shouted. 'Have you come here to torture us before the appointed time?' Some distance from them a large herd of pigs was feeding. The demons begged Jesus, 'If you drive us out, send us into the herd of pigs.' He said to them, 'Go!' So they came out and went into the pigs, and the whole herd rushed down the steep bank into the lake and died in the water. Those tending the pigs ran off, went into the town and reported all this, including what had happened to the demon-possessed men. Then the whole town went out to meet Jesus. And when they saw him, they pleaded with him to leave their region" (Matthew 8:28-34).

5 Donna Leinwand, "Sniper Case could be Among Deadliest," *USA TODAY*, 8 November, 2002 (McLean, Virginia: Gannett Co. – online at www.usatoday.com).

6 "Chronology of the Case," *USA TODAY*, 8 November, 2002 (McLean, Virginia: Gannett Co. – online at www.usatoday.com).

7 Francis MacNutt, *Deliverance from Evil Spirits* (Grand Rapids, Michigan: Chosen Books, A Division of Baker Book House Co., 1995), 67.

8 "You shall not bow down to them or worship them; for I, the LORD your God, am a jealous God, punishing the children for

the sin of the fathers to the third and fourth generation of those who hate me, but showing love to a thousand [generations] of those who love me and keep my commandments" (Deuteronomy 5:9-10).
"The LORD is slow to anger, abounding in love and forgiving sin and rebellion. Yet he does not leave the guilty unpunished; he punishes the children for the sin of the fathers to the third and fourth generation" (Numbers 14:18).

[9] Alexander M. Bielakowski, "Causalities," in *The Encyclopedia of the American Civil War: A Political, Social, and Military History – Volume 1*, David S. Heidler and Jeanne T. Heilder, eds. (Santa Barbara, California: ABC-CLIO, 2000), 373-374.

[10] J. L. Scott, *45th Virginia Infantry*, 2nd ed. (Lynchburg, Virginia: H. E. Howard, Inc., 1989) - available through Farnsworth House, Gettysburg, Pennsylvania.

Chapter 11 — Faith, Hope, and Trust

[1] "I desire to speak to the Almighty and to argue my case with God" (Job 13:3).

Chapter 12 – The Spirit-Filled Life

[1] "I [Jesus] am come that they might have life, and that they might have *it* more abundantly" (John 10:10, KJV).

[2] "Do you not know that your body is a temple of the Holy Spirit, who is in you, whom you have received from God? You are not your own; you were bought at a price. Therefore honor God with your body" (I Corinthians 6:19-20).

[3] See also Luke 4:33-35: "In the synagogue there was a man possessed by a demon, an evil spirit. He cried out at the top of his

voice, 'Ha! What do you want with us, Jesus of Nazareth? Have you come to destroy us? I know who you are—the Holy One of God!' 'Be quiet!' Jesus said sternly. 'Come out of him!' Then the demon threw the man down before them all and came out without injuring him."

4 "Submit yourselves, then, to God. Resist the devil, and he will flee from you" (James 4:7).

5 Robert H. Stein, *The Method and Message of Jesus' Teachings* (Philadelphia: The Westminster Press, 1978), 100.

6 "Jesus went through all the towns and villages, teaching in their synagogues, preaching the good news of the kingdom and healing every disease and sickness" (Matthew 9:35).
" When Jesus landed and saw a large crowd, he had compassion on them and healed their sick" (Matthew 14:14).

7 "People were also bringing babies to Jesus to have him touch them. When the disciples saw this, they rebuked them. But Jesus called the children to him and said, 'Let the little children come to me, and do not hinder them, for the kingdom of God belongs to such as these. I tell you the truth, anyone who will not receive the kingdom of God like a little child will never enter it' " (Luke 18:15-17).
"Great crowds came to him, bringing the lame, the blind, the crippled, the mute and many others, and laid them at his feet; and he healed them. The people were amazed when they saw the mute speaking, the crippled made well, the lame walking and the blind seeing. And they praised the God of Israel. Jesus called his disciples to him and said, 'I have compassion for these people; they have already been with me three days and have nothing to eat. I do not want to send them away hungry, or they may collapse on the way.' His disciples answered, 'Where could we get enough bread in this remote place to feed such a crowd?' 'How many loaves do you have?' Jesus asked. 'Seven,' they replied, 'and a few small fish.' He told the crowd

to sit down on the ground. Then he took the seven loaves and the fish, and when he had given thanks, he broke them and gave them to the disciples, and they in turn to the people. They all ate and were satisfied. Afterward the disciples picked up seven basketfuls of broken pieces that were left over. The number of those who ate was four thousand, besides women and children" (Matthew 15:30-38).

8 "'Teacher,' he declared, 'all these I have kept since I was a boy.' Jesus looked at him and loved him. 'One thing you lack,' he said. 'Go, sell everything you have and give to the poor, and you will have treasure in heaven. Then come, follow me'" (Mark 10:20-21). "But I have prayed for you, Simon, that your faith may not fail. And when you have turned back, strengthen your brothers" (Luke 22:32).
"'Where have you laid him?' he asked. 'Come and see, Lord,' they replied. Jesus wept. Then the Jews said, 'See how he loved him!' But some of them said, 'Could not he who opened the eyes of the blind man have kept this man from dying?' Jesus, once more deeply moved, came to the tomb. It was a cave with a stone laid across the entrance. 'Take away the stone,' he said. 'But, Lord,' said Martha, the sister of the dead man, 'by this time there is a bad odor, for he has been there four days.' Then Jesus said, 'Did I not tell you that if you believed, you would see the glory of God?' So they took away the stone. Then Jesus looked up and said, 'Father, I thank you that you have heard me. I knew that you always hear me, but I said this for the benefit of the people standing here, that they may believe that you sent me.' When he had said this, Jesus called in a loud voice, 'Lazarus, come out!' The dead man came out, his hands and feet wrapped with strips of linen, and a cloth around his face. Jesus said to them, 'Take off the grave clothes and let him go'" (John 11:34-44).

9 "If I speak in the tongues of men and of angels, but have not love, I am only a resounding gong or a clanging cymbal" (I Corinthians 13:1).

10 "But I tell you: Love your enemies and pray for those who persecute you" (Matthew 5:44).

11 "The teachers of the law and the Pharisees brought in a woman caught in adultery. They made her stand before the group and said to Jesus, 'Teacher, this woman was caught in the act of adultery. In the Law Moses commanded us to stone such women. Now what do you say?' They were using this question as a trap, in order to have a basis for accusing him. But Jesus bent down and started to write on the ground with his finger. When they kept on questioning him, he straightened up and said to them, 'If any one of you is without sin, let him be the first to throw a stone at her.' Again he stooped down and wrote on the ground. At this, those who heard began to go away one at a time, the older ones first, until only Jesus was left, with the woman still standing there. Jesus straightened up and asked her, 'Woman, where are they? Has no one condemned you?' 'No one, sir,' she said. 'Then neither do I condemn you,' Jesus declared. 'Go now and leave your life of sin'" (John 8:3-11).

12 "Jesus said, 'Father, forgive them, for they do not know what they are doing.'" (Luke 23:34).

13 "If your brother sins against you, go and show him his fault, just between the two of you. If he listens to you, you have won your brother over. But if he will not listen, take one or two others along, so that 'every matter may be established by the testimony of two or three witnesses.' If he refuses to listen to them, tell it to the church; and if he refuses to listen even to the church, treat him as you would a pagan or a tax collector" (Matthew 18:15-17).

14 Ravi Zacharias, "The Fingerprints on Your Soul," *Just Thinking,* Winter 2003: 1-7, (Norcross, GA: Ravi Zacharias International Ministries, 2003), 7.

15 "He called his twelve disciples to him and gave them authority to drive out evil spirits and to heal every disease and sickness. . .

Go rather to the lost sheep of Israel. As you go, preach this message: 'The kingdom of heaven is near.' Heal the sick, raise the dead, cleanse those who have leprosy, drive out demons. Freely you have received, freely give"(Matthew 10:1,6-8).

16 "He told them, 'The secret of the kingdom of God has been given to you'" (Mark 4:11).

17 The Faith of the Centurion: "When Jesus had entered Capernaum, a centurion came to him, asking for help. 'Lord,' he said, 'my servant lies at home paralyzed and in terrible suffering.' Jesus said to him, 'I will go and heal him.' The centurion replied, 'Lord, I do not deserve to have you come under my roof. But just say the word, and my servant will be healed. For I myself am a man under authority, with soldiers under me. I tell this one, "Go," and he goes; and that one, "Come," and he comes. I say to my servant, "Do this," and he does it.' When Jesus heard this, he was astonished and said to those following him, 'I tell you the truth, I have not found anyone in Israel with such great faith.' Then Jesus said to the centurion, 'Go! It will be done just as you believed it would.' And his servant was healed at that very hour" (Matthew 8:5-10, 13; see also Luke 7:1-10).
The Faith of the Canaanite Woman: "Leaving that place, Jesus withdrew to the region of Tyre and Sidon. A Canaanite woman from that vicinity came to him, crying out, 'Lord, Son of David, have mercy on me! My daughter is suffering terribly from demon-possession.' Jesus did not answer a word. So his disciples came to him and urged him, 'Send her away, for she keeps crying out after us.' He answered, 'I was sent only to the lost sheep of Israel.' The woman came and knelt before him. 'Lord, help me!' she said. He replied, 'It is not right to take the children's bread and toss it to their dogs.' 'Yes, Lord,' she said, 'but even the dogs eat the crumbs that fall from their masters' table.' Then Jesus answered, 'Woman, you have great faith! Your request is granted.' And her daughter was healed from that very hour" (Matthew 15:21-28).

[18] Jesus Walks on the Water: "Immediately Jesus made the disciples get into the boat and go on ahead of him to the other side, while he dismissed the crowd. After he had dismissed them, he went up on a mountainside by himself to pray. When evening came, he was there alone, but the boat was already a considerable distance from land, buffeted by the waves because the wind was against it. During the fourth watch of the night Jesus went out to them, walking on the lake. When the disciples saw him walking on the lake, they were terrified. 'It's a ghost,' they said, and cried out in fear. But Jesus immediately said to them: 'Take courage! It is I. Don't be afraid.' 'Lord, if it's you,' Peter replied, 'tell me to come to you on the water.' 'Come,' he said. Then Peter got down out of the boat, walked on the water and came toward Jesus. But when he saw the wind, he was afraid and, beginning to sink, cried out, 'Lord, save me!' Immediately Jesus reached out his hand and caught him. 'You of little faith,' he said, 'why did you doubt?'" (Matthew 14:22-31).

[19] *The American Heritage Dictionary of the English Language*, 3rd ed., s.v. "presumption," (Houghton Mifflin Company, 1992).

[20] A Sick Woman: "A woman who had been subject to bleeding for twelve years came up behind him and touched the edge of his cloak. She said to herself, 'If I only touch his cloak, I will be healed.' Jesus turned and saw her. 'Take heart, daughter,' he said, 'your faith has healed you.' And the woman was healed from that moment" (Matthew 9:20-22; see also Mark 5:25-34 and Luke 8:43-48).

[21] John Wesley, "notes for James 2:24," *John Wesley's Notes on the Whole Bible*, in *Bible Explorer Version 2.0 Deluxe* (San Jose, California: Epiphany Software, 1999).

[22] William Barclay, "The Proof of Faith (James 2:20-26)," *Barclay's Daily Study Bible – New Testament Commentary* (Louisville, Kentucky: Westminster John Knox Press, 1975), in *Bible Explorer Version 2.0 Deluxe* (San Jose, California:

Epiphany Software, 1999).

[23] *Microsoft Encarta Encyclopedia 2000*, s.v. "Dead Sea."

[24] John R. W. Stott, *Human Rights & Human Wrongs: Major Issues for a New Century* (Grand Rapids, Michigan: Baker Books, 1999), 146.

[25] David B. Barrett, George T. Kurian, and Todd M. Johnson, "Bangladesh, India, Nicaragua, United States, Uzbekistan, Zimbabwe" *World Christian Encyclopedia: A Comparative Survey of Churches and Religions in the Modern World – Volume 1*, 2nd ed. (New York: Oxford University Press, 2001), 97, 359, 543, 772, 793, 821.

[26] See also I Corinthians 4:1-2: "Now it is required that those who have been given a trust must prove faithful."

[27] "Do not store up for yourselves treasures on earth, where moth and rust destroy, and where thieves break in and steal" (Matthew 6:19).

[28] "Praise our God, O peoples, let the sound of his praise be heard; he has preserved our lives and kept our feet from slipping" (Psalms 66:8-9).

[29] The following scriptures also relate to God sustaining life:
"The Spirit of God has made me; the breath of the Almighty gives me life" (Job 33:4).
"Man's days are determined; you have decreed the number of his months and have set limits he cannot exceed" (Job 14:5).
"The God who made the world and everything in it is the Lord of heaven and earth and does not live in temples built by hands. And he is not served by human hands, as if he needed anything, because he himself gives all men life and breath and everything else" (Acts 17:24-25).
"In the sight of God, who gives life to everything, and of Christ

Jesus, who while testifying before Pontius Pilate made the good confession, I charge you to keep this command without spot or blame until the appearing of our Lord Jesus Christ" (I Timothy 6:13-14).

30 See the book of Job and Luke 22:31-32: "Simon [Peter], Satan has asked to sift you as wheat. But I have prayed for you, Simon, that your faith may not fail. And when you have turned back, strengthen your brothers."

31 "But when he, the Spirit of truth, comes, he will guide you into all truth. He will not speak on his own; he will speak only what he hears, and he will tell you what is yet to come" (John 16:13).

32 Williams, *Renewal Theology: God, the World and Redemption*, 68.

33 "I love those who love me, and those who seek me find me" (Proverbs 8:17).

Chapter 13 — Spirit-Filled Ministry

1 "When the Son of Man comes in His glory, and all the angels with Him, he will sit on His throne in heavenly glory. All the nations will be gathered before Him, and he will separate the people one from another as a shepherd separates the sheep from the goats. He will put the sheep on His right and the goats on His left. Then the King will say to those on His right, 'Come, you who are blessed by my Father; take your inheritance, the kingdom prepared for you since the creation of the world. For I was hungry and you gave me something to eat, I was thirsty and you gave me something to drink, I was a stranger and you invited me in, I needed clothes and you clothed me, I was sick and you looked after me, I was in prison and you came to visit me.' Then the righteous will answer Him, 'Lord, when did we see you hungry and feed you, or thirsty and give you something to drink?

When did we see you a stranger and invite you in, or needing clothes and clothe you? When did we see you sick or in prison and go to visit you?' The King will reply, 'I tell you the truth, whatever you did for one of the least of these brothers of mine, you did for me'" (Matthew 25:31-40).

2 "But Jesus often withdrew to lonely places and prayed" (Luke 5:16).

3 "I thank God that I speak in tongues more than all of you" (I Corinthians 14:18).

4 "He who speaks in a tongue edifies himself" (I Corinthians 14:4).

5 "But thou *art* holy, *O thou* that inhabitest the praises of Israel" (Psalms 22:3, KJV).

6 "There are different kinds of gifts, but the same Spirit. There are different kinds of service, but the same Lord. There are different kinds of working, but the same God works all of them in all men. Now to each one the manifestation of the Spirit is given for the common good" (I Corinthians 12:4-7).

7 W. George Selig and Alan A. Arroyo, *Loving Our Differences: Building Successful Family Relationships* (Virginia Beach, Virginia: CBN Publishing, 1989).

8 Many organizations incorporate the DISC survey in their personality testing materials. One good interpretative version of the survey is: Adult DISC Survey, © 1995, 2000 by In His Grace, Inc., 3006 Quincannon Lane, Houston, Texas 77043-1201.

9 "He who prophesies edifies the church. I would like every one of you to speak in tongues, but I would rather have you prophesy. He who prophesies is greater than one who speaks in tongues, unless he interprets, so that the church may be edified"

(I Corinthians 14:4-5).

10 Jack Deere, *Surprised by the Power of the Spirit* (Grand Rapids, Michigan: Zondervan Publishing House, 1993).

11 "And we pray this in order that you may live a life worthy of the Lord and may please Him in every way: bearing fruit in every good work, growing in the knowledge of God, being strength- ened with all power according to His glorious might so that you may have great endurance and patience, and joyfully giving thanks to the Father, who has qualified you to share in the inheri- tance of the saints in the kingdom of light" (Colossians 1:10-12). "We ought always to thank God for you, brothers, and rightly so, because your faith is growing more and more, and the love every one of you has for each other is increasing" (II Thessalonians 1:3).

12 John Stott uses the term "complementarity" to describe the rela- tionship between men and women, particularly between husband and wife. See *Our Social & Sexual Revolution: Major Issues for a New Century*, 3rd ed. (Grand Rapids, Michigan: Baker Rooks, 1999), 111-113.

13 Charles Colson, "Working-Class Heroes," *BreakPoint online Commentary #020902* (Merrifield, Virginia: Prison Fellowship Ministries - BreakPoint with Charles Colson, online at www.breakpoint.org, 2 September, 2002).

14 Henri J. M. Nouwen, *In the name of Jesus: Reflections on Christian leadership* (New York: The Crossroad Publishing Company, 1989), 63.

15 Paul A. Cedar, *Strength in Servant Leadership* (Waco, Texas: Word Books, 1987), 157.

16 "It was just before the Passover Feast. Jesus knew that the time had come for Him to leave this world and go to the Father. Having loved His own who were in the world, He now showed

them the full extent of His love. . . . so He got up from the meal, took off his outer clothing, and wrapped a towel around his waist. After that, He poured water into a basin and began to wash His disciples' feet, drying them with the towel that was wrapped around Him (John 13:1, 4-5).

Chapter 14 – Living Reflections of Christ

[1] The Apostle Paul said: "I have fought the good fight, I have finished the race, I have kept the faith. Now there is in store for me the crown of righteousness, which the Lord, the righteous Judge, will award to me on that day—and not only to me, but also to all who have longed for His appearing" (II Timothy 4:7-8).

[2] "The LORD is compassionate and gracious, slow to anger, abounding in love. He will not always accuse, nor will He harbor His anger forever; He does not treat us as our sins deserve or repay us according to our iniquities. For as high as the heavens are above the earth, so great is His love for those who fear Him; as far as the east is from the west, so far has He removed our transgressions from us" (Psalms 103:8-12).

[3] "Neuroblastoma is one of the most common solid tumours of early childhood usually found in babies or young children. The disease originates in the adrenal medulla or other sites of sympathetic nervous tissue. The most common site is the abdomen (near the adrenal gland) but can also be found in the chest, neck, pelvis, or other sites. Most patients have widespread disease at diagnosis." Children's Cancer Web, s.v. "Neuroblastoma" (http://www.cancerindex.org/ccw/about, September 24, 2002).

[4] Moses kills the Egyptian: "One day, after Moses had grown up, he went out to where his own people were and watched them at their hard labor. He saw an Egyptian beating a Hebrew, one of his own people. Glancing this way and that and seeing no one, he killed the Egyptian and hid him in the sand" (Exodus 2:11-12).

David and Bathsheba: "One evening David got up from his bed and walked around on the roof of the palace. From the roof he saw a woman bathing. The woman was very beautiful, and David sent someone to find out about her. The man said, 'Isn't this Bathsheba, the daughter of Eliam and the wife of Uriah the Hittite?' Then David sent messengers to get her. She came to him, and he slept with her. (She had purified herself from her uncleanness.) Then she went back home. The woman conceived and sent word to David, saying, 'I am pregnant.' . . . In the morning David wrote a letter to Joab and sent it with Uriah. In it he wrote, 'Put Uriah in the front line where the fighting is fiercest. Then withdraw from him so he will be struck down and die.' So while Joab had the city under siege, he put Uriah at a place where he knew the strongest defenders were. When the men of the city came out and fought against Joab, some of the men in David's army fell; moreover, Uriah the Hittite died. . . . After the time of mourning was over, David had her brought to his house, and she became his wife and bore him a son. But the thing David had done displeased the LORD" (II Samuel 11:3-5, 14-17,27).

Printed in the United States
62791LVS00001BA/1-96

9 781594 675010